Buddhist Culture in Far East Asia

Buddhist Culture in Far East Asia

Dr. S.S. Tiwari

Mahaveer & Sons
(Publishers & Distributors)
New Delhi-110002

Buddhist Culture in Far East Asia

First Published 2011

ISBN 978-81-8377-276-1

Published by :

MAHAVEER & SONS

(Publishers & Distributors)

H-2/16, Ansari Road, Darya Ganj,
(Near Shiv Mandir) New Delhi-110002
E-mail : mahaveersonspub@rediffmail.com
Ph. 011 23242069, Mob. 09899608339

PRINTED IN INDIA

Published by Sh. Seema Sharma for Mahaveer & Sons. Publishers and Distributors H-2/16 Ansari Road, Near Shiv Mandir, Daryaganj, New Delhi-110002, Printed at Himanshu Printers, Delhi.

Preface

Buddhism is one of the oldest world religions. It was started by an Indian prince named Siddhartha who was born 544 years before Christ. He renounced his family and kingdom and studied and practiced all the spiritual teachings of that time, until one day, he vowed not to move from his seat under a Bodhi tree until he discovered the truth of all existence. He did this by examining the nature of his own mind. Buddhist philosophy deals extensively with problems in metaphysics, phenomenology, ethics, and epistemology. The Buddha's general outlook has been described as neither ontological nor metaphysical, but empirical. He assumed an unsympathetic attitude toward speculative and religious thought in general. A basic idea of the Buddha is that the world must be thought of in procedural terms, not in terms of things or substances. The Buddha advised viewing reality as comprised of dependently originated phenomena; Buddhists view this approach to experience as avoiding the two extremes of reification and nihilism.

Buddhism can be regarded as either a practical philosophy or a belief-based religion. In the South and East Asian cultures in which Buddhism developed, the distinction between philosophy and religion did not exist. As such, the Western need to classify Buddhism as one or the other is somewhat spurious and may be a mere semantic problem. Proponents of the view that Buddhism is a philosophy argue (a) that Buddhism is non-theistic, having no particular use for the existence or non-existence of a god or gods; and (b) that religion entails theism. However, both prongs of this argument are contested by proponents of the alternative view, that Buddhism is a religion.

Buddhism is broadly recognized as being composed of two major branches: 1. Theravada, which has a widespread following in Southeast Asia and 2. Mahayana (including Pure Land, Zen, Nichiren Buddhism, Shingon, Tibetan Buddhism and Tendai), found throughout East Asia. It should be noted that in some methods of classification, Vajrayana is considered a third branch. While Buddhism remains most popular within these regions of Asia, both branches are now found throughout the world. Buddhist schools disagree on what the historical teachings of Gautama Buddha were, so much so that some scholars claim Buddhism does not have a clearly definable common core. Significant disagreement also exists over the importance and canonicity of various scriptures. Various sources put the number of Buddhists in the world between 230 million and 500 million.

Contents

1

BUDDHIST CULTURE IN JAPAN

Buddhism was introduced in Japan in the sixth century AD (538 AD). Prince Shotoku (574-621 AD) who was a regent to the female Emperor Suiko and a sincere Buddhist gave the first imperial patronage to Buddhism and initiated the cultural exchange with China. Japan had close cultural contact with Korea and introduced Chinese culture and Buddhism through that country. Before the introduction of Buddhism, the people of Japan had practiced Shinto since the ancient time.

The word 'Shinto' means 'the way of gods' and it is concerned with the worship of the imperial and family ancestors as well as with nature-worship and society. It had neither any official scripture, nor any moral code or any idealistic philosophy. However, Shinto believes in 'living communion' of men with gods or spirits, animals and trees, rocks and streams. It stands for a harmonious cooperation between Man and the rest of the Nature. In Japan, Shinto was at that time their religion, or rather their way of life. The only concern was with ritual purity. Kami or Gods were felt to be everywhere and were worshipped and prayed to as beneficent forces. Shinto still remains in the Japanese people today.

When the great cultural wave came from China through Korea to Japan, it could not sweep away Shinto. Shinto lived on all through the centuries despite changes in the political organizations due to the immense influences of Chinese Confucianism. The

Japanese people soon developed the concept of Gods of Shinto that were simply the local manifestation of universal Buddhist principles and deities. The two religions became institutionally intertwined. Shinto focused on adapting to life in this world and on a simple merging of man into the natural environment around him.

On the other hand, Buddhism was concerned with the relation of the individual soul to the limitless cosmos and the afterlife, stressing their escape from the endless cycle of painful existences through enlightenment or salvation. In Japan there were three levels of understanding: the idea of Buddhism was concerned about the other world, and the concept of Shinto was towards nature in daily life, and Confucianism dealt with political systems and ethical concepts of the society. The Japanese people felt no sense of conflict between these different religions and philosophies. Each has its own position and its own power in their way of life.

The introduction of Buddhism brought about a radical change in the minds of Japanese people who got a new message of compassion and salvation. With this developed a new idealistic philosophy viewed with awe, a new type of worshipping of the decorated images of the Buddha with artistic demonstration in ceremonies and elaborated performance of rituals. In that century (6th AD), the image-making was started and many Buddhist relics and statues were created that resulted in the construction of many temples of Japan after Buddhist monks, artisans and other immigrants came from Korea. Though this first spread of Indian culture in Japan may be indirect, Buddhist teachings and philosophy gave a great impact on Japanese life and culture.

INDIAN INFLUENCE ON JAPANESE CULTURE

After having introduced Buddhism, a large number of Buddhist Sanskrit words were introduced into Japanese language. Most of them can be looked for in the former Sanskrit words that retained their original forms. Some of the proper nouns have completely lost the original meaning of Sanskrit but only retains the sound. The Buddhist Sanskrit words still have a significance of existence and occupy a great portion of the lifestyle and thought in Japanese culture.

For example, the words which are still remaining are as follows: Butsuda or Buddha, Bosatsu or Bodhisattva, Amida or Amitabha, Bonten or Brahman, Miroku or Maitreya, Monju or Manjusri, Yasya or Yaksa, Ashura or Asura, Daruma or Dharma, Naraku or Naraka, Namu or Namas, Shaba or Saha, Danna or Dana, Kesa or Kasaya, Sotobha or Stupa, etc. According to the 'Nihonshoki' which is the oldest history book of Japan, there are a large number of words which were adopted into Japanese words not only Buddhist terms but also the words which are usually used in their daily life, such as Kawara (roofing tile) or kapala, Hachi (pot) or patra, Hata(flag) or pata, Biwa or Vina, etc.

Although they did not know Sanskrit, they were familiar with the Indian Siddham letters, which was called "sittan" in Japan. In Japanese temples and cemeteries many tablets written in Siddham letters can be found. Japanese letters (Hiragana and Katakana) were constructed on the basis of Chinese characters. However, there is a great difference between them. The Chinese letters are ideographic but Japanese letters are phonetic like the Indian letters.

The Japanese letters were arranged in the same order as that of Sanskrit. Indian legends were also introduced into Japanese literature. One of them is the legend of Rsyasringa. This legend, which is very famous in the Mahabharata and other literary works, was incorporated into the Buddhist scriptures, and transmitted into Japan. There was a saint in the drama under the name of Ikkaku Sennin or Ekasringa (unicorn) which is preserved and adopted into the famous Kabuki drama "Narukami'. Other Indian legends are found in several stories of the "Konjakumonogatari" which derived from Jataka (the stories of the previous lives of the Buddha) in Pali as well as Avadana in Sanskrit.

Along with Buddhism, Indian gods were introduced into Japan. These gods started to be worshipped later in Buddhist rituals.

For example, Indra, originally the god of thunder and the most popular of all gods in the Rig-veda, was adored by the Japanese people under the name of Taishakuten (literally, Emperor of Gods). Ganesha, the Indian god of wisdom, who has a head of elephant with human body, was worshipped under the name of Shoten (literally, Holy God) as one who gives happiness, especially in business and love affairs. In Japan the figures of two Ganeshas, male and female, embracing each other are often found. Naga, the god of serpent was worshipped by sailors, is called Ryujin in Japanese. Vaishravana (Kubera) is equivalent to Bishamonten as the god of fortune in Japan. Even in Shinto, we can find a strong Indian influence which is still remaining in the present day.

The following gods are worshipped in the Shinto Shrines.

- Suiten (water-god), which is a Shinto name, is widely worshipped by the people in down-town Tokyo. It was originally Varuna (water-god in India) and introduced into Tantra Buddhism, and then adopted by Shinto.
- Benten (literally, Goddess of Speech) is equivalent to Sarasvati in India. The Benten shrines can be found in many places along the seacoast and around the ponds and lakes. In the shrine, the figure that a woman plays Biwa(Vina) is installed.
- Daikoku, a god of fortune (literally, god of great Darkness or Blackness) is a favourite god among the general people. The original name in Sanskrit is Mahakala, another name for Shiva, the mightiest god in Hinduism. The figure of Daikoku wears Japanese robe and holds a wooden hammer with a gentle smiling face in the Japanese shrines
- Kichijoten, the goddess of beauty, is equivalent to "Lakshmi" in India. In the sixth century, Buddhism was introduced through Korea, and the new style of painting was brought in with many other new crafts. The most prominent example of early Buddhist paintings is found on the panels of the Tamamushi-

no-Zushi shrine which was made in the reign of the Female Emperor Suiko, and is still preserved in the Golden Hall of the Horyuji temple, near Nara.

In the 8th Century, painting underwent new and noticeable development under the influence of the Indian chiaroscuro style, introduced from the Tang Dynasty of China. The best example of this style can be seen in the fresco of the Horyuji temple. The style closely resembles the wall paintings of the cave temples of Ajanta in India. The court dance and music (called "Bugaku" and "Gagaku") which were introduced into Japan in around 7th century, directly by Bodhisena, the Indian monk, and Fu-Ch'e, a Vietnamese, are preserved in their original form to this early day. The original form of musical performance is neither preserved in India at present, nor in other Asiatic countries.

It is a unique cultural property found only in Japan. From the time it was first introduced into this country, the court dance and music was given careful attention and protection by the Imperial Household. This art has been preserved through centuries as a ceremonial dance which is performed on various national celebrations and for visiting foreign diplomats. The formal stage for this art is found only in the Imperial Palace. Thus, considering such instances mentioned above, it could apparently be understood that India in her unique way has greatly influenced Japanese thought and culture that exists even today. If you want to discover thriving communities of Japanese Buddhism and Zen these days, your best bet is probably a trip to Los Angeles, New York City or Berlin, but most certainly not to Japan.

While people in the West have embraced "all things Zen," Japanese culture has moved on to more modern pastures. One of the quickest ways for a westerner to sound like a real wacko to your average Japanese person is to explain that you practice Japanese Buddhism and Zen meditation. To the Japanese ear, the earnest daily practice of Japanese Zen Buddhism is something akin to being involved in Civil War reenactments in America - it's odd, historical and makes one seem rather "out of touch." The disinterest in the role that Japanese Buddhist beliefs have played in Japanese history is related, on the whole, to the lowly place that Japan religion now holds.

And while Japanese Buddhism isn't strictly speaking a religion, it's a spiritual outlook all the same, which contrasts strongly with the affirmative materialism that now dominates Japanese culture. In much the same manner that school children in New England are herded onto buses and driven to Plymouth Plantation each fall to learn how the pilgrims made cornbread, Japanese high school students are brought to the local Japanese Buddhist temple and are made to sit zazen (sitting meditation on a cushion) and learn what a stark and disciplined life that Japanese Buddhist monks have (no cell phones or computer games!).

Much of the interest in Zen Japanese Buddhism in the West is not directly related to the work of Japanese Buddhists (an exception would be the U.S. lectures of Japanese Zen master D.T. Suzuki), but largely the result of American Beat writers like Gary Synder (who studied Zen in Japan in the 1950s) and others like Jake Kerouac and Alan Ginsberg who discovered in Buddhism a "religion" of sorts that made very few moral demands on them in the way that the Judeo-Christian tradition does. It was the writings of the Beat writers on Japanese Buddhism in particular that the bohemians and hippies of the 1960s latched onto as they rejected much of the traditions, religions and beliefs of Western culture.

In some ways the decline of Zen Japanese Buddhism is also occurring in neighboring South Korea, but in the case of Korea this is due to nearly half the population converting to Christianity since the end of World War II. The Japanese, in contrast, have shown a stubborn resistance to embracing the Christian faith. While it's true that Japan is not, strictly speaking, a Buddhist country - it has been shaped as well by the native Shinto religion, ancestor worship and Confucian ethical teachings - one can declare that the Japanese people now live, in the words of Catholic Pope John Paul II, as practical atheists.

In the years 1906 and 1913, a member of the German expedition team, Albert von Le Coq, was astounded by the beauty of the ultramarine decorating the walls of the Kizil Grottoes.

"...the extravagant use of a brilliant blue – the well-known ultramarine which, in the time of Benvenuto Cellini, was frequently employed by the Italian painters, and was bought at double its weight in gold."

The ultramarine that he praised in his book, the deep shade of blue reminiscent of the sky, was realized by the use of the precious mineral, lapis lazuli, which raw stone is said to be produced only in Afghanistan. The word "lapis lazuli" is the combination of the Latin word "lapis" meaning "stone," and the Arabic word "lazuli" meaning "sky" or "blue." The stone had been brought all the way from the west, where present Afghanistan is. It was the abundant use of this stone, deemed highly precious throughout history, which surprised Le coq.

Le Coq was surprised also by the fact that "there was ... not the slightest sign in the paintings of any East Asiatic influences" in the Kizil grottoes. Despite its geographic proximity to China, the Buddhist art there did not show any Chinese elements, but more Indian and Persian (Iranian) influence. For instance, at the time of excavation, Frieze murals with clear Sasanian (A.D.226^ÿ651) influence ran to the right and left of the great podiums, representing in pearl medallions, two Sasanian ducks facing one-another and carrying together in their beaks a jeweled necklace. Many such works created in the Indian/ Persian style following "late antique principles" were seen among the Buddhist art of the Kizil grottoes, and Le Coq praises them as the "most interesting, and artistically perfect paintings."

The great Sasanian Empire ruled the Iranian Plateau and Mesopotamia, and during its peak era, the empire is said to have extended power over Afghanistan as well. The Kizil Grottoes was a ruin "full of surprises" that presented strong influence of the distant western lands such as Persia and India, through abundant use of Afghanistan lapis lazuli0and the Persian style art.

THE STYLE AND STRUCTURE OF THE KIZIL GROTTOES

The Kizil Grottoes run along the Cliffs on the Northern Shore of Muzalt River() sixty-seven kilometers west of Kucha. Because written records or dated inscriptions have not been found providing hints on when the grottoes were begun, there is no standard theory on this point. Thus, a there is no standard theory on this point. A wide range of theories exist from those setting the beginning of the grottoes at third century, to those that do so at fifth century. However, researchers generally agree that the grottoes were probably abandoned at the beginning of eighth century after the Tang influence reached the area.

A little also is known about when the murals in the Kizil grottoes were painted. However, the German team proposed a theory categorizing the arts in the Kizil Grottoes into at least two styles, which remains prevalent to this day. The Murals Belonging to the First Phase() are characterized by use of reddish pigments. Furthermore, the lines in the paintings are drawn carefully, and shades blend smoothly in the gradations used in order to give three-dimensional appearance to the paintings. On the other hand, Murals Belonging to the Second Phase feature bluish pigments achieved by addition of lapis lazuli, and great jumps exist between the levels of shades in the gradations used to give three dimensional appearance to the body parts of the figures featured in the paintings.

As will be discussed below, many works in the Kizil Grottoes belong to style 2. Let us now consider the floor plans of the grottoes. There are three main styles; namely, the center pillar caves, rectangular caves, and monastic caves, but the plan with the most unique features are the Center Pillar Caves This floor plan consists of three areas; namely, the main room, the center pillar, and the corridor. The composition of the murals on the walls is mostly the same. The structure of the center pillar caves follows a worshipping procedure such as the one mentioned below, and functions as sort of a stage device for this procedure.

Those who enter the cave will first reminisce Buddha's past lives deeds in the main room, and whilst doing so, worship the main icon, Sakyamuni, on the centre pillar. Secondly, the individual will circle the corridor, heading right, and worships the center pillar in doing so. In the back corridor, the individual will view Sakyamuni's nirvana scene, and there, think of how his own life is destined to a Buddha-less world. Upon exiting the corridor, the worshipper will see the future Buddha Maitreya painted on the wall above the main room entrance. On the side walls of the main room, murals of various themes are painted, such as the Jâtaka depicting stories of Sakyamuni's past lives, the Illustrated Biographies of His Life, which depict the episodes from his own life, and the Preaching Scenes or featuring the different occasions after Buddha's enlightenment where he preached.

In the style characteristic to the Kizil grottoes, the vault ceilings of the main room are divided into diamond blocks, decorated with themes such as the Jâtaka and the Preacghing Scenes. The popular style for the front wall of the main pillar is to create a niche with a seated Buddha image and to cover the entire wall with stucco mountain-scape. In some cases, vestige of large scale standing image remains on the front wall. However, the images are long lost, and their original appearance remains a mystery. On the left, right, and the back of the center pillar are corridors with low ceilings, and Images of Donors, monks and stupas adorn the corridor walls.

On the back wall of the corridor behind the center pillar are either Painted Nirvana Images or stucco figures of the same theme. The Kâúyapa Image with memorable tree leaf patterns and facial expression, also painted on this wall, were originally part of the nirvana scene on the back wall of the back corridor. These images represent Mahâkâúyapa who arrived late at the scene of Buddha's nirvana, and thus failed to be there at the moment of his death. Furthermore, on the half circle above the entrance of the main room are drawn Maitreya preaching in Tucita Heaven.

KIZIL GROTTOES

The members of the German expedition team that conducted a major survey of the Kizil Grottoes, including Le Coq, left not only written records of the murals and cave structures, but also records of various nature such as measured floor plans of the caves, photographs, records on the condition of the caves, and colored sketches and line drawings of the murals. Especially, Grunwedel's Line Drawings, created by pressing thin paper directly on the paintings, are of great value and became an important material for the thorough researches by himself and Waldschmidt. Le Coq and the team members also cut out murals from the Kizil Grottoes.

The process was to "cut round" the designated area "with a very sharp knife – care being taken that the incision goes right through the surface-layer – to the proper size for the packing-cases," carefully cutting "the boundary line in curves or sharp angles to avoid going through faces or other important parts of the picture." Then, they would make a hole with "the pickaxe in the wall at the side of the painting to make space to use the fox-tail saw," and when the condition of the surface layer was bad, they would press boards covered with felt firmly onto the painting as they were being cut out.

The Paintings that the German Teams Brought Home in this method are cut into small parts due to such procedures. As a result, the walls in the Kizil grottoes are left scarred with countless blank areas where the paintings have been cut out, and where the members quit in middle of the process, with straight cuts. The paintings cut out in such processes were carried back to Germany together with Sculptures, Painted Boards, and manuscripts; a magnificent harvest for the German team, over any that they achieved in the past excavations. The result of this excavation was compiled into reports such as the seven volume Die Buddhistische Spätantike in Mittelasien, and contributed greatly to researches on the Kizil Grottoes.

KUMÂRAJÎVA'S LEGACY IN TRANSMITTING GREATER VEHICLE BUDDHISM TO EASTERN ASIA

The Kizil Grottoes are located in the present districts of Kuche and Baicheng, the former ruling grounds of the ancient kingdom of Kucha, where historically Buddhism prospered the most among the areas on the Silk Road's Northern route. Kucha at the time was a Buddhist kingdom crowded with temples and monks. The fourth century manuscript, *Chu-san-zang-ji-ji*, records how there were "over ten thousand monks in Kucha," "countless extravagantly decorated temples," and "palaces adorned with images of standing Buddha, just like temples." Furthermore, the manuscript records that there were three nunneries in Kucha with daughters of kings and nobles, and that the city functioned as one great Buddhist center in Central Asia.

It is not clear when Buddhism entered Kucha, but from what one can tell from Chinese records, already at the end of third century to the beginning of fourth century, many monks from this area seems to have been translating Buddhist canons in China. Kumârajîva (Jiumoluoshi, date of birth and death unknown) made his entrance into history around such times. Praised as one of the most famous historical figures representing Kucha, his major accomplishments are concentrated in the period between the first half of the fourth century and the first half of the fifth century. Kumârajîva, who was born a son of the royal princess of Kucha, had an Indian father. At a young age, he and his mother entered Buddhist priesthood.

He then studied small vehicle Buddhism, and at Gandhara (Kashmir, Jibin) located northwest of India, he encountered large vehicle Buddhism. Upon returning to Kucha, he dedicated himself to promoting large vehicle Buddhism, and thus was greatly admired. His fame reached past the Kucha borders, and rang throughout the Central Asian nations. *Kao-seng-chuan* book two records; "the western nations all knelt at Kumârajîva's sacred wisdom. During the annual lecture, the kings all lowered themselves before his seat, and let him step on their backs as he ascended the steps. Thus was the extent to which he was admired." Later, due to strong requests from the Chinese who heard of his fame, he would participate in the translation of sutras in Chang'an.

Chinese translations of sutras did exist in China before Kumârajîva entered Chang-an. However, these translations were achieved by simply applying vocabularies from Lao-Zhuang philosophy indigenous to China. Soon the Chinese began to realize the shortcomings of studying Buddhist canons in this manner, and began to desire translation by foreign monks with deep understanding of Buddhist vocabularies and teachings in the original texts. Thus, Kumârajîva was chosen as the perfect candidate, for not only had he acquired Sanscrit during his studies in India, but also was thoroughly familiar with greater vehicle Buddhism.

Whilst instructing his students who are said to have exceeded three thousand, he continued to translate greater vehicle Buddhist canons such as the *Smaller Sukhâvatîvyûha Sutra*, *Pañcavi úatisâhasrikâ Prajñâpâramitâ Sutra*, *Vimalakirti Sutra*, and *Mahâprajñâpâramitaœastra*. His translation of the Lotus Sutra especially, was used beyond the many other past translations. Due to Kumârajîva's superb translations, greater vehicle Buddhism spread throughout Eastern Asia, and soon propagated to the distant eastern land of Japan.

The fact that Kumârajîva's translation continues to be used in the present day Japan shows the enormity of his achievement in the full-scale propagation of greater vehicle Buddhism to the East. Not only Chinese Buddhism, but also Buddhism in nations belonging to the same strand, such as Japan, receives benefit from Buddhist culture, which was passed from west to east along the Silk Road, and Kucha, the Buddhist kingdom that prospered there. Buddhism originated in India in the 6th century BC. It consists of the teachings of the Buddha, Gautama Siddhartha. Of the main branches of Buddhism, it is the Mahayana or "Greater Vehicle" Buddhism which found its way to Japan.

Buddhism was imported to Japan via China and Korea in the form of a present from the friendly Korean kingdom of Kudara (Paikche) in the 6th century. While Buddhism was welcomed by the ruling nobles as Japan's new state religion, it did not initially spread among the common people due to its complex theories. There were also a few initial conflicts with Shinto, Japan's native religion. The two religions were soon able to co-exist and even complement each other. During the Nara Period, the great Buddhist monasteries in the capital Nara, such as Todaiji, gained strong political influence and were one of the reasons for the government to move the capital to Nagaoka in 784 and then to Kyoto in 794.

Nevertheless, the problem of politically ambitious and militant monasteries remained a main issue for the governments over many centuries of Japanese history. During the early Heian Period, two new Buddhist sects were introduced from China: the Tendai sect in 805 by Saicho and the Shingon sect in 806 by Kukai. More sects later branched off the Tendai sect. Among these, the most important ones are mentioned below:

In 1175, the Jodo sect (Pure Land sect) was founded by Honen. It found followers among all different social classes since its theories were simple and based on the principle that everybody can achieve salvation by strongly believing in the Buddha Amida. In 1224, the Jodo-Shinshu (True Pure Land sect) was founded by Honen's successor Shinran. The Jodo sects continue to have millions of followers today.

In 1191, the Zen sect was introduced from China. Its complicated theories were popular particularly among the members of the military class. According to Zen teachings, one can achieve self enlightenment through meditation and discipline. At present, Zen seems to enjoy a greater popularity overseas than within Japan.

The Lotus Hokke or Nichiren sect, was founded by Nichiren in 1253. The sect was exceptional due to its intolerant stance towards other Buddhist sects. Nichiren Buddhism still has many millions of followers today, and several "new religions" are based on Nichiren's teachings.

Oda Nobunaga and Toyotomi Hideyoshi fought the militant Buddhist monasteries (especially the Jodo sects) at the end of the 16th century and practically extinguished Buddhist influence on the political sector. Buddhist institutions were attacked again in the early years of the Meiji Period, when the new Meiji government favored Shinto as the state religion and tried to separate and emancipate it from Buddhism. Nowadays about 90 million people consider themselves Buddhists in Japan. However, the religion does not directly affect the everyday life of the average Japanese very strongly. Funerals are usually carried out in a Buddhist way, and many households keep a small house altar in order to pay respect to their ancestors.

To some extent, Japanese Buddhism can be thought of as a series of imports from China. Over the centuries, starting as early as 500 C.E., both lay devotees and monks traveled to the mainland, bringing back with them layer after layer of Buddhist teachings and practices along with other Chinese cultural traditions. At the same time however, as the religion developed in Japan, it often did so along paths not followed on the mainland.

The official story of the arrival of Buddhism to Japan states that a political delegation arrived from Korea in 538 C.E. Among the gifts it brought for the Emperor were a bronze Buddha image, some sutras, a few religious objects and a letter warmly praising the most excellent Dharma. After initial opposition, the gifts were accepted, and a temple was built to house the objects. However, an epidemic which ravaged the land was interpreted as bringing the wrath of the indigenous kami (Japanese Shinto deities) down on the nation. This led to the objects being thrown into a canal and the temple being destroyed.

Nevertheless, during the course of the next half century, Japan witnessed the firm establishment of Buddhism as a religion officially recognized and actively supported by the imperial court, thus overcoming doubts about its efficacy as a means of preventing disease, and also overcoming the fear of the national kami. In these early days, the most important aspect with regard to the flow of Chinese culture into Japan was the introduction of the Chinese script. This provided the means for the Japanese (who did not possess an indigenous writing system of their own) to assimilate the vast tradition of Chinese classics, and the Chinese version of the Buddhist canon. Only very few imported Chinese texts were translated into Japanese; most have continued throughout their history to be used in their original version.

The main three characteristics of the arrival of Buddhism in Japan are as follows.

Firstly, it did not come to Japan on a popular level, but was only accepted by the imperial court and then disseminated in the country from the top. Often, Buddhist faith in Japan is connected with absolute devotion to a leader with emphasis on veneration of the founders of sects, and the majority of sects keep close relations to the central governmental authority of their times.

Secondly, Buddhism was often associated with magic powers, and was used by the court as a means of preventing or curing disease, bringing rain and abundant crops etc.

Thirdly, Buddhism did not replace the indigenous kami, but always recognized their existence and power. This led to numerous varieties of Shinto-Buddhist amalgamation, in which often the kami were considered manifestations of the Buddhas. This is typical of how Buddhism favours harmonious coexistence with indigenous beliefs, and it was to be a similar story when Buddhism subjugated local gods and spirits in Tibet a few centuries later.

During the course of the development of Buddhism in Japan, the prevailing tendency is to search for fulfillment and ultimate truth, not in any transcendental sphere, but within the structure of secular life, neither denying nor repressing man's natural feelings, desires or customs. This perhaps explains why many Japanese arts and skills are pervaded by Buddhist spirituality. Well known examples being the tea ceremony, the arts of gardening, calligraphy and the No play.

The initial period saw the introduction onto Japanese soil of the six great Chinese schools, including the Hua-Yen and Lu, that became respectively the Kegon and Ritsu in Japanese. In terms of geography, the six sects were centered around the capital city of Nara, where great temples such as the Todäiji and Hokkeji were erected. However, the Buddhism of this early period – later known as the Nara period – was not a practical religion, being more the domain of learned preists whose official function was to pray for the peace and prosperity of the state and imperial house.

This kind of Buddhism had little to offer the illiterate and uneducated masses, and led to the growth of "people's priests" who were not ordained and had no formal Buddhist training. Their practice was a combination of Buddhist and Taoist elements, and the incorporation of shamanistic features of the indigenous religion. These figures became immensely popular, and were a source of criticism towards the sophisticated academic and bureaucratic Buddhism of the capital.

HEIAN PERIOD (794-1185)

In 794, the imperial palace of Japan moved to Kyoto, and it is from this date that important changes and developments take place which result in the emergence of a more characteristically Japanese form of Buddhism. Two schools – the Tendai and the Shingon – particularly came to the fore, in time supplanting the other established schools, and laying the foundations for future developments. Two monks, Saicho (767 – 822) and Kukai (774 – 835), effected this change which so decisively affected the future of Japanese Buddhism. By their comprehensive syntheses of the Chinese doctrine, two systems of teaching and practice were created, which effectively furnished all the essentials for the entire further development of Japanese Buddhism.

Saicho, the founding father of the Tendai School, entered the sangha at an early age. After years of study and practice, he became especially partial to the teachings of the Chinese grand master Chih-

I and the T'ien-t'ai School, which were based on the Lotus Sutra. In 804, he went to China, and returned with an improved knowledge of various teachings and practices, along with many sutras. He established his base on Mount Hiei, and received permission to ordain two novices every year. Official recognition of his Tendai sect soon followed, and it became one of the two dominating schools of Japanese Buddhism during the Heian period.

The teachings of Chih-I form a far-reaching synthesis of Buddhist tradition inspired by the Lotus Sutra, and Saicho was to add three further elements: the practice of Chinese Ch'an; the commandments of the Mahayana which are based in essentials on the Bonmokyo, and parts of the esoteric teaching of the "True Word", Chen-yen (Shingon in Japanese). All this helped to make a decisive step away from the academic Buddhism of the early period, to a revived active kind of religion based on belief. An essential element in the doctrine of the Tendai was the teaching in the Lotus Sutra that the possibility of salvation is given to all.

Kukai and his secret doctrine, known as the True Word, Shingon, had a mysterious radiance, which encouraged the formation of legends about him. During his early studies in Buddhism, Taoism and Confucianism he came to know one of the principal texts of the esoteric canon, the Mahavairocana Sutra, but did not reach a deeper understanding of it. In 804, he traveled to China where all his doubts and questions with regard to the sutra were resolved; he returned to Japan with many new skills and instructions to impart. He founded his headquarters on Mount Koya on the Kii peninsular. His career was successful to the extent that he was allowed to build a Shingon temple in the emperor's palace, where he performed esoteric rituals and ceremonies. In 835, Kukai sitting in deep meditation fell into complete silence.

In the eyes of his devotees he is not dead, but still sits in timeless meditation on Mount Koya. Esoteric practices were very influential to the point that they dominated the Heian period, and had a decisive influence on the subsequent Kamakura period. Even the more philosophical Tendai School adopted esoteric rituals in order to make it more popular with the general population, whilst figures such as Kukai succeeded by means of esoteric rites in making rain after a time of drought, giving Buddhist esotericism a magical attraction. Towards the end of the Heian, the dissemination of more popular devotional forms of Buddhism began, which were mainly derived from the Pure Land cult of Amitabha (Amida in Japanese).

This was connected with the somewhat pessimistic philosophy of a deteriorating "final period of the dharma", which became widespread during this time. The devotional cults basically propounded the notion that salvation was only possible through the intercession of buddhas and bodhisattvas, for example through the recitation and repetition of simple formula such as the Namu-Amida-butsu (the Nembutsu – "thinking on the Buddha"). There were other faith-based doctrines during this time, the most noteworthy being the belief in the bodhisattva Jizo, who dispenses help to beings on all levels of existence and it is still alive today.

KAMAKURA PERIOD (1185-1333)

From the end of the 11th century, a new military aristocracy in the provinces increasingly evaded the control of the central government, culminating in war between the Taira and Minamoto families. The latter were victorious and thereby acquired absolute power of the country, setting up a military government in Kamakura in the vicinity of present-day Tokyo. Minamoto-no Yoritomo received the title of Shogun with supreme military and police power, thus transferring rule from the court aristocracy to those of the warrior class (samurai). Inevitably, this was to change the whole cultural climate. This new climate did not favour the study of abstruse philosophy or the performance of elaborate rituals, so more robust and generally accessible teachings became the order of the day.

The *Tendai* and *Shingon* schools declined, and more earthy democratic movements such as Zen and the devotional schools advanced. The first of the three great traditions of Kamakura

Buddhism, the doctrine of the Pure Land, continued the development which had begun in the Heian period. There was the founding of an independent Japanese sect of the Pure Land known as *Jodo-shu* by Genku (1133-1212), better known as Honen. He decided that Enlightenment was no longer achievable by the strength man alone, and that the only possible way was to surrender to Buddha Amida and rebirth into the *Western Paradise Pure Land.* New in Honen's philosophy was that, while he recognized the scholastic apparatus of Mahayana philosophy, he concentrated on an intensified religious feeling which found expression in the simple invocation of the name Namu-Amida-Butsu, stamped by unshakeable faith in rebirth into Amida's paradise.

Honen's successor, Shinran-Shonin (1173-1262) founded the *True Sect of the Pure Land, Jodo-shinshu,* which is the largest Buddhist sect in Japan today. In his chief work written in 1224, he explains that the doctrine, practice, belief and realization are all given by Amida Buddha and that nothing depends on man's "own power" (jiriki). Instead, everything depends on the "power of the other" (tariki), namely that of the Buddha Amida. Shinran emphasized that the recitation of the Namu-Amida-butsu was simply the expression of thankfu joy for having received everything from Amida. It is worth noting that Shinran was a monk who decided to take a wife, with which he had five children, and thus he symbolizes a decisive turn in Japan towards lay Buddhism.

He stressed that obedience to the Buddhist commandments and the performance of good deeds were not necessary to obtain deliverance; in fact it is precisely the bad man who can be assured of rebirth in Amida's paradise if he wholeheartedly appeals to Amida. While belief in Amida proceeds from the "strength of the other" (tariki), Zen Buddhism teaches that man can come to deliverance and Enlightenment only from his own strength (jiriki). Zen (Chinese Ch'an, from Pali, jhana and Sanskrit, dhyana) places supreme emphasis on self-power: on the active mobilization of all one's energies towards the realization of the ideal of enlightenment.

There had been contacts between Japan and Zen doctrine since the 7th century. However, a lasting tradition that concentrated on Zen practice and led to the formation of a separate sect, was first created by the Tendai monk Eisai (1141-1215). During his studies in China, he had been introduced to the practice and doctrine of a branch of Zen which went back to Lin-chi (called Rinzai in Japanese), and on his return to Japan he started to disseminate the new doctrine. Eisai established firm relations with the new military government in Kamakura and the military caste that held sway there. They found the simple, hard and manly discipline of Zen more to their taste than the ritual and dogma of the old schools. In contrast to this, Zen Buddhism was greeted with less enthusiasm by the intellectual elite of cities such as Kyoto.

There, established practice was represented by Tendai, Shingon and Pure Land with their beautiful rituals. The fierce demands of Zen, with its emphasis on personal effort and the promise of enlightenment rather than heaven, seemed rebarbative and disturbing to the elite. Eisai is also linked to the introduction of tea drinking in Japan, which in time was to lead to the creation of the "tea-way" which, though non-religious, was strongly influenced by the spirit of Zen and the Tea Ceremony. In general, the monks involved in the transmission of Zen from China to Japan also transmitted Neo-Confucian values and ideas, which were themselves strongly influenced by Ch'an Buddhism and Hua-yen philosophy.

The Zen masters added a Confucian moral to Buddhist spirituality, which appealed to the new warrior-class of the Kamakura. For many centuries, the big Rinzai temples in Japan were centres of Chinese learning in general, and Neo-Confucianism in particular. Furthermore, the Rinzai school is closely associated with Japanese arts and the "ways" – the aforementioned "tea way", the "flower way", the "way of archery" and others. A second Chinese school of Zen, the Ts'ao-tung (Soto in Japanese), introduced to Japan by Dogen (1200-1253). After four years of training in China under Master Ju-ching, Dogen returned to Japan in 1227, and eventually established the Eihei-ji temple in a remote province, which to this day remains one of the two main temples of the Japanese Soto Zen school.

The foundation of Dogen's Zen is the constantly emphasized principle that practice does not lead to Enlightenment, but is carried out *in the state of being Enlightened*; otherwise it is not practice. In a logically constructed picture of the world, he equates all being – the believer, his practice and the world – with the present moment, the moment of enlightenment. Striving for enlightenment would therefore be going astray. Dogen's chief work was the Shobogenzo (The Eye and Treasury of the True Dharma). After Pure Land and Zen, the final great reformer and sect-founder of the Kamakura period was Nichiren (1222-82). After studying in Kamakura and training in Tendai doctrine and practice, he came to the conclusion that the highest, all-embracing truth lay in the Lotus Sutra, known in Japan as the Myoho-renge-kyo, the fundamental canonical text of the Tendai sect.

However, Nichiren thought that for the simple ordinary person, Tendai dogma and the reading of the Lotus Sutra were too difficult. He proclaimed that the title, Myoho-renge-kyo, was the essence of the whole sutra, and that it was in fact identical with the state of Enlightenment of Shakyamuni Buddha. It was therefore sufficient to utter the title and find oneself in the state of highest enlightenment. This condition gave rise spontaneously to morally right behaviour, so that it was necessary for the state and society that all should follow the practice of the "invocation of the title."

Two issues isolated Nichiren: the militant style of his presentation, and his insistence that the Lotus Sutra should inform the practice of government. He constantly made his views public, and the hot worded language which he used spared neither secular nor Buddhist establishments, and led to his eventual banishment to the island of Izu. He was soon pardoned, but his continued attacks on institutions so provoked government and clergy that he was sentenced to be executed. According to legend, the axe which was raised to behead him was struck by lightning. Off the hook, he again went into exile and further developed his writings. When he finally returned to the mainland, he devoted himself to his missionary activity and to the training of monks on Mount Minobu, until today the main temple of the Nichiren sect. In recent times, certain branches of Nichiren have been connected to nationalistic tendencies within Japan.

Later Periods

The demise of the Kamakura regime inaugurated a new era of internal strife and fighting in Japan, which was to last into the seventeenth century. It also signaled the end of the truly creative phase of Japanese Buddhism. A slide into stagnation occurred, which was to broadly last until the end of the nineteenth century. According to the twentieth century Zen writer D.T. Suzuki, after the Kamakura period "what followed was more or less the filling-in and working out of details."

In the 14th and 15th centuries, the privileged relations of the Rinzai Zen sect with the military government permitted it to gain tremendous wealth. This led to the creation of what is known as the "Culture of the Five Mountains" which constitutes the summit of Japanese Zen culture. It included all the arts, such as architecture, painting, calligraphy and sculpture, as well as printing, gardening and medicine. Ikkyu (1394-1481), a priest of the Rinzai sect, was particularly known for his unconventional character, and he was an accomplished poet, calligrapher and painter.

The Tokugawa Shogunate was to rule Japan from its bastion in Edo (Tokyo) for over two and a half centuries. It was to be the longest period of peace, and for the most part, prosperity in the history of the country. This was basically achieved by closing the country to the outside world, and establishing a regime of inflexible authoritarian control that created stability and order, but stifled all creative change and innovation. The Buddhist clergy was under the strict control of the government, and it was forbidden to found a new sect or build a new temple without special permission.

The Shogunate encouraged the Buddhist clergy of the sects in scholarly pursuits, hoping thereby to divert them from politics. Therefore a huge amount of learned literature was produced, and by the second half of the seventeenth century, editions of the Buddhist canon appeared, the most influential being that by Tetsugen of the new Obaku-shu sect.

Obaku-shu had been founded by the Chinese master Yin-yuan Lung-ch'i, a Rinzai Zen priest. It added a new flavour to Japanese Zen, not only by its syncretism (it contained elements of Pure Land Buddhism), but also by the introduction of rituals, customs and a new architectural style imported from Ming China.

From the Zen school during this period, a few influential figures did emerge, the poet Basho and the Rinzai Zen masters Bankei and Hakuin being chief among them. Matsuo Basho (1644-94) was a poet who consciously transformed the practice of poetry into an authentic religious way; many of his finest poems (seventeen syllable *haiku* form) are thought to succinctly catch the elusive, often melancholy magic of the passing moment, and thereby express the true spirit of Zen. Bankei (1622-93) was an iconoclast who challenged orthodox Zen teaching. He spent many years intensively pursuing Enlightenment, and then at last he realized that he had been in possession of what he had been seeking all along, and decided that the term Un-born best described it. He thereafter advocated that people simply awaken to the unborn in the midst of everyday affairs, and he won himself a large audience which did not go down well with the Zen establishment.

Hakuin (1685-1768) is considered to be the restorer of the Rinzai sect in modern times. He revived the use of the koan, statements of Zen masters that are used as problems set to novices in Zen monasteries. They cannot be solved by rational thinking, and are designed to help open the mind to Enlightenment. Hakuin invented many new koans himself, adapted to the need of the times, in that they do not presuppose any scholarly knowledge of the Chinese Zen classics. His most famous koan being, "The sound produced by the clapping of two hands is easy to perceive, but what is the sound produced by one hand only?"

The restoration of the imperial regime in 1868 signaled the end of Japanese isolation. The pressure on Japan to reopen her doors simply becoming too great. There followed a temporary persecution of Buddhism when Shinto was made a state cult, however Buddhism was too firmly established in the affections of the Japanese people for this to last for long, and its religious freedom was effectively soon regained. For the first time in centuries, contact was made with other Buddhist countries, along with Western ones as well, and this served to encourage Buddhist scholarship, and various Buddhist universities were established by the first half of the twentieth century.

During the last 50 years, the evolution of Buddhism has been closely linked to Japan's history. The grip of the government during the Second World War over Buddhist institutions was rigid, and any writings in which Buddhism was placed above the authority of the state or the emperor were suppressed. The only opposition to this came from the Soka-gakkai, founded in 1930 as a non-religious society of teachers, and they were severely persecuted. Since the end of the war, Buddhism in Japan has once again revived, and there has been the foundation of many new sects, along with an ongoing reinvigoration as a result from sustained contacts with other peoples and cultures. Japanese Zen has also been successfully exported to many Western countries, in particular North America.

Buddhism was brought to Japan from China at different periods by various individuals whose studies and practice differ widely. Buddhism as practiced in Japan has been shaped by Japanese cultural practices and values and has developed differently from Buddhism practiced elsewhere in Asia. In Japan, Zen Buddhism has become one of the major forms of Buddhist practice and is the most well-known form of Japanese Buddhism outside of Japan.

Buddhism was first introduced into Japan from Korea in the year 522. As a foreign religion, it first met with resistence but it was recognized in 585 by emperor Yomei. During the period of government of Prince Shotoku (593-621) it was the official religion of Japan. Shotoku fostered the study of Buddhist scriptures and founded Horyu-ji in Nara among other temples. During this period it was primarily the Sanron school that spread.

During the Nara period (710-794) there were already six schools of Buddhism in Japan: Kosha, Hosso, Sanron, Jojitsu, Ritsu and Kegon. It was firmly established in the imperial house which expecially took the teachings of the Kegon school as the basis of its government. The "Sutra of Golden Light "was of particular importance.

During the Heian period (794-1184) the Tendai and Shingon schools gained influence and became the dominant forms of Buddhism in Japan and became the *de facto* tate religion. Around the middle of the 10th century Amidism began to spread and in the Kamakura period (1185-1333) it was organized into the Jodo-shu and Jodo-shinshu. In 1191 Zen came to Japan and has remained until today the most vital form of Japanese Buddhism, two main schools are Soto and Rinzai.

In the 13th century the Nichiren school emerged. In the 19th century Shintoism was elevated to the state religion. After the Second World War there was a renaissance of Buddhism in Japan and a whole series of popular movements have arisen: Soka Gakkai, Rissho Koseikai and Nipponzan Myohoji, to name a few, which have adapted Buddhism to modern times.

Buddhism began with the experiences of a man who is known mainly as the Buddha (Butsu - the enlightened one, Shakyamuni — the sage of the Shakya clan, Siddhartha Gautama —personal name) (b 563 B.C. died at age 84). The philosophy/religion is based on his teachings after his experience of being enlightened [*satori*–(*kenshô jobutsu* "seeing one's own true nature") enlightenment – awakening – an understanding of the entire universe, emptiness and phenomena are one. *satoru*– to know.] It is often not considered a religion because there is no god. There are powerful beings who are petitioned for assistance in reaching this goal but they are not identified as gods.

The term *butsu*or buddha is used to refer to anyone who is aware or enlightened as to the true nature of existence. All people are *hotoke* — buddhas.Shakyamuni is the historical buddha for this age. Kâshyapa — buddha of past ages (there are 6 buddhas of earlier epochs). Maitreya (Miroku) — future buddha, associated with the attribute of wisdom. The main ideas of the philosophy are to be found in the Taishô issaikyô (Tripitaka, three baskets). The Japanese is a modern version of the Buddhist canon which consists of 1) Vinaya — pitaka accounts of origins of Buddhism, 2) sutra-pitaka — teachings of the Buddha, 3) abhidharma-pitaka — compendium of buddhist psychology and philosophy.

Three main sutras:

- Lotus sutra – transcendental nature of Buddha and possibility of universal liberation. Discourse of the Buddha at Vulture Peak.
- Heart Sutra – "form is no other than emptiness, emptiness is no other than form" *Maka hanya haramita shingyo*. Essential teaching of non-duality.
- Diamond Sutra - all phenomena are not ultimate reality but rather illusions, projections of one's own mind.

Two main branches of Buddhism developed over time through the transmission of Buddhist teachings to other cultures. They are similar in many respects in understanding of Buddha's teaching and differ mainly with respect to the goal of Buddhist practice. Mahayana defines the goal as the liberation of all beings and Hinayana focuses on one's own liberation. As a result, Mahayana has identified individuals (*bodhisattva* and *rakan*) who have delayed their own liberation from *samsara* and assist others in their practice.

Hinayaya, sometimes referred to as Theravada after the remaining school in this branch, is found in Burma, Thailand, Vietnam. Mahayana is found in Tibet, Mongolia, China, Korea, Japan.

rakan (*lohan, arhat*) individual who has attained enlightenment by own effort.

bosatsu (*bodhisattva*) — a being who seeks buddhahood through special practice of perfect virtues but renounces complete entry into nirvana until all beings are saved — exhibits compassion (*karuna*) and insight or wisdom (*prajna*). There are 6 transcendental perfections (*parmitas*) that identify a *boddhisattva*:: generosity, discipline, patience, energy, meditation, wisdom. Latter four additional ones were added: right method or means, vow, manifestation of 10 powers, knowledge of the true definition of all dharmas (laws).

Four Great Bodhisattva:

- Jizo (Kshitigarbha) "womb of the earth" venerated as a savior from the torments of hell, especially for children and as a protector of travelers. Currently identified as a protector of aborted fetuses. The only bodhisattva depicted as a monk.
- Fugen (Samantabhadra) Represents the power of wisdom to overcome all obstructions. He is depicted riding on an elephant. He is the protector of all those who teach the dharma and is an embodiment of the wisdom of essential sameness.
- Monju (Manjushri) "He who is noble and gentle" He is the embodiment of wisdom.

There are some basic ideas of Buddhism found in all schools. The goal of spiritual practice is *nirvana* — 'extinction' the goal of spiritual practice, release for the cycle of rebirths and entry into a new mode of existence. Overcoming desire, hatred and delusion, freedom from the determining effect of karma. In Mahayana this also means a oneness with the absolute, freedom from attachment to delusion, and the affects of desires. It is the cessation of suffering. In Hinayana, there are two types: 1) can be attained before death, 2) attained at death.

Three attributes of everything existing:

1. Non-self (*anatman*) no self exists in the sense of a permanent eternal integral and independent substance with individual existence. (In Hinduism, this non-self is the real immortal self of human beings which is part of the larger realism of the universe. The ego is transitory, changeable and prone to suffering.)
2. Impermanence (*anitya*) fundamental property of everything. It is the basis of life.
3. Suffering (*duhkha*) suffering characterizes all things. It arises because of desire, craving.

gôKarma — the universal law of cause and effect. The effect of actions is necessarily one or more rebirths that together constitute the cycle of existence. The effect of an action, which can be of the nature of body, speech or mind, is not primarily determined by the act itself but rather particularly by the intention of the action. It is the intention of actions that cause a karmic effect. When a deed cannot be carried out but the intention toward it exists, this alone produces an effect. Only a deed that is free from desire, hate and delusion is without karmic effects. In order to be liberated from the cycle of rebirth, one must refrain from both 'good' and 'bad' deeds. It is not deterministic and you cannot predict the future based on actions.

shôji (*samsara*) the world in which we live governed by the cycle of rebirth, journeying, the phenomenal world, the chain of existence.

hô (*dharma*) — law of karmically determined rebirth.

mayoi (*maya*, delusion) — deception, illusion, appearance, belief in something that contradicts reality

Sambô - Three Jewels (Refuges) 1. Buddha, 2. Dharma 3) Sangha. These are the way a person can become free of the effect or karma.

Amida (Amitâbha) another way of referring to Buddha.

mara — murder, destruction, death.

chakra body energy system points where soul and body connect, centers of consciousness.

dana — gift, alms, donation, voluntary giving material energy or wisdom to others.

swastika — a Buddhist symbol.

mantra — a technique for concentration and meditation, involving the repetition of syllables such as the *nembutsu*..

SCHOOLS OF BUDDHISM IN JAPAN

- Kegon (School of the Flower Garden) established at Todaiji in Nara brought to Japan from China by Shen-hsiang (Shinshô)around 740. Established the relationship of Buddhism to the state.
- Shingon (School of the True Word) founded in Japan by KûKai (Kôbô Daishi) (774-835) settled on Mt Koya. Truth is passed secretly from teacher to student. The three secrets: body, speech and mind, are the ways in which the student can come to understand the truth. KûKai introduced the Shinto deities into Buddhism. *Ryobu-shintô*: Shintô gods were shown to be manifestations of Buddhist saints.
- Tendai (Celestial Platform) Chinese T'ien-Tai brought to Japan by Saichô, established at Mt Hiei in 8th century. No difference between the Chinese and Japanese forms of Buddhism which is based on the Lotus Sutra. The temple on Mt. Hiei founded by Ennin in Kyoto is the main location for this school.

- Nichiren Shu "School of the Lotsu of the Sun" founded by Nichiren (1222-1282) Teaching is based on the Lotus sutra. The recitation of "namu myoho renge kyô" if said with complete devotion can realize buddhahood. The school venerates the three mysteries: the *mandala (go-honzon), daimoku* the title of the sutra itself and third the *kaidan,* a sacred shelf. Numerous schools have developed in Japan based on Nichiren's teaching. One of the most important of these in modern Japan is Sôka Gakkai – founded in 1930 by Makiguchi Tsunesaburo (1871-1944) a follower of Nichren Buddhism. An aggressive form of Buddhism that actively seeks converts (*shokubutsu*). The leader was arrested for refusal to participate in Shintô rites. It is known as NSA (Nichiren Shoshu America) and founded but later separated from the political party Kômeito.
- Jôdô (Pure Land) established by Honen (1133-1212) one of the schools of the "easy path" or *tariki* (outside assistance, as compared to Zen and other schools which rely on *jiriki* or one's own efforts) based on faith and reliance on the Buddha through recitation of the *nembutsu*: *"namu amida butsu"* There are 5 pure lands which correspond to the 5 directions. The pure land is a stage before entering nirvana, after which it is not possible to retrogress. These are states of mind not places.
- Jôdô Shin Shu (New School of Pure Land) founded by Shinran (1173-1262) Honganji and Otani temples are the main branches of this school. This school has dropped monasticism. Its followers may marry. Liberation is to be attained exclusively through the help and grace of Buddha Amida.
- Zen – no ritual, no texts. Zen practices meditation as a means to enlightenment.

Daruma (Bodhidharma) First Chinese Ch'an (Zen) patriarch, 28th after Shakyamuni Founded the school in China in the 6th century and is considered an important person in the development of Japanese practice. In Japan there are two main schools Rinzai and Soto. They are similar in teachings but differ slightly in practice. Rinzai zen uses the *kôan* as a major teaching technique but Soto zen emphasizes *mokushô* (no reliance on words) and the practice of *dokusan* (meeting of a zen student with the master) has died out.

- Rinzai Enni Ben'in (Shoichi Kokushi 1202-1280) founder. He went to China to study and returned in 1241, established Tofukji in 1255, Kenninji in Kyoto. This school has two main lineages Yôgi and Oryo Musô Soseki – (1275-1351) wandering monk, aboot of Tenryu-ji most known for garden design. Daito Kokushi –(Myôcho Shûhô) founder of Daitokuji in Kyoto in 1319.
- Sôtô Dôgen Zenji (1200-1253) Eiheiji (1243) brought the practice to Japan.
- Obaku – this school is a subsidiary of Rinzai and has one temple, Manpuku-ji in Uji. Founded in the 17th century, mainly known for its relationship to *osencha* (style of tea ceremony).

Three Pillars of Zen:

- *dai gidan* – 'great doubt' - state of perplexity, inquiry, self-questioning.
- *dai funshi* – inflexible determination to dispel 'great doubt'
- *dai shinkon* – 'great root of faith'

Terms for Important Concepts in Zen:

- *zazen*- meditative practice, a state of thought-free, alertly wakeful attention. Sitting in this manner brings the mind f the sitter to a state of totally contentless wakefulness from which in a sudden breakthrough of enlightenment the sitter can realize his/her own true nature. All delusions are eliminated.

- *Seiza* – sitting in silence, sitting on one's heels on the floor.
- *Sanmai* – non-dualistic consciousness, the experiencing 'subject' becomes one with the experienced 'object.'
- *kû* (*shunyata*) void, emptiness.
- *kyô* (sutra) – prose texts of the teachings of the Buddha. In Zen they are primarily chanted rather than analyzed and discussed
- *dôjô* – room for practice of zen or other spiritual-practice trainings.
- *enso* – circle – symbol of truth, reality.
- *kôan* – a paradox, which transcends the logical or conceptual and points to the natured of ultimate reality. It is not a riddle. It requires a leap to another level of comprehension. It has been used since the 10th century as a training technique.
- *komusô* – wandering monk (depicted with flute and bamboo hat) follower of the Fuke school of Zen established in Kamakura by Kakushin. This school has been prohibited in the Meiji period.
- *anjin* – "peace of mind" *Zazen* leads to this.
- *roshi* – master, teacher of Buddhism.
- *niwa zume* – the time in which a person who has requested admittance to a monastery after initial rejection is left standing at the gate.

U.S. TEACHERS OF ZEN

Zen is probably the best known form of Buddhism in the United States and this is due to the work of two teachers: Suzuki Daisetsu Teitaro (1876-1966) a lay follower fo shaku Sôen of Enjaku-ji in Kamakura. He received zen training but was not confirmed as a Zen master. His books published in English did much to spread interest in Zen in the U.S. and Suzuki Shunryû (1905-1971) Sôtô school He came to the U.s. in 1958 and founded several Zen Centers including the center in San Francisco and at Tassajara, California.

2

Buddhist Culture in Korea

South Korea, officially the Republic of Korea (ROK) and often referred to as Korea is a country in East Asia, occupying the southern half of the Korean Peninsula. Also known as the "Land of the Morning Calm", it is neighbored by China to the west, Japan to the east and borders North Korea to the north. Its capital is Seoul, the second largest metropolitan city in the world and a major global city. South Korea lies in a temperate climate region with a predominantly mountainous terrain. Its territory covers a total area of 100,032 square kilometers and has a population of almost 50 million, making it one of the most densely populated regions in the world. South Korea is a presidential republic consisting of 16 administrative divisions.

Archaeological findings indicate that the Korean Peninsula was occupied by humans as early as the Lower Paleolithic period. Korea first began with the founding of Gojoseon kingdom in 2333 BCE by Dangun, making it one of the oldest civilizations in the world. Following the unification of North and South States period under Goryeo 936 AD, Korea went through the Goryeo and Joseon Dynasty as one nation until the end of the Korean Empire in 1910. After liberation and division, South Korea was established in 1948 as a democracy. Following the Korean War, the South Korean economy grew significantly, transforming the country into a major global economy.

South Korea is a developed country with a high standard of living. It has the fourth largest economy in Asia and the 15th largest in the world. It is also the second largest advanced economy in Asia, classified by the IMF and CIA. South Korea is one of the world's top ten exporters, and is a leader in technologically advanced goods such as electronics, automobiles, ships, machinery, petrochemicals and robotics, headed by Samsung, LG and Hyundai-Kia. South Korea is a member of the United Nations, WTO, OECD and G-20 major economies. It is also a founding member of APEC and the East Asia Summit, and a major non-NATO ally of the United States. More recently, South Korean culture has gained international interest, a trend known as the Korean wave.

Korea, South, officially known as the Republic of Korea, country in northeastern Asia that occupies the southern portion of the Korean Peninsula. South Korea is bounded on the north by North Korea; on the east by the Sea of Japan; on the southeast and south by the Korea Strait, which separates it from Japan; and on the west by the Yellow Sea. It has a total area of about 98,480 sq km (about 38,023 sq mi), including numerous offshore islands in the south and west, the largest of which is Cheju (area, 1829 sq km/ 706 sq mi). The state of South Korea was established in 1948 following the post-World War II partitioning of the peninsula between the occupying forces of the United States in the south and the Union of Soviet Socialist Republics (USSR) in the north. The capital and largest city of South Korea is Seoul.

In order to understand Korean Buddhism, we must first take a look at its history. Introduced from China in 372 A.D., Buddhism combined with indigenous Shamanism. During the Three Kingdoms period, Buddhism slowly developed. After the unification of the peninsula in 668 by Shilla, the golden age of the unified Shilla Period (668-935) was followed by ritualistic Koryo (935-1392). Persecution ran high in the Choson Period as Neo Confucianism gained the favour of the ruling families. In 1945, after thirty-six years, the Japanese colonization of Korea came to an end: Korean Buddhism underwent a renewal.

SHAMANISM AND BUDDHISM

When Buddhism was first introduced to Korea from China in 372 A.D., Shamanism was the indigenous religion. Shamanism is the ancient religion of animism and nature-spirit worship. The origin of Shamanism in Korea is unknown. It is based on the belief that human beings as well as natural forces and inanimate objects al possess spirits. Since Buddhism was not seen to be in conflict with the rites of nature worship, it was able to naturally blend in with Shamanism. And so many of the special mountains believed to be the residence of spirits in pre-Buddhist times soon became the sites of Buddhist temples.

Korean Shamanism regarded three spirits with special reverence and importance: the Mountain Spirit, *Sanshin* (who is usually depicted as an old man with a tiger at his feet), *Toksong*, or the *Recluse*, and *Ch'ilsong* (the spirit of the seven stars, the Big Dipper). Buddhism accepted and absorbed these three spirits and, even today, special shrines are set aside for them in most temples. The Mountain Spirit, in particular, receives due veneration following the ceremonies honoring the Buddha in the main hall. This is in case the local mountain spirits, on whose land the temple stands, should become angry. And thus Chinese Buddhism blended with Korean Shamanism to produce a unique form: Korean Buddhism. As in other Buddhist countries, the fundamental teachings of the Buddha remained the same, even though the form was uniquely Korean.

THE THREE KINGDOMS PERIOD

In the 4th century A.D., at the time when Buddhism was first introduced to Korea, the Korean peninsula was divided into three separate kingdoms: Koguryo, Paekje and Shilla. Buddhism arrived first in the northern kingdom of Koguryo and gradually spread to Paekje, in the southwest, finally reaching southeastern Shilla in the 5th century A.D.

KOGURYO

In 372 A.D., a monk was invited from China to the northern Kingdom of Koguryo. He brought Chinese texts and statutes with him. Buddhism was quickly accepted by the Koguryo royalty and their subjects. The Buddhism in China at that time, was elementary in form. The people believed in the law of cause and effect - "as you sow, so shall you reap" - and the search for happiness. This simple philosophy had much in common with the indigenous Shaman beliefs and may have been a reason for the quick assimilation of Buddhism by the people of Koguryo.

PAEKJE

Buddhism was carried from Koguryo to the southwestern kingdom of Paekje in 384 A.D. and there, too, the royal family received it. The teaching seems to have been similar to that in Koguryo. King Asin (392-450 A.D.), for example. Proclaimed that Korean "people should believe in Buddhism and seek happiness".

During the reign of King Song (523-554 A.D.) there is record of a monk, Kyomik, returning from India with new texts. He is considered the founder of one of the main schools of Buddhism of that period. Beginning to 530 A.D., Korean monks traveled to Japan to teach the Japanese people about Buddhism. Architects and painters often accompained the monks. These craftsmen constructed great temples in Japan.

KAYA

For a short time, a small, separate federation known as Kaya emerged. Situated on the southern coast between mighty Paekje and fast-growing Shilla, Jaya could not repel an invasion in the mid-sixth century. And thus the federation fell before reaching full maturity and was annexed to Shilla.

SHILLA

In Shilla, it was the common people who were first attracted to Buddhism. Among some of the aristocrats, there was considerable resistance to the new culture. It was only after the martyrdom of Ich'adon, during the reign of King Pophung (514-540) in 527 A.D., that Buddhism gradually became recognized as the national religion of Shilla. Ich'adon was a prominent court official. One day he presented himself to the king and announced that he had become a Buddhist.

The king had him beheaded. When the executioner cut off his head, milk poured out instead of blood. Paintings of this miracle can be seen on temple walls (at Haein-sa Temple for example). A stone monument in the National Museum of Kyongju honors Ich'adon's death. King Chinhung (540-575 A.D.) particularly encouraged the growth of Buddhism. During his reign, a special training institution, the *Hwarangdo*, was formed. Selected young men were trained physically and spiritually according to Buddhist principles so that they could govern and defend the nation.

Towards the end of his life, King Chinhung became a monk. (Several Silla kings were ordained and their queens and families often followed the example and entered monasteries.) The arts flourished during the Shilla Period. Some of the finest statues-Sokgur-am Buddha in Kyongju for example - were made a huge temple, Hwangnyong-sa was built during this period.

This temple was the center of Buddhism of Shilla. Many famous monks emerged from this temple, including Won-gwang (531-630 A.D.), Cha-jang (608-686 A.D.), Won-hyo (617-686 A.D.), and Ui-sang (620-660 A.D.). Won-hyo, a great scholar, was born in a simple family. He renounced his religious life in order to better serve the people. Married for a short time to a princess, he had one son. As a scholar, he wrote many important treatises. His philosophy revolved around the unity and the interrelatedness of all things. Searching for a teacher at that time, many monks went to China to study Buddhism. Won-hyo and his close friend, Ui-sang, also set out for China together. Both wanted to study Buddhism there.

On the way to China Won-hyo awoke one evening thirsty and searching around, he found a container with delicious cool water in it. His thirst quenched, he went back to sleep. In the morning, he found that the vessel from which he drank the delicious water was a human skull. At that moment he realized that everything depends on the mind and attained enlightenment. Realizing that it was no longer necessary for him to go to China in search of a teacher, he returned home. Master Ui-sang continued the journey. After ten years studying in China under a great master, Ui-sang offered a special gift to his teacher: a poem in the shape of a seal which, when written down, geometrically represented infinity.

This poem contained the essence of the Avatamsaka Sutra (an extremely long text explaining the universe) and it is one of the greatest offerings of the Korean people to the world. During the Shilla Period, the people were so devoted that some kings became Buddhists and took on Buddhist names and gave them to members of their families. Places too, were renamed according to the places famous at the time of the Buddha. It is interesting to note that incense was introduced from China during this period. The people, not knowing its use, thought it magical and so employed it for curing disease!

BUDDHISM FROM UNIFIED SHILLA PERIOD TO TODAY

UNIFIED SHILLA PERIOD (668-935 A.D.)

In 668 A.D., Shilla conquered the other kingdoms and Buddhism became the central cultural force uniting the peninsula. This period came to be known as the Unified Shilla Period. Various rituals were developed and performed as spiritual requests for protection from foreign invasion. National sentiment was strong and the people worked hard for unity and understanding and everything ended towards the realization of the patriotic aspirations of the people. From the very beginning, Korean Buddhism developed using the unified approach - the "One Mind," the universal interrelatedness of everything - as taught be Won-hyo.

Throughout the Unified Shilla Period, Buddhism continued to prosper and grow both academically and culturally. During this era some of the finest Korean Art were created: the main temples of Korea were built, pagodas were erected; beautiful statues fashioned - all of this was of profound significance to the country's Buddhist Heritage. The famous rock statue of the Buddha in Sokgur-am cave in Kyongju was carved in 732 A.D.; today it still evokes a sense of wonder.

The Avatamsaka Sutra and the Lotus Sutra were much studied while the people worshipped Amitabha (the Buddha of Light) and Avalokitesvara Bodhisattva (the Bodhisattva of Compassion). Towards the end of the Unified Shilla Period, the Ch'an School (Son of Korean, Zen in Japanese) was introduced from China and this added a new dimension to Korean Buddhism. Meditation and direct experience were emphasized over concentration on studying the texts. Nine different schools emerged and they were known as the Nine Mountains of Son.

KORYO (935-1392 A.D.)

After the glory of Shilla faded, the Koryo Dynasty assumed power in the 10th century A.D. Buddhism continued to be the national religion, with the kings establishing shrines and temples throughout the country. However, excessive focus was placed on rituals and this created an unfavorable atmosphere for spiritual development. In an attempt to purify and renew the spiritual aspect of Buddhism, several monks struggled against the ritualistic trend.

One of these monks was Master Ui-chon (1055-1101 A.D.), son of King Munjong (1047-1083 A.D.) who collected about 4,000 volumes of Buddhist texts while studying in China; from these texts the Tripitaka Korean was produced. This eminent Koryo monk emphasized the importance of bringing Contemplative Son (Zen) and Textual (Avatamsaka) traditions together under a Chinese school, Tientai (Ch'ont'ae, in Korean). The formation of this school gave new life to Koryo Buddhism.

Buddhism remained the dominant intellectual influence during the latter past of the Koryo Dynasty. Confucianism, introduced to the peninsula at the same time as Buddhism, had not yet gained much popularity. Master Chi-nul (1158-1210), usually known as Pojo-kuksa, became the leading monk of Korea. He founded Songgwang-sa temple on Mt. Chogye, and this large temple remained the headquarters of the Son sect for over 300 years. The nine school of Son (Zen) were unified by Mater Tae-go (1301-1382 A.D.) under the name Chogye which has remained the main sect to this day.

CHOSON (1392-1910 A.D.)

With the downfall of the Koryo Dynasty in 1392 A.D., Buddhism slowly declined as the new rulers of the Choson Dynasty adopted Neo-Confucianism. Prior to this, many Buddhist monks had become overly involved in politics, resulting in royal strife. The new interest in Confucianism led to the oppression and restriction of Buddhism by some Choson kings. Temples could not be built near towns and had to be constructed in the mountains; many temples were pulled down; monks were looked down on and, for some years, not permitted to enter the capital city.

While some kings persecuted Buddhism, the common people continued to go to the temples. At the beginning of the Choson Dynasty, geomancers were consulted in order to find the ideal site for a new capital. They chose an ancient place called "Hanyang" which was then renamed "Seoul" and which has been the center of culture and learning for the peninsula since that time. The name means "capital" in Korean and was probably derived from the ancient Indian place most dear to the Buddha: Sravasti. In Chinese, "Sravasti" became "Sarobol" and finally "Seoul" in Korean.

In the late 16th century A.D., during the Japanese invasion by the armies of Hideyoshi, Buddhism came to the country's rescue. At the age of 72, Master So-san (1520-1604 A.D.) and his disciple Sa-myong (1544-1610 A.D.), led a band of 5,000 Buddhist monks against the people's respect for Buddhism. Following the defeat of Hideyoshi invasion, his disciple, Master Sa-myong, was sent as chief delegate to Japan and in 1604, he completed a peace treaty.

MODERN TIMES

In 1910, the Choson Dynasty came to an end with the annexation of the country to Japan. During the Colonial Period, Buddhism was greatly favored and supported by the Japanese government. However, the celibate sects were discouraged and monks were encouraged to take wives. Heads of temples were appointed by the Japanese occupation authorities. Unfortunately, during this period, many Buddhist art treasures were taken to Japan; even today the Buddhists, in co-operation with the Korean government, are negotiating with Japan in order to have these stolen treasures returned to Korea.

After liberation in 1945, the celibate ordained members of the main sect of Korean Buddhism, Chogye, superseded the married monks who had taken over the main temples during the Japanese Occupation. Large numbers of men and women were ordained and there was a great revival of Korean Buddhism. Recently, many new temples and centers have opened in the town. Programs for people of all ages include learning to chant, studying, all night meditation classes, and social gatherings. About half the population of Korea is Buddhist. Most Koreans, even though they may not call themselves Buddhists, maintain a Buddhist view of life and the afterworld.

FEATURES OF KOREAN BUDDHISM

Let us now consider four special features of Korean Buddhism:

Characteristics:

1. Bodhisattva Principles

From the beginning, the way of the Bodhisattva became a central feature in the development of Korean Buddhism. A

Bodhisattva is a being who postpones his or her own final enlightenment in order to help all beings, for she is the perfection of altruism, perfect in wisdom and compassion. Bodhisattvas are the embodiment of the Six Perfections: Generosity, Good Conduct, Vigor, Patience, Meditation and Wisdom. Initially, generosity is considered the most important perfection for the negation of the self: the first step on the spiritual path. Eventually all are interrelated and equally important on the path to becoming a Bodhisattva.

Let us look at a practical example of the intermingling of these six perfections. As long as giving is selfish, it is not truly generous. However, in order to practice perfect generosity, one must practice the other perfections. One has to observe good conduct in order to give a pure gift. Then patience is necessary in order to choose the time and determination so that you do not give up. Finally meditation helps you to let go of your greed, so that you can offer the gift selflessly and wisdom helps you to choose the "right" gift! Just as all are linked in generosity, each one is related to the other in all aspects of our life. Perfection in these factors lead to a perfect being: one who lives for all.

With the advent of Buddhism these values became fundamental and central to the Korean way of life. The youth corp (Hwarangdo) of the Unified Shilla period (seep.14) lived according to these ideas, and the teachings of the great Korean masters all emphasized the importance of the Bodhisattva path. In Korean temples, there are many statues and painting of Bodhisattvas representing various aspects of compassion and wisdom. Throughout the history of Korean Buddhism, different Bodhisattvas have been especially popular at different times: Maitreya, the Future Buddha, and Avalokitesvara, the Bodhisattva of Compassion, in particular. Special shrines were built for them or they were placed in the main Buddha hall next to the principal statue.

2. Unification

Buddhism was the force which originally brought the people of the peninsula together forming the Unified Shilla Period. After the unification in 668 A.D., social harmony, so necessary to maintaining defense, was fostered by Buddhism. Buddhist monks led the Korean people against the Japanese in the sixteenth century. Great Buddhist writers promoted this unity by amalgamating the different schools and teaching "Returning to the One Mind", "All is One" or "One Mindedness" (Won-hyo). Peace, harmony and unity became the foundation of Korea's spirit and her strong patriotism.

3. Openness

Although Buddhism has always mixed with local culture, in Korea this is especially true. For example, Buddhism was open to Shamanism and Confucianism. Even today, new elements are constantly being added. A lot of music has entered Buddhist life nowadays. There are Buddhist songs and concerts as well as singing groups. There also seems to be a growing vogue for Buddhist themes woven into modern stories; many old stories have been made into plays for television and movies.

4. The Mundane

From early on in history, Korean Buddhism emphasized mundane benefits over spiritual benefits for the people - the monks of course, being primarily interested in spiritual growth. The people, constantly threatened by invaders and calamities, were much drawn to a teaching promising present prosperity rather than future salvation.

Korea has a long and distinguished cultural history. The Koreans are one of ethnic family speaking one language. Linguistic and anthropological studies as well as legendary sources clearly distinguish Koreans from the Chinese and the Japanese. Koreans were a homogeneous people by the beginning of the christian era. The Korean people struggled successfully for millennia to maintain cultural and political identity despite the influence of neighboring countries. Koreans all speak and write the same language, which has been a crucial factor in strong national identity. Korean arts possess several distinguishing characteristics that create a unique style of its own.

Korean art respects nature. In traditional korea, the typical family was large with several generations usually living together. With modernization, however, such large families are disappearing. Koreans have traditionally believed that a man must first cultivate himself and manage his family properly before he can govern the nation. Order at home is maintained through obedience to superiors that is, children obeying parents, the wife the husband, the servants the master, and so on. This Confucian decorum has dominated Korean life and way of thinking over the centuries and is still respected in all forms of human relations.

Koreans still place great emphasis on filial piety to parents and ancestors, fidelity to spouse and faithfulness to friends, loyalty to the ruler and respect for teachers. Korea's most ancient religions are Shamanism, Buddhism and Confucianism. All these played an important role in the country's early cultural development and have greatly influenced thought and behavior. During the Three Kingdoms period, the Korean people were actively acquiring classical cultural traditions of both the East and the West.

Confucianism and Taoism were being introduced from China, and Buddhism from far away as India and Central Asia. Because of its unique geographical location, Chinese culture filtered into Japan through Korea; a common cultural sphere of Buddhism and Confucianism was thus established between the three countries. Ethnically, Koreans belong to the Mongolian race, but for centuries the people have maintained their own unique language, culture and customs.

CULTURE

Korean culture has blossomed during her long history. Though affected by other Asian cultures, its roots lie deep within the creative Korean psyche, and it has tended to spread rather than be encroached upon. Japan especially has adopted many Korean ideas and customs. The delicate styling and fine craftsmanship of celadon pottery well illustrates the refinement of the culture, even from as far back as the Three Kingdoms period. Korea has also spawned some great inventors; its first printing systems predate Gutenberg's, the famous 'Turtle Ship' was the first ever iron-clad battleship, and the Korean alphabet, devised by a group of scholars in the 15 century, was so effective that it remains largely unchanged today.

The reasons behind Korea's rapid economic development can be found in this innate creativity. Buddhism has played a powerful role in Korean art. A large number of excellent examples of Korean artwork and architecture can be found in Buddhist temples and paintings. During the Choson Dynasty, Confucianism became a leading inspiration for the noblemen to whom the arts of calligraphy and painting were essential. They have left a legacy of fine brush work from which contemporary artists have benefited from.

TRADITIONAL ART

Korea has a long and distinguished cultural history. The current trend in Korean art is the harmonious combination of traditional and modern styles, revealing the historical roots and influences of Korean art.

PAINTING

Tomb murals from the Three Kingdoms Period are the earliest examples of Korean painting. Mythological beasts such as dragons and flying horses show an imaginative and creative spirit. Throughout the Unified Shilla and Koryo Periods, Buddhism prevailed in every field of life, thus leaving a rich collection of icon paintings. In the late Koryo Dynasty, ink and brush paintings of the four "noble plants", (the cherry blossom, orchid, chrysanthemum, and bamboo), which symbolized traditional virtues, became popular.

The artists of the Choson Dynasty produced innovative embodying the Korean spirit and perspective. There are humorous animal pictures, scroll paintings of dreamlike, mist-clad mountains, and insightful sketches of everyday life done in brush and ink.

Paintings with folk custom and nature themes flourished in the latter half of the 18th century.

CALLIGRAPHY

Calligraphy, the art of brush writing, is a traditional art form in Korea which has exerted a strong influence on social and cultural life and is still highly respected today.

ARCHITECTURE

Four factors have shaped traditional Korean architecture: religion, the availability of materials, the natural landscape, and an aesthetic preference for simplicity. Gently sloping roof lines and sturdy, undecorated pillars characterize its simplicity, harmony, and practical utility. Korea has many original wooden and stone structures, some dating back over a thousand years. There are also many skillful reproductions. Traditional architectural designs are also incorporated in many modern buildings throughout the country.

POTTERY

One of the most significant achievements in Korean art, the perfection of celadon, was accomplished during the Koryo Dynasty. Korean artisans developed a superbly controlled glaze that was both beautiful and unique because it fully utilized the properties of Korea's rich clay. The highest praise is given to the color of the glaze - a delicate kingfisher green celadon inlaid with a pictorial underglaze which is called sanggamch'ongja and occupies a central position in Koryo celadons. The motifs and decorations found on the celadon are additional reasons for its great popularity among art lovers.

MODERN ART

With its characterisitic blend of the traditional and modern, and the balance of influences from east and west, Korean contemporary art has surged in popularity. Most artists try to be accessible to their audience, and there are many exhibitions and galleries in any major city.

MUSEUMS

Visiting the museums of a country is a valuable opportunity to see its historic treasures and cultural legacies. As in other countries with long histories, many national, municipal and university museums, as well as a number of private institutions, preserve Korea's colorful past.

TRADITIONAL PERFORMANCE

Koreans have always had a deep love for music and dance. Traditional Korean dance and musical performances can be a memorable part of visiting Korea.

Korean Buddhism is distinguished from other forms of Buddhism by its attempt to resolve what it sees as inconsistencies in *Mahayana* Buddhism. Early Korean monks believed that the traditions they received from foreign countries were internally inconsistent. To address this, they developed a new holistic approach to Buddhism. This approach is characteristic of virtually all major Korean thinkers, and has resulted in a distinct variation of Buddhism, which is called *Tongbulgyo* ("interpenetrated Buddhism") by Korean scholars. Korean Buddhist thinkers refined their predecessors' ideas into a distinct form.

As it now stands, Korean Buddhism consists mostly of the *Seon* lineage. *Seon* has a strong relationship with other *Mahayana* traditions that bear the imprint of Chinese *Ch'an* teachings, as well as the closely related Japanese *Zen*. Other sects, such as the *Taego*, the modern revival of the *Cheontae* lineage, the "Jingak" order (a modern esoteric sect), and the newly formed *Won*, have also attracted sizable followings. When Buddhism was originally introduced to Korea from Former Qin which was governed by Tibettans in 372, or about 800 years after the death of the historical Buddha, Shamanism was the indigenous religion.

As it was not seen to conflict with the rites of nature worship, it was allowed to blend in with Shamanism. Thus, the mountains that were believed to be the residence of spirits in pre-Buddhist times became the sites of Buddhist temples. Korean Shamanism held three spirits in especially high regard: Sanshin (the Mountain Spirit), Toksong (the Recluse) and Chilsong (the Spirit of the Seven Stars, the Big Dipper). Korean Buddhism accepted and absorbed these three spirits and, even today, special shrines are set aside for them in many temples. The Mountain Spirit receives particular recognition in an attempt to appease the local mountain spirits, on whose land the temple stands. This blend of Buddhism and Shamanism became known as Korean Buddhism, although the fundamental teachings of the Buddha remained.

Though it initially enjoyed wide acceptance, even being supported as the state ideology during the Goryeo period, Buddhism in Korea suffered extreme repression during the Joseon Dynasty, which lasted for several hundred years. During this period, Neo-Confucian ideology overcame the prior dominance of Buddhism. Only after Buddhist monks helped repel a Japanese invasion at the end of the 16th century did the persecution of Buddhism and Buddhist practitioners stop. Buddhism in Korea remained subdued until the end of the Joseon period, when its position was strengthened somewhat by the Japanese occupation, which lasted from 1910 to 1945.

After World War II, the Seon school of Korean Buddhism once again gained acceptance. As Christianity has become increasingly influential in Korea, it is estimated that the declining proportion of the religious population among self-professed Buddhist community in South Korea now accounts for about 23% of the country's population. In officially atheist North Korea, Buddhists make up 2% of the population.

BUDDHISM IN THE THREE KINGDOMS

When Buddhism was introduced to Korea in the 4th century CE, the Korean peninsula was politically subdivided into three kingdoms: Goguryeo in the north, Baekje in the southwest, and Silla in the southeast.

GOGURYEO

In 372 the monk Sundo was sent by Fujian of Former Qin which was governed by Tibettans to the court of the King Sosurim of Goguryeo. He brought texts and statues with him and the Goguryeo royalty and their subjects quickly accepted his teachings. The Buddhism in China was in a rudimentary form, consisting of the law of cause and effect and the search for happiness. This had much in common with the predominant Shamanism, which likely led to the quick assimilation of Buddhism by the people of Goguryeo.

BAEKJE

In 384, the Serindian monk Marananta arrived in Baekje and the royal family received the similar strain of Buddhism he brought. King Asin proclaimed, "people should believe in Buddhism and seek happiness."

GAYA

A small, separate federation called Gaya emerged for a short time on the southern coast between Baekje and the fast growing Shilla. It fell to an invasion in the mid sixth century before reaching maturity, however, and was annexed by the Silla.

SILLA

Buddhism did not enter the kingdom of Silla until the 5th century. The common people were first attracted to Buddhism here, but there was resistance among the aristocrats. In 527, however, a prominent court official named Ichadon presented himself to King Pophung and announced he had become Buddhist. The king had him beheaded, but when the executioner cut off his head, it is said that milk poured out instead of blood. Paintings of this are in the temple at Haein-sa and a stone monument honoring his martyrdom is in the National Museum of Kyongju.

During the reign of the next king, King Chinhung, the growth of Buddhism was encouraged — eventually being recognized as the national religion of Silla. Additionally, selected young men were physically and spiritually trained at Hwarangdo according to Buddhist principles to be able to defend the kingdom. King Chinhung later became a monk himself. Many Korean Buddhist monks traveled to China in order to study Buddhism in the late Three Kingdoms Period, especially in the late 6th century. The monk Banya is said to have studied under the Tiantai master Zhiyi, and Gyeomik of Baekje and travelled to India to learn Sanskrit and study Vinaya.•

Monks of the period brought back numerous scriptures from abroad and conducted missionary activity throughout Korea and Japan. The date of the first mission to Japan is unclear, but it is reported that a second detachment of scholars was sent to Japan upon invitation by the Japanese rulers in 577. The strong Korean influence on the development of Buddhism in Japan continued through the Unified Silla period; only in the 8th or 9th century did independent study by Japanese monks begin in significant numbers.

Several schools of thought developed in Korea during these early times:

- The Samnon school focused on the Indian *Mâdhyamika* (Middle Path) doctrine,
- The Gyeyul school was mainly concerned with the study and implementation of moral discipline (*úîla*), and
- The Yeolban school, which was based in the themes of the *Mahâparinirvâna-sûtra*

Toward the end of the Three Kingdoms Period, the Wonyung school was formed. It would lead the actualization of the metaphysics of interpenetration as found in the Huayan jing and soon was considered the premier school, especially among the educated aristocracy. This school was later known as Hwaeom (*Huayan* in Chinese) and was the longest lasting of these "imported" schools. It had strong ties with the Beopseong, the indigenous Korean school of thought.

The monk Jajang is credited with having been a major force in the adoption of Buddhism as a national religion. Jajang is also known for his participation in the founding of the Korean sangha, a type of monastic community. Another great scholar to emerge from the Silla Period was Won-hyo. He renounced his religious life to better serve the people and even married a princess for a short time and had a son. He wrote many treatises and his philosophy centered on the unity and interrelatedness of all things. He set off to China to study Buddhism with a close friend, Ui-sang, but only made it part of the way there.

The legend is that Won-hyo awoke one night very thirsty, found a container with cool water, drank, and returned to sleep. The next morning he saw the container from which he had drunk was a human skull and he realized all enlightenment depended on the mind. He saw no reason to continue to China, so he returned home. His companion, Ui-sang, continued to China and after studying ten years, offered a poem to his master in the shape of a seal that geometrically represents infinity. The poem contained the essence of the Avatamsaka Sutra. Buddhism was so successful during this period that many kings converted and cities/places were even renamed after famous places during the time of Buddha.

BUDDHISM IN THE UNIFIED SILLA PERIOD (668–918)

In 668, the kingdom of Silla succeeded in unifying the whole Korean peninsula, giving rise to a period of political stability that lasted for about one hundred years. This led to a high point in the scholarly studies of Buddhism in Korea. In general, the most popular areas of study were *Wonyung*, *Yusik* (*Weishi*; "consciousness-only"; the East Asian form of *Yogâcâra*), *Jeongto* (Pure Land), and the indigenous Korean *Beopseong* ("dharma-nature school"). The monk Wonhyo taught the "Pure Land"-practice of *yeombul*, which would become very popular amongst both scholars and laypeople, and has had a lasting influence on Buddhist thought in Korea.

His work, which attempts a synthesis of the seemingly divergent strands of Indian and Chinese Buddhist doctrine, makes use of the *essence-function* (*che-yong*) framework, which was popular in native East Asian philosophical schools. His work was instrumental in the development of the dominant school of Korean Buddhist thought, known variously as *Beopseong*, *Haedong* ("Korean") and later as *Jungdo* ("Middle way"). Wonhyo's friend Uisang went to Changan, where he studied under Huayan patriarchs Zhiyan (600–668) and Fazang (643–712).

When he returned after twenty years, his work contributed to *Hwaeom* and became the predominant doctrinal influence on Korean Buddhism, together with Wonhyo's *tong bulgyo* thought. *Hwaeom* principles were deeply assimilated into the Korean meditational school, the Seon school, where they made a profound effect on its basic attitudes. Influences from Silla Buddhism in general, and from these two philosophers in particular, even crept "backwards" into Chinese Buddhism. Wonhyo's commentaries were very important in shaping the thought of the preeminent Chinese Buddhist philosopher Fazang, and Woncheuk's commentary on the *SaCdhinirmocana-sûtra* had a strong influence in Tibetan Buddhism.

As was the case in Tang China, as well as the Nara and early Heian period in Japan, which are roughly contemporary to the Silla period, the intellectual developments of Silla Buddhism also brought with them significant cultural achievements in many areas, including painting, literature, sculpture, and architecture. During this period, many large and beautiful temples were built. Two crowning achievements were the temple Bulguksa and the cave-retreat of Seokguram. Bulguksa was especially famous for its jeweled pagodas, while Seokguram was known for the beauty of its stone sculpture.

A new epoch in Korean Buddhism began during the latter Silla period with the birth of schools of *Seon* in Korea. In China, the movement toward a meditation-based view of practice, which came to be known as *chan*, had begun during the sixth and seventh centuries, and it was not long before the influence of the new meditational school reached Korea, where it was known as *Seon*. Meaning "meditation," the term is more widely known in the West in its Japanese variant *zen*. Tension developed between the new meditational schools and the previously existing academically oriented schools, which were described by the term *gyo*, meaning "learning" or "study."

Kim Kiaokak(630–729), a prince who became a monastic came to the region of Anhui to Mount Jiuhua in China. Many Chinese buddhists believe he was indeed the transformation body of Kcitigarbha. Two uncles sent by his mum and wife to call him back also became a monastic there. His well-preserved, dehydrated body were seen at the monastery he built on Mount Jiuhua today. The two uncles, unable to resist wine and meat as they were official before becoming monastics, practise in another place in the mount. People built the palace of the two saints in their practise place to memorize them. Many buddhists visited there.

Beomnang (fl. 632–646), said to be a student of the Chinese master Daoxin (580–651), is generally credited with the initial transmission of *Seon* into Korea. *Seon* was popularized by Sinhaeng (704–779) in the latter part of the eighth century and by Doui (died 825) at the beginning of the ninth century. From then on, many Koreans studied *Chan* in China, and upon their return established their own schools at various mountain monasteries with their leading disciples.

Initially, the number of these schools was fixed at nine, and Korean *Seon* was termed the "nine mountains" (*gusan*) school at the time. Eight of these were of the lineage of Mazu Daoyi (709–788), as they were established through connection with either him or one of his eminent disciples. The one exception was the Sumi-san school founded by Ieom (869–936), which had developed from the *Caotong* lineage.

BUDDHISM AS STATE RELIGION IN THE GORYEO PERIOD (918–1392)

Initially, the new Seon schools were regarded by the established doctrinal schools as radical and dangerous upstarts. Thus, the early founders of the various "nine mountain" monasteries met with considerable resistance, repressed by the long influence in court of the Gyo schools. The struggles which ensued continued for most of the Goryeo period, but gradually the Seon argument for the possession of the true transmission of enlightenment would gain the upper hand.

The position that was generally adopted in the later Seon schools, due in large part to the efforts of Jinul, did not claim clear superiority of Seon meditational methods, but rather declared the intrinsic unity and similarities of the Seon and Gyo viewpoints. Although all these schools are mentioned in historical records, toward the end of the dynasty, Seon became dominant in its effect on the government and society, and the production of noteworthy scholars and adepts. During the Goryeo period, Seon thoroughly became a "religion of the state," receiving extensive support and privileges through connections with the ruling family and powerful members of the court.

Although most of the scholastic schools waned in activity and influence during this period of the growth of Seon, the *Hwaeom* School continued to be a lively source of scholarship well into the Goryeo, much of it continuing the legacy of Uisang and Wonhyo. In particular the work of Gyunyeo (923–973) prepared for the reconciliation of Hwaeom and Seon, with Hwaeom's accommodating attitude toward the latter. Gyunyeo's works are an important source for modern scholarship in identifying the distinctive nature of Korean Hwaeom. Another important advocate of Seon/Gyo unity was Uicheon.

Like most other early Goryeo monks, he began his studies in Buddhism with Hwaeom. He later traveled to China, and upon his return, actively promulgated the *Cheontae* (or *Tiantai* in Chinese) teaching, which became recognized as another Seon school. This period thus came to be described as "five doctrinal and two meditational schools" (*ogyo yangjong*). Uicheon himself, however, alienated too many Seon adherents, and he died at a relatively young age without seeing a Seon-Gyo unity accomplished. The most important figure of Seon in the Goryeo was *Jinul* (1158–1210). In his time, the sangha was in a crisis of external appearance and internal issues of doctrine.

Buddhism had gradually become infected by secular tendencies and involvements, such as fortune-telling and the offering of prayers and rituals for success in secular endeavors. This kind of corruption resulted in the profusion of increasingly larger numbers of monks and nuns with questionable motivations. Therefore, the correction, revival, and improvement of the quality of Buddhism were prominent issues for Buddhist leaders of the period. Jinul sought to establish a new movement within Korean Seon, which he called the *"samâdhi and prajñâ society"*, whose goal was to establish a new community of disciplined, pure-minded practitioners deep in the mountains. He eventually accomplished this mission with the founding of the Seonggwangsa monastery at Mt. Jogye.

Jinul's works are characterized by a thorough analysis and reformulation of the methodologies of Seon study and practice. One major issue that had long fermented in Chinese *Chan*, and which received special focus from Jinul, was the relationship between "gradual" and "sudden" methods in practice and enlightenment. Drawing upon various Chinese treatments of this topic, most importantly those by Zongmi (780–841) and Dahui (1089–1163), Jinul created a "sudden enlightenment followed by gradual practice" dictum, which he outlined in a few relatively concise and accessible texts.

From Dahui, Jinul also incorporated the *gwanhwa* method into his practice. This form of meditation is the main method taught in Korean Seon today. Jinul's philosophical resolution of the Seon-

Gyo conflict brought a deep and lasting effect on Korean Buddhism. The general trend of Buddhism in the latter half of the Goryeo was a decline due to corruption, and the rise of strong anti-Buddhist political and philosophical sentiment. However, this period of relative decadence would nevertheless produce some of Korea's most renowned Seon masters.

Three important monks of this period who figured prominently in charting the future course of Korean Seon were contemporaries and friends: Gyeonghan Baeg'un (1298–1374), Taego Bou (1301–1382) and Naong Hyegeun (1320–1376). All three went to Yuan China to learn the *Linji* (*Imje* in Korean) *gwanhwa* teaching that had been popularized by Jinul. All three returned, and established the sharp, confrontational methods of the Imje School in their own teaching. Each of the three was also said to have had hundreds of disciples, such that this new infusion into Korean Seon brought about considerable effect.

Despite the Imje influence, which was generally considered to be anti-scholarly in nature, Gyeonghan and Naong, under the influence of Jinul and the traditional *tong bulgyo* tendency, showed an unusual interest in scriptural study, as well as a strong understanding of *Confucianism* and *Taoism*, due to the increasing influence of Chinese philosophy as the foundation of official education. From this time, a marked tendency for Korean Buddhist monks to be "three teachings" exponents appeared.

A significant historical event of the Goryeo period is the production of the first woodblock edition of the Tripitaka, called the Tripitaka Koreana. Two editions were made, the first one completed from 1210 to 1231, and the second one from 1214 to 1259. The first edition was destroyed in a fire, during an attack by Mongol invaders in 1232, but the second edition is still in existence at Haeinsa in Gyeongsang province. This edition of the Tripitaka was of high quality, and served as the standard version of the Tripitaka in East Asia for almost 700 years.

SUPPRESSION UNDER THE JOSEON DYNASTY (1392–1910)

The Buddhist establishment at the end of the Goryeo period had become ridden with excesses. There were too many monks and nuns, a large percentage of whom were only in the sangha as a means of escaping taxation and/or government service. There were also far too many temples being supported, and too many elaborate rituals being carried out. The support of Buddhism had become a serious drain on the national economy. The government itself was suffering from rampant corruption, while also struggling with wars on its northern and eastern borders. Moreover, a new and rapidly growing *Neo-Confucian* ideological movement of stridently anti-Buddhist inclination gained political power.

In 1388, an influential general named Yi Seonggye (1380–1400) carried out a coup d'etat, and established himself as the first ruler of the Joseon Dynasty under the reign title of *Taejo* in 1392 with the support of this Neo-Confucian movement. Subsequently, Buddhism was gradually suppressed for the next 500 years. The number of temples was reduced, restrictions on membership in the sangha were installed, and Buddhist monks and nuns were literally chased into the mountains, forbidden to mix with society. Joseon Buddhism, which had started off under the so-called "five doctrinal and two meditational" schools system of the Goryeo, was first condensed to two schools: Seon and Gyo. Eventually, these were further reduced to the single school of Seon.

Despite this strong suppression from the government, and vehement ideological opposition from Korean Neo-Confucianism, Seon Buddhism continued to thrive intellectually. An outstanding thinker was *Giwha* ((Hamheo Deuktong) 1376–1433), who had first studied at a Confucian academy, but then changed his focus to Buddhism, where he was initiated to the *gwanhwa* tradition by *Muhak Jacho* (1327–1405). He wrote many scholarly commentaries, as well as essays and a large body of poetry. Being well-versed in Confucian and Daoist philosophies, Giwha also wrote an important treatise in defense of Buddhism, from the standpoint of the intrinsic unity of the three teachings, entitled the *Hyeon jeong non*. In the tradition of earlier philosophers, he applied *che-yong* ("essence-function") and *Hwaeom* (*sa-sa mu-ae*, "mutual interpenetration of phenomena").

Common in the works of Joseon scholar-monks are writings on Hwaeom-related texts, as well as the *Awakening of Faith, Sutra of Perfect Enlightenment, Úûrangama-sûtra, Diamond Sutra* and the *Heart Sutra*. The Jogye order instituted a set curriculum of scriptural study, including the above-mentioned works, along with other shorter selections from eminent Korean monks, such as Jinul. During the Joseon period, the number of Buddhist monasteries dropped from several hundred to a mere thirty-six. Limits were placed on the number of clergy, land area, and ages for entering the sangha. When the final restrictions were in place, monks and nuns were prohibited from entering the cities.

Buddhist funerals, and even begging, were outlawed. However, some rulers occasionally appeared who looked favorably upon Buddhism and did away with some of the more suppressive regulations. The most noteworthy of these was the Queen Munjeong, who, as a devout Buddhist, took control of the government in the stead of her young son Myeongjong (r. 1545–67), and immediately repealed many anti-Buddhist measures. The queen had deep respect for the brilliant monk *Bou* (1515–1565), and installed him as the head of the Seon school.

One of the most important reasons for the restoration of Buddhism to a position of minimal acceptance was the role of Buddhist monks in repelling the Japanese invasions of Korea, which occurred between 1592 and 1598. At that time, the government was weak from internal squabbles, and was not initially able to muster strong resistance to the incursion. The plight of the country encouraged some leaders of the sangha to organize monks into guerrilla units, which enjoyed some instrumental successes. The "righteous monk" movement spread during this eight-year war, finally including several thousand monks, led by the aging *Seosan Hyujeong* (1520–1604), a first-rate Seon master and the author of a number of important religious texts. The presence of the monks' army was a critical factor in the eventual expulsion of the Japanese invaders.

Seosan is also known for continuing efforts toward the unification of Buddhist doctrinal study and practice. His efforts were strongly influenced by Wonhyo, Jinul, and Giwha. He is considered the central figure in the revival of Joseon Buddhism, and most major streams of modern Korean Seon trace their lineages back to him through one of his four main disciples: *Yu Jeong* (1544–1610); *Eongi* (1581–1644), *Taeneung* (1562–1649) and *Ilseon* (1533–1608), all four of whom were lieutenants to Seosan during the war with Japan. The biographies of Seosan and his four major disciples are similar in many respects, and these similarities are emblematic of the typical lifestyle of Seon monks of the late Goryeo and Joseon periods.

Most of them began by engaging in Confucian and Daoist studies. Turning to Seon, they pursued a markedly itinerant lifestyle, wandering through the mountain monasteries. At this stage, they were initiated to the central component of Seon practice, the *gong'an*, or *gwanhwa* meditation. This *gwanhwa* meditation, unlike some Japanese *Zen* traditions, did not consist of contemplation on a lengthy, graduated series of deeper *kôans*. By contrast, the typical Korean approach was that "all *gong'an* are contained in one" and therefore it was, and still is, quite common for the practitioner to remain with one hwadu during his whole meditational career, most often Zhaozhou's *"mu."*

Buddhism during the three centuries, from the time of Seosan down to the next Japanese incursion into Korea in the late nineteenth century, remained fairly consistent with the above-described model. A number of eminent teachers appeared during the centuries after Seosan, but the Buddhism of the late Joseon, while keeping most of the common earlier characteristics, was especially marked by a revival of Hwaeom studies, and occasionally by new interpretations of methodology in Seon study. There was also a revival, during the final two centuries, of the *Pure Land* (*Amitâbha*) faith. Although the government maintained fairly tight control of the sangha, there was never again the extreme suppression of the early Joseon.

BUDDHISM DURING THE JAPANESE OCCUPATION (1910–1945)

The Japanese occupation from 1910 to 1945 brought great suffering on the Korean people as a whole, and to the Korean sangha in particular, as it had to comply with an extensive set of Japanese regulations. Japanese Buddhists demanded the right to proselytize in the cities, lifting the five-hundred year ban on monks and nuns entering cities. The formation of new Buddhist sects, such as *Won Buddhism*, and the presence of Christian missionaries during this period led to further turbulence in traditional Korean Buddhism.

The Japanese Buddhist custom of allowing Buddhist priests to marry contradicted the lifestyle of Korean Buddhist monks and nuns, who traditionally lived in celibacy. The Japanese occupational authorities encouraged this practice, appointed their own heads of temples, and had many works of art shipped to Japan. Negotiations for the repatriation of Korean Buddhist artworks are still ongoing.

BUDDHISM AND WESTERNIZATION (1945–PRESENT)

When Korea was liberated from Japanese occupation in 1945, the celibate monastics of what has become the main sect of Korean Buddhism, Chogye or Jogye, began to take over for the married monks who ran the temples during the occupation. This order sees itself as the primary representative of traditional Korean Buddhism in existence.

SOUTH KOREA

Starting in the 1950s, Syngman Rhee and others worked to further divide and weaken the Buddhist Sangha in the country. Rhee campaigned in 1954 against the so-called "Japanized Buddhists". Western education and scholarship, and the empowerment of women and the poor, caused divisions among Koreans. Specifically, a deep rift opened between married priests and celibate monks. The differences were so great that fistfights over the control of temples became frequent. Monks, mostly belonging to the celibate Jogye order, threatened to kill themselves.

Many of them were against the Japanized Buddhists. As the Buddhist riots continued, the influence of Buddhism lessened. Buddhism continued to lose followers to Christian missionaries, who were able to capitalize on these weaknesses. President Park Chung Hee unsuccessfully attempted during his rule (1961–1979) to settle the dispute by building a pan-national Buddhist organization. However, he did succeed in allying himself with the celibate faction of the sangha. In the 1980s, President Chun Doo-hwan also used politics and intrigue to attack Buddhism. He sent troops to raid temples, and had hundreds of monks arrested and tortured.

During the 1990s, conflicts between the South Korean government and Buddhist leaders, and Christian denominations continued. The government accused Buddhist monks of immorality and some Christians used this to forward their missionary work. Some religious gatherings have even turned violent, with statues of Buddha and Dangun, the founder of Korea, being vandalized. There was also a rash of temple burnings in the 1980s and 1990s, and attacks on Buddhist artwork have continued. In one instance, a Christian minister used a microphone on a cord as a bolo weapon and smashed temple paintings and a statue. In other instances, red crosses have been painted on temple walls, murals, and statues. Buddha statues have also been decapitated.

Furthermore, students at Buddhist universities report aggressive attempts to convert them to Christianity on campus, especially near campus temples. On and off, sectarian tensions between Christians and Buddhists occasionally rises due to what was seen by a tendency of the government officials–many of whom are Christians to tilt the political balance in favour of Christians over Buddhists which has occasionally led to discontent over some quarters.

Of particular note was after Lee Myung-bak's ascendency to Presidency, Buddhists drew flak over the high proportion of Christians favouring over Buddhists in the public sector–particularly the cabinet whereby there were 12 Christian ministers to only one Buddhist minister within his cabinet among other reported incidences.

NORTH KOREA

The regime in North Korea actively discouraged the practice of religion, including Buddhism. Currently, the country claims to boast about 10,000 active adherents of Buddhism. As with other religions in the country, Buddhists came under the close scrutiny of the country's government–including worship at Buddhist temples by monks, through the state-sponsored Korea Buddhist Federation. Nevertheless, Buddhists in North Korea reportedly fared better than other religious groups–particularly Christians, who were said to often face persecution by the authorities, and Buddhists were given limited funding by the government to promote the religion, given that Buddhism played an integral role in traditional Korean culture.

CURRENT SITUATION

The Seon school, which is led by the dominant Jogye order, practices disciplined traditional Seon practice at a number of major mountain monasteries in Korea, often under the direction of highly regarded masters. Modern Seon practice is not far removed in content from the original practice of Jinul, who introduced the integrated combination of the practice of Gwanhwa meditation with the study of selected Buddhist texts. The Korean sangha life is markedly itinerant: while each monk has a "home" monastery, he will regularly travel throughout the mountains, staying as long as he wishes, studying and teaching in the style of whatever monastery is housing him.

The Korean monastic training system has seen a steadily increasing influx of Western practitioner-aspirants in the second half of the twentieth century. Currently, Korean Buddhism is in a state of slow transition. While the reigning theory behind Korean Buddhism was based on Jinul's "sudden enlightenment, gradual cultivation," the modern Korean Seon master, Seongcheol's revival of Hui Neng's "sudden enlightenment, sudden cultivation" has taken Korean Buddhism by storm.

Although there is resistance to change within the ranks of the Jogye order, with the last three Supreme Patriarchs' stance that is in accordance with Seongcheol, there has been a gradual change in the atmosphere of Korean Buddhism. According to many recent local news, Christian persecution of Buddhism has increased in recent years. Recently Christians have been destroying temples, statues of the Buddha, and 'praying for the destruction of all Buddhist temples, and persecuting Buddhist monks. Some South Korean Buddhists have denounced what they view as discriminatory measures against them and their religion by the administration of President Lee Myung-bak, which they attribute to Lee being a Christian.

The Buddhist Jogye Order has accused the Lee government of discriminating against Buddhism and favoring Christianity by ignoring certain Buddhist temples but including Christian churches in certain public documents. In 2006, according to the *Asia Times*, "Lee also sent a video prayer message to a Christian rally held in the southern city of Busan in which the worship leader prayed feverishly: 'Lord, let the Buddhist temples in this country crumble down!'"

Further, according to an article in *Buddhist-Christian Studies*: "Over the course of the last decade a fairly large number of Buddhist temples in South Korea have been destroyed or damaged by fire by misguided Christian fundamentalists. More recently,

Buddhist statues have been identified as idols, and attacked and decapitated in the name of Jesus. Arrests are hard to effect, as the arsonists and vandals work by stealth of night." A 2008 incident in which police investigated protesters who had been given sanctuary in the Jogye temple in Seoul and searched a car driven by Jigwan, executive chief of the Jogye order, led to protests by Buddhists who claimed police had treated Jigwan as a criminal.

3

Buddhist Culture in East-Russia

Historically, Buddhism was incorporated into Russian lands as early as the late 16th century, when Russian explorers travelled to and settled in Siberia and what is now the Russian Far East. It is also believed that Indian King Ashoka had sent monks to spread Buddhism all over the world including Siberia. Mongolian and Tibetan lamas first appeared on the eastern shores of Lake Baikal in the middle of the 17th century and quickly spread Buddhism in the area. Later in that century Buddhism emerged as the dominant religion in Tuva. The Kalmyks who migrated from China to the lower reaches of the Volga River in the later half of the 17th century also professed Buddhism.

Tsarist authorities were fairly tolerant with respect to Buddhists. Later, religious centers - Buddhist monasteries, or datsans - appeared in other areas of Buryatia, too. Within a short time most of the Buryats living east of Lake Baikal were converted to Buddhism. In 1764, Zayaagiyn Damba Darjaa, the high priest of the Tsongol datsan - the oldest in the Baikal region - became head of the entire Buddhist clergy with the title Bandida Khamba Lama.

KALMYKS

In the late sixteenth century the Kalmyks were converted to Buddhism by Mongolian lamas in Dzungaria (China). In the seventeenth century, they moved to the lower reaches of the Volga

River, retaining their religion. At that time the Kalmyks gained access to the first works of Buddhist literature translated from the Tibetan language. The main form of Buddhism in Russia is the Gelukpa school of Tibetan Buddhism. Although Tibetan Buddhism is most often associated with the peoples of Tibet, in the north the school spread into southwestern and northern China, Mongolia, and finally Russia. In the south, it took hold in Bhutan and parts of northern India and Nepal.

BURYATIA, TUVA

Afterwards, it began to spread into the geographically and culturally adjacent Russian constituent regions known today as: Amur Oblast, Buryatia, Chita Oblast, Tuva Republic, and Khabarovsk Krai. There is also Kalmykia, another constituent republic of Russia that is in fact the only Buddhist region in Europe, perhaps paradoxically located to the north of the Caucasus. Buddhism has been in Russia for four centuries. In the second half of the XVIIth century Buryats were incorporated into Russia. Beginning from 1727 when the treaty determining the borders between Russia and Manchu-Chinese empires was signed the Buryats started the official development within the Russian state.

In Czarist Russia, where Orthodoxy was the predominant state religion, Buddhists were subjected to certain restrictions. Buddhist monks (lamas) were made dependent on the local police and were subordinated to the chief provincial board. The regulations for the lamaist clergy, introduced in 1853, established the almost despotic reign of officials under the czar.

The latter made the most important assignments concerning even the clerical posts; in official documents the Buddhists like all non-Orthodox Christians were called "otherbelievers", or "the followers of the alien belief" (Russian: *inovertsi*) and the religious problems of the Buddhist were the concern of a special department for foreign religions. Nevertheless, Buddhism began spreading among the Buryats in the 17th century and became an essential and significant element of social, spiritual and material life of most Buryat ethnic groups, and has played a great role in their political and spiritual consolidation. This process of consolidation was stimulated by the formation of a centralized system of the Buryat Buddhist religious administrative structure.

KALACHAKRA TANTRA AND WEST

The spread of the Shambhala myth and the Kalachakra Tantra in the West has a history of its own. It does definitely not first begin with the expulsion of the lamas from Tibet (in 1959) and their diaspora across the whole world, but rather commences at the beginning of the twentieth century in Russia with the religious political activity of an ethnic Buryat by the name of Agvan Dorjiev.

He was convinced that the union of Tibet with Russia would provide the Highlands with an extremely favorable future, and was likewise able to convince the hierarchy upon the Lion Throne of the merits of his political vision for a number of years. He thus advanced to the post of Tibetan envoy in St. Petersburg and at the Russian court. His work in the capital was extremely active and varied. Since the end of the 19th century Buddhism had become fashionable among the Russian high society.

PETER BADMAYEV

Tibetan medical doctor Peter Badmayev was head of the most famous private hospital in St. Petersburg. There the cabinet lists for the respective members of government were put together under his direction. R. Fülöp-Miller has vividly described the doctor's power-political activities: "In the course of time medicine and politics, ministerial appointments and 'lotus essences' became more and more mingled, and a fantastic political magic character arose, which emanated from Badmajev's sanatorium and determined the fate of all Russia.

The miracle-working doctor owed this influence especially to his successful medical-political treatment of the Tsar. Badmajev's mixtures, potions, and powders brewed from mysterious herbs from the steppes served not just to remedy patient's metabolic disturbances; anyone who took these medicaments ensured himself an important office in the state at the same time".

BUDDHIST TEMPLE IN ST. PETERSBURG

For this "wise and crafty Asian" too, the guiding idea was the establishment of an Asian empire with the "White Tsar" at its helm. Buryats had received initiations into the Time Tantra from the Ninth Panchen Lama which were supposed to have been of central significance for Russias future vision. At the center of Agvan Dorjiev 's activities in Russia stood the construction of the Buddhist temple in St. Petersburg. The shrine was dedicated to the Kalachakra deity.

A painter by the name of Nicholas Roerich, who later became a fanatic propagandist for Kalachakra doctrine, produced the designs for the stained-glass windows. Work commenced in 1909. In the central hall various main gods from the Tibetan pantheon were represented with statues and pictures, including among others Dorjiev's wrathful initiation deity, Vajrabhairava. Regarding the décor, it is perhaps also of interest that there was a swastika motif which the Bolsheviks knocked out during the Second World War. Stalinist secret police agents tried to oppress all religious groups, leading to a decline in Buddhism.

Tibetan Buddhism is primarily practiced by the indigenous peoples in various regions of central and eastern Russia, except for a few Russian converts based mainly in the larger cities such as St. Petersburg or Moscow, where there is greater access to urban Buddhist centers or similar facilities. The other major form of Buddhism found in Russia is the more commonly known Mahayana Buddhism, primarily practiced by the Vietnamese or Chinese immigrant communities based mainly in the large cities.

The Russian Federation and Austria are the only two European states today that recognize Buddhism as an "official", though not necessarily "state religion" in their respective countries. On top of that, Russia also recognizes it, along with Islam, Judaism, and of course Orthodox Christianity, as native to Russian soil in the 1993 Constitution of the Russian Federation. All other religious groups are unrecognized, and must officially register and be subject to rejection by the state. There are a few dozen Buddhist university-monasteries throughout Russia, but concentrated in the Russian Far East and Siberia, known in Russian as Datsans. Adherents to Buddhism account for approximately 700,000 in the Russian Federation, about 0.5% of the total population.

IVOLGA MONASTERY

Organizations: The highest authority for Russian Buddhists is the Central Buddhist Board based in the Ivolga Datsan in the Buryat. (A permanent office in Moscow is concerned with external relations). The congress of clergy and laity convenes once in four years and elects the members of the Board. Head of the Central Buddhist Board is Bandida Khambo-lama. Russian Buddhism is representative of the Gelugpa school ("the School of Virtue"), which is a branch of Tibetan Buddhism in the Mahayana tradition, that is, "the broad path" of salvation from endless rebirth in the world of suffering. Russian Buddhism has a number of specific ritual peculiarities that have taken shape over the course of history.

Historically it has been marked by the prevalence of rural lamas living outside datsans because of the nomadic way of life. To some extent, this tradition has survived to this day. In keeping with tradition, six major holidays, khurals, are celebrated annually and are attended by a large number of people who bring various gifts to datsans as well as money and food for lamas.

HOLIDAYS

Tsagaalgan is a holiday celebrated on the eve of the lunar New Year, which usually falls in February. This khural is devoted to the twelve miracles of Buddha during his dispute with six preachers of heresy. Services and a series of religious rites are conducted to mark the occasion. Buddhists, dressed in their best clothes, come to pray together for well-being and more happiness. On the eve of the New Year, a solemn evening ritual is performed during which food is served to the doksheetsi, the protectors of the faith.

This involves the ritual burning of Dugzhub, a magic pyramid of paper and wood; according to a Buddhist belief, a ritual fire consumes all evil thoughts. A long note from a big white conch proclaims the first day of the lunar New Year. A traditional service is held to celebrate the Sagaan Sar ("white month") holiday. In the main temple lamas, replacing one another, pray for fifteen days for peace and goodness.

The khural Duyn-khor, a second major holiday, lasts three days in April. It is dedicated to the preaching of the sacred teaching of Kalachakra. The third major holiday is Gandun-Shunserme, devoted to the birth and enlightenment of Buddha and his attainment of nirvana. It is celebrated in early summer. The fourth holiday Maidari is dedicated toMaidari, the Buddha of the future (Maitreia). It is always celebrated for two days in midsummer. People spend the first day in many hours of devout prayer. On the second day the gilded statue of Maidari is solemnly carried out of the temple and placed on a chariot twined with silk ribbons. It is surrounded by lamas in ceremonial dress.

A green horse of plaster is harnessed to the chariot, and the procession sets off around the datsan. This ceremony symbolizes Maidari's tour of the universe and the spread of his grace throughout it. Several thousand people gather in the datsan for the procession. Akharang, a big copper shield, is struck with a mallet, and its sounds can be heard far away. There is a fanfare, the drums roll, and conchs are blown. The procession stops at every turn of the monastery walls for a reading of sacred Scriptures.

Many Buddhists attending the procession try to approach the chariot, to hold onto its beam and harness, and to throw money at the feet of the statue of Maidari. The last two khurals are celebrated with less splendor, but they also attract large crowd of believers. Lhabab Düisen, marked in autumn, is devoted to the Buddha's return from the thirty-third heaven. The holiday Zula is dedicated to the passing away of the father of Lamaism,Bogdo Tsongkhapa. A thousand candles are lit during the service.

During the khurals prayers are said in honor of the protectors of the faith and for well-being and peace on earth. Lamas who live in monasteries observe the Dulva, a traditional moral and ethical code. Depending on the level of ordination, they participate in services and philosophical discussions and perform special religious rites at the people's request. Recently, in addition to Buryats, Kalmyks, and Tuvinians, more and more Russians, Ukrainians have been attending Buddhist services. Previously, they all went to pray at the Ivolga datsan, but today, with the 1991 reopening of the temple in Leningrad, followers of Buddhism from the Europe an part of the country will travel there, too.

BUDDHISM IN SCIENCE

In Russia, academic Buddhist studies began from the middle of the 19th century. By the end of the century, the Russian Buddhological School had won international prestige. With the discovery of Buddhist manuscripts in Central Asia at the beginning of the 20th Century, a new stage in the study of Buddhism began. The Central Asian, Sak and Uyghur Buddhist texts with their Chinese and Tibetan translations have been published. The international series *Bibliotheca Buddhica*, founded in Russia by S.F. Oldendurg and F.I. Tsherbatsky became the center of Buddhist studies; attracting the greatest scholars of the world: L. de La Vallee Poussen, Max Walleser, Sylvan Levi and others.

From 1897 to 1937, the most important Buddhist texts in Sanskrit, Tibetan and Uyghur on Buddhist philosophy, logic, etc. were printed in a 30-volume series. In 1960, V.N. Toporov published a translation of *Dhammapada*, becoming the 31st volume, and A.I. Vostrikov's book *The Tibetan Historical*

Literature became the 32nd. Many of the works published, particularly on Buddhist logic, have been regarded as unsurpassed. In the enormous volume of buddhological works, the quantitative contribution of Russian scientists has been rather modest, but their qualificative aspect is of high value.

In 1985 with the publication of the *Monuments of the Indian Texts from Central Asia* by G.M. Bongard-Levin and M.I. Vorobyova-Desyatovskaya the edition of this series was continued. Later on a few other publications appeared. Among them one can mention the study and the translation from Sanskrit of the first part of the *Abhidharmakosa* done by V.I. Rudoi, the translation from the Pali of the *The Questions of Milinda* (Milindapanhi) carried out by A.V. Paribok and also the publication of the work by the Chinese author Huei Tsyao: *Biographies of the Distinguished Monks*(Gao Sen Chuan) carried out by M.E.Ermakov.

At present Buddhism is studied at research centers in Moscow, St. Petersburg, as well as in Ulan-Ude, Elista and Kyzyl. The buddhologists in Moscow concentrate their efforts on the role of the Buddhist cult as well as the place and role of Buddhism in social and political life of Asian countries, and its influence on the culture and traditions of oriental peoples. In St. Petersburg, scholars are mainly engaged in deciphering ancient Indian inscriptions and textological research in the field of Buddhist art and old Uyghur, Tibetan, Mongolian and Chinese texts and treatises.

In buddhological studies —mainly pursuing the fields of sinology and indology— notable achievements have been made; whereas in the fields of Tibetan and Mongolian studies, the scope of research has not been so broad. Nevertheless, all the buddhological studies are closely interrelated. A great many texts in the Tibetan language, translated from Sanskrit, are accessible now; though their original texts in Sanskrit have been lost. Therefore the value of these Tibetan texts becomes all the more significant. The fact that in Russia, there is a living tradition of Tibetan Buddhism, spread among Buryats, Kalmycks and Tyvanians, greatly contributed to the development of Tibetan and Mongolian studies, and within their frame to the buddhological studies.

BUDDHISM IN BURYATIA

Buddhism in Buryatia, a region in Central Asia and Southern Siberia, which was the northern-most point of the spread of Buddhism. The Buryats were, and are still are the largest Buddhist population in Russia. The Buryats, Kalmyks and the Tuvans are the three Buddhist nationalities in Russia, historically belonging to the common Mongolian spiritual realm and to the Tibetan and Mongolian cultural and religious tradition of the great Central Asian civilization. Tibetan religious and cultural influence has been playing, up to now, an important role in the culture and history of these peoples. In the beginning, Buddhist monasteries were the centers, not only of culture and learning, but in fact they became moral and ethical regulators of everyday life of Buryat families. Buddhism stimulated the formation of the nation's intellectual potential.

There appeared different monastic educational faculties with many learned monks and scholars. Among them we can mention Agvan Dorjiev (1857-1930), one of the tutors of the 13th Dalai Lama, who was his representative in the Russian court and played a great role in Tibet's international political life, establishing various relations between Tibet and Russia. By the beginning of the century, Buddhism had become quite strong and this caused the anxiety on the part of the Christian church. In order to adapt the Buddhist teaching and church to the rapidly developing and changing world, Agvan Dorjiev and some prominent Buryat scholars initiated a modernization movement among Buddhist clergy and intellectuals, proclaiming the necessity of combining the Buddhist philosophy with the best achievements of Western culture and civilization.

The movement has gained a wide scope in Buryatia. It was due to the fact of mutual interest of both: the Buddhist clergy wanted to preserve somehow the church, by means of modification, whereas local intelligentsia regarded Buddhist ideas as a cultural and social basis for further national development after being freed from pagan elements. Though "modernists" played an important role in the national liberation movement of Buryats and promoted national and cultural autonomy of Buryats within the Russian Federation and establishing of the Buryat-Mongolian Autonomous Republic after the revolution, still the movement was doomed to failure because it was unrealistic to expect gaining self-administration for Buryat people by means of religious reforms and revival of national culture neither before the revolution nor after it.

The attempt of these "modernists" to emphasize similarity of ideas in Marxism and early Buddhism also failed. This movement is all the more noteworthy because no comparable developments took place in Tibetan Buddhism until after the confrontation with Chinese communism in 1949. By 1935 there were about 45 or 46 Buddhist temples and monasteries in Buryatia. In Europe systematic and large-scale buddhological studies started from the middle of the XIXth

century when the main canonical texts of the southern Buddhism were introduced into academic turnover and there emerged their translations in the English language in the series of "Sacred texts of the Buddhists" and "Sacred books of the East", which served as resources for further broad and diverse studies. In Russia academic Buddhist studies began from the middle of the XIXth century. Already by the end of the century the Russian Buddhological School had won international prestige. With the discovery of the Buddhist manuscripts in Central Asia in the beginning of the XXth century a new stage in the study of Buddhism began.

The Central Asian, Sak and Uigur Buddhist texts with their Chinese and Tibetan translations have been published. The international series "Bibliotheca Buddhica" founded in Russia by S.F. Oldendurg and F.I. Tsherbatsky became the center of Buddhist studies which attracted the greatest scholars of the world L. de La Vallee Poussen, Max Walleser, Sylvan Levi and others. Beginning with 1897 and up to 1937 the most important Buddhist texts in Sanskrit, Tibetan and Uigur on Buddhist philosophy, logic, etc. were printed in 30 volumes within this series. In 1960 V.N. Toporov published the translation of "Dhammapada", which became the 31st volume, and A.I. Vostrikov's book "The Tibetan historical literature" - the 32nd.

Many of the works published, particularly on Buddhist logic, have been regarded unsurpassed. In the enormous volume of Buddhological works the quantitative contribution of the Russian scientists is rather modest, but their qualificative aspect is of high value. In 1985 with the publication of the "Monuments of the Indian texts from Central Asia" by G.M. Bongard-Levin and M.I. Vorobyova-Desyatovskaya the edition of this series was continued. Later on a few other publications appeared.

Among them one can mention the study and the translation from Sanskrit of the 1st part of the "Abhidharmakosa" done by V.I. Rudoi, the translation from the Pali of the "The questions of Milinda" (Milindapanhi) carried out by A.V. Paribok and also the publication of the work by the Chinese author Huei Tsyao "Biographies of the distinguished monks" (Gao sen chuan) carried out by M.E. Ermakov. At present Buddhism is studied at the research centers in Moscow, St. Petersburg and Tartu, as well as in Ulan-Ude, Elista and Kyzyl.

The buddhologists in Moscow concentrate their efforts on the role of the Buddhist cult as well as the place and role of Buddhism in social and political life of Asian countries, and its influence on the culture and traditions of oriental peoples. In St. Petersburg scholars are mainly engaged in deciphering ancient Indian inscriptions and textological researches in the field of Buddhist art and old Uigur, Tibetan, Mongolian and Chinese texts and treatises. In the buddhological studies which were pursued mainly in the field of sinology and indology notable achievements have been made, whereas in the field of Tibetan and Mongolian studies the scope of research has not been so wide. Nevertheless all the buddhological studies are closely interrelated.

A great many texts in the Tibetan language translated from Sanskrit are accessible now though their original texts in Sanskrit have been lost. Therefore the value of the Tibetan texts becomes all the more significant. The fact that in Russia there is the living tradition of the Tibetan Buddhism, spread among Buryats, Kalmycks and Tyvanians, greatly contributed to the development of Tibetan and Mongolian studies and within their frame to the Buddhological studies. Though one should state quite precisely that implied in this case is the study of a modern European type.

In the Buddhist monasteries there was their own system of study of Buddhism owing to which we dispose at present of a large layer of the written legacy of the peoples of Central Asia in Tibetan and Mongolian which is the main resource for Buddhist studies and is an independent object for study within our other projects. Buddhism in Buryatia Buryatia is one of the Buddhist regions of Central Asia and South Siberia, which was the extreme point of the spread of Buddhism northwards. The Buryats were and still are the largest Buddhist population in Russia. The Buryats, Kalmycks and the Tyvanians are the three Buddhist nationalities in Russia historically belonging to the common Mongolian spiritual realm and to the Tibetan and Mongolian cultural and religious tradition of the great Central Asian civilization.

Tibetan religious and cultural influence has been playing up to now an important role in the culture and history of these peoples. In the second half of the XVIIth century Buryats were incorporated into Russia. Beginning from 1727 when the treaty determining the borders between Russia and Manju-Chinese empires was signed the Buryats started the official development within the Russian state. In the tsarist Russia, where Orthodoxy was the predominant state religion, Buddhists' activities were subjected to certain restrictions. Buddhist monks (lamas) were made dependent on the local police and were subordinated to the chief provincial board. The Regulations for the lamaist clergy, introduced in 1853, made legal the despotic reign of tsarist officials.

The latter made the most important assignments concerning even the clerical posts; in official documents the Buddhists were called "the followers of the alien belief" (inovertsi) and the religious problems of the Buddhist were the concern of a special Department for foreign religions. Nevertheless Buddhism that began spreading among Buryats in 17th century became an essential and significant element of social, spiritual and material life of most of Buryat ethnic groups, has played a great role in their political and spiritual consolidation. This process of consolidation was stimulated by the formation of a centralized system of the Buryat Buddhist religious administrative structure. With the increase of the number of Buddhist temples their role in social and economic life of the Buryat society was constantly growing.

At the beginning Buddhist monasteries were the centers not only of culture and learning, but in fact they became moral and ethical regulators of everyday life of Buryat families. Buddhism stimulated the formation of the nation's intellectual potential. There appeared different monastic educational faculties with many learned monks and scholars. Among them we can mention Agvan Dorjiev (1857-1930), one of the tutors of the 13th Dalai Lama, who was his representative at the Russian court and played a great rôle in the international political life, establishing various relations between Tibet and Russia.

By the beginning of the century Buddhism has become quite strong and this caused the anxiety on the part of the Christian church. In order to adapt the Buddhist teaching and church to the rapidly developing and changing world A. Dorjiev and some prominent Buryat scholars initiated a modernization movement among Buddhist clergy and intellectuals, proclaiming the necessity of combining the Buddhist philosophy with the best achievements of Western culture and civilization. The movement has gained a wide scope in Buryatia.

It was due to the fact of mutual interest of both: the Buddhist clergy wanted to preserve somehow the church by means of modification, whereas local intelligentsia regarded Buddhist ideas as a cultural and social basis for the further national development after being freed from pagan elements. Though "modernists" played an important role in national liberation movement of Buryats and promoted national and cultural Autonomy of Buryats within the Russian Federation and establishing of the Buryat-Mongolian Autonomous Republic after the revolution, still the movement was doomed to failure because it was unrealistic to expect gaining self-administration for Buryat people by means of religious reforms and revival of national culture neither before the revolution nor after it.

The attempt of "modernists" to emphasize similarity of ideas in Marxism and early Buddhism also failed. This movement is all the more noteworthy because no comparable developments took place in Tibetan Buddhism until after the confrontation with Chinese communism in 1949. By 1935 in Buryatia there were about 45 or 46 Buddhist temples and monasteries. Antireligious and atheistic policy of the Soviet government was the reason of a complete annihilation of all the Buddhist churches and the clergy.

As a result of it nowadays we face the break of cultural and historical links between the generations and the breaking of spiritual and ethic succession of traditions, the loss of the indigenous script. This is vividly testified by the bibliography. During these years buddhological researches in Buryatia gave the foremost attention to atheistic education, critical analyses of social role of lamaist church in the history of Buryat society. Now we witness the active process of Buddhist restoration and revival, Buddhist temples are being built practically anew. But the process of reviving of spiritual values appears to be more difficult and complicated, because the loss of spiritual and ethic succession of traditions between the generations can't be restored.

Buddhist Studies in Buryatia 1991 was the year when 250 years ago the Russian government has officially recognized the Buryat Buddhist church and gave some privileges to its clergy. Of course, this is a short historical period in the general history of a nation. But it revealed the fact that we don't know much about the early history, the first steps of Buddhist dissemination on the territory of Buryatia. We don't have enough materials and sources for studying this period of history, that the primary sources written in classic Mongolian script have not yet been studied and translated.

This was a result of the fact that the history, development and problems of Buryat Buddhism in the former USSR were of interest only for a relatively small group of professionals. Buddhological researches in Buryatia have ancient traditions going back to Russian classic oriental studies. They have received a new stimulus with the appearance in 1967 of a special department of Buddhist studies at the former Institute of social sciences, now Institute of Mongolian, Tibetan and Buddhist studies.

The scholars of the Department and of the Institute have published a series of monographs and collected works devoted to various aspects of Buryat Buddhism, such as its cult structure and its special features in Buryatia, interrelationship of Buddhism with traditional Central Asian beliefs, the process of Buddhist assimilation of ancient Mongolian, Buryat and Tibetan beliefs, the influence of Buddhism on spiritual culture of these peoples, the role of Buddhist church in different historical periods, Buddhist philosophy, Buddhist art, Buddhist literature, critical study of different Buddhist written sources, their translation and publication, etc.

Buddhological researches include not only Buryat Buddhism, but the whole Central and Eastern Asian regions and are carried on the basis of different oriental languages. Buddhist Bibliography Now we are working out a number of electronic resources that are aimed at upgrading Oriental Studies in Buryatia. These include several projects on cataloging archives, Tibetan and Mongolian collections of the DOMX, subject bibliographies on Buryat ethnography (this one has been presented for the 1998 PNC meeting) and the Bibliography under discussion. Bibliography on Buddhism and Buddhist Studies in Russia and Buryatia presents the works on Buddhism published during 1737-1991 in Russia.

The draft version of the Bibliography includes about 2,500 items. Among them there are monographs, articles and papers printed in different periodicals and collected works. All of them are now being input into computer. Electronic Buddhist Bibliography is supposed to be published on-line during the year 1999. Of course, it will be further developed. The database provides easy and convenient access to resources it contains. Its structure has been developed for supplying more related information and services than any printed or card catalog can give. For example, there are additional tables that contain extensive information on authors, periodicals, publishing houses, thematic series. It provides also subject systematization.

4

BUDDHIST CULTURE IN VIETNAM

Buddhism came to Vietnam as early as the second century CE through the North from central Asia and via Southern routes from India. Buddhism in Vietnam is made up of both Mahayana and Theravada schools, but the more prominent is Mahayana. Buddhism in Vietnam has had a symbiotic relationship with Taoism, Chinese spirituality, and the indigenous Vietnamese religion.

The majority of Buddhist practitioners focus on devotional rituals rather than meditation. Buddhism is not practiced the same as in other Asian countries and does not contain the institutional structures, hierarchy, or sanghas that exist in other traditional Buddhist settings. Due to this observation the estimate that 80% of the Vietnamese population is Buddhist is questionable, but does however show that many Vietnamese define their spiritual needs using a Buddhist worldview.

FOUNDATION

Buddhism came to Vietnam in the first or second century CE through the North from central Asia and via the South from India trade routes. By the end of the second century, Vietnam developed a major Buddhist centre (probably Mahayana) in the region, commonly known as the Luy Lâu centre, now in the B¯c Ninh province, north of the present day Hanoi city. Luy Lâu was the capital of Giao ChÉ, (the former name of Vietnam), and was a popular place visited by many Indian Buddhist missionary monks to China.

The monks followed the sea route from the Indian sub-continent to China used by Indian traders. A number of Mahayana sutras and the Agamas were translated into Chinese script at that centre, including the Sutra of Forty-Two Chapters and the Anapanasati. Over the next 18 centuries Vietnam and China shared many common features of cultural, philosophical and religious heritage. This was due to geographical proximity to one another and Vietnam being annexed twice by the Chinese. Vietnamese Buddhism has been greatly influenced by the development of Mahayana Buddhism in China, with the dominant traditions of Pure Land and Ch'an/Zen. Theravada Buddhism would become incorporated through the annexation of the Khmer land and khmer people.

DEVELOPMENT

During the Đing Dynasty (968-980) Buddhism was recognized by the state as an official religion (~971) suggesting that the current kings at the time held Buddhism in high regard. The Early Lê Dynasty (980-1009) would follow a similar path. Reasons for growth of Buddhism during this time are contributed to an influx of educated monks, a newly independent state needing an ideological basis on which to build a country and the development of Confucianism. Buddhism became more prominent during the Lý Dynasty (1009-1225) beginning with the founder Lý Thái TÕ who was raised in a pagoda (Buddhist temple).

All of the kings during the Ly Dynasty supported Buddhism as a state religion and this continued into the Tr§n Dynasty (1225-1400) where Buddhism later developed in combination with Confucianism. Buddhism fell out of favor during the Later Lê Dynasty and would grow under the NguyÅn Dynasty. A Buddhist revival (Chan Hung Phat Giao) started in 1920 in an effort to reform and develops institutional Buddhism, which continues today. Under Communist rule many religious practices in Vietnam Buddhism were suppressed. However a government sanctioned and approved United Buddhist Church was created in the North.

In the South, the Unified Buddhist Church was created and opposed the communist government. Since ĐÕi MÛi (1986) many reforms have allowed Buddhism to be practiced further. It was not until 2007 that Pure Land Buddhism, the largest type of Buddhism practiced in Vietnam, was officially recognized as a religion by the government.

PRACTICE

Normally it is believed that the differing schools of Buddhism are incompatible and cannot practice together. However within Vietnam followers practice differing traditions without any problem or without contradiction. Although Vietnamese Buddhism does not have a strong centralized structure, the practice is similar throughout the country at almost any temple. Gaining merit is the most common and essential practice in Vietnamese Buddhism with a belief that liberation takes place with the help of Buddhas and bodhisattvas.

Buddhist monks commonly chant sutras, recite Buddhas' names (Amitabha most notably, doing repentance and praying for rebirth in the Pure Land). Meditation is not always a common daily practice. The Lotus Sutra and Amitabha Sutra are the most commonly used sutras. Most sutras and texts have come from China and have been translated into Sino-Vietnamese (Han –Viet) rather than the vernacular making them largely incomprehensible to most practitioners.

Three services are practiced regularly at dawn, noon, and dusk. They include sutras (mainly devotional), reciting dharanis and Buddha's name, and circumambulation (walking meditation). Laypeople at times join the services at the temple and some devout Buddhist practice the services at home. Special services such as Sam Nguyen/Sam Hoi (confession / repentance) take place on the full moon and new moon each month. Chanting the name of Buddha is one way of repenting and purifying bad karma.

PURE LAND

Pure Land Buddhism is the most widespread form of Buddhism within Vietnam. It is common for practitioners to recite sutras, chants and dharanis looking to gain protection from bodhisattvas or Dharma-Protectors. It is a devotional practice where those practicing put their faith into Amitabha Buddha (V. A Di Đà Ph-t). Followers believe they will gain rebirth in the Pure Land by chanting Amitabha's name.

The Pure Land is where one can more easily gain enlightenment since suffering does not exist. Many religious organizations have not been recognized by the government however in 2007, with 1.5 million followers, The Vietnamese Pure Land Buddhism Association (TËnh ĐÙ Cý S) Ph-t HÙi ViÇt Nam) received official recognition as an independent and legal religious organization.

ZEN IN VIETNAM

ThiÁn Buddhism (ThiÁn Tông) is the Vietnamese name for the school of Zen Buddhism. Thien is ultimately derived from Chan Zong, itself a derivative of the Sanskrit "Dhyâna". The traditional account is that in 580, when an Indian monk named Vinitaruci (Vietnamese: Tì-ni-ða-lýu-chi) traveled to Vietnam after completing his studies with Jianzhi Sengcan, the third patriarch of Chinese Zen. This would be the first appearance of Vietnamese Zen, or Thien (thiÁn) Buddhism.

The sect that Vinitaruci and his lone Vietnamese disciple founded would become known as the oldest branch of Thien. After a period of obscurity, the Vinitaruci School became one of the most influential Buddhist groups in Vietnam by the 10th century, particularly under the patriarch V¡n-H¡nh (died 1018). Other early Vietnamese Zen schools included the Vo Ngon Thong (Vô Ngôn Thông), which was associated with the teaching of Mazu, and the Thao Duong (Th£o ĐýÝng), which incorporated nianfo chanting techniques; both were founded by Chinese monks.

A new school was founded by King Tr§n Nhân Tông (1258–1308); called Trúc Lâm (Bamboo Grove) school, which evinced a deep influence from Confucian and Taoist philosophy. Nevertheless, Trúc Lâm's prestige waned over the following centuries as Confucianism became dominant in the royal court. In the 17th century, a group of Chinese monks led by Nguyên ThiÁu introduced the Ling school (Lâm T¿). A more domesticated offshoot of Lâm T¿, the LiÅu Quán school, was founded in the 18th century and has since been the predominant branch of Vietnamese Zen.

CONTROVERSY OVER ZEN

Some scholars argue that Zen (ThiÁn) in Vietnam is an invented tradition and that the Zen schools have played more of an elite rhetorical role than a role of practice. The ThiÁn UyÃn T-p Anh (Outstanding Figures in the Vietnamese Zen Community) has been the dominant text used to legitimize the Zen Buddhist lineage and history within Vietnam.

However Cuong Tu Nguyen's "Zen in Medieval Vietnam: A Study and Translation of the Thien Tap Anh" (1997) gives a critical review of how the text has been used to create a history of Zen Buddhism that that is "fraught with discontinuity". Current day Buddhist practices are not reflective of a Zen past is that in modern day Vietnam the common practices are more focused on ritual and devotion than the Zen focus on meditation. Nonetheless, we are seeing an increased population in Zen today.

THERAVADA

The southern part of present day Vietnam was originally occupied by the Cham people and the Khmer people who followed both a syncretic Saiva-Mahayana Buddhism and Theravada Buddhism. The Đ¡i ViÇt annexed the land occupied by the Cham during conquests in the 15th century, and by the 18th century had also annexed the southern portion of the Khmer Empire resulting in the current borders of Vietnam. From that time onward, the dominant Đ¡i ViÇt, followed the Mahayana tradition while the Khmer continued to practise Theravada.

In the 1920s and 1930s, there were a number of movements in Vietnam for the revival and modernization of Buddhist activities. Together with the re-organization of Mahayana establishments, there developed a growing interest in Theravadin meditation as well as the Pali Canon. These were then available in French. Among the pioneers who brought Theravada Buddhism to the ethnic Đ¡i ViÇt was a young veterinary doctor named Lê Vãn Gi£ng. He was born in the South, received higher education in Hanoi, and after graduation, was sent to Phnom Penh, Cambodia, to work for the French government.

During that time he became especially interested in Theravada Buddhist practice and in 1940, upon an invitation from a group of lay Buddhists led by Mr. NguyÅn Vãn HiÃu, he went back to Vietnam in order to help establish the first Theravada temple for Vietnamese Buddhists, at Go Dua, Thç Đéc (now a district of HÓ Chí Minh City). The temple was named Bíu Quang (Ratana Ramsyarama). The temple was destroyed by French troops in 1947, and was later rebuilt in 1951.

At Bíu Quang temple, together with a group of Vietnamese bhikkhus (monks), who had received training in Cambodia, such as Venerables ThiÇn Lu-t, Bíu Chõn, Kim Quang and Gioi Nghiem, Venerable HÙ Tông began teaching the Dhamma in their native Vietnamese. He also translated many Buddhist materials from the Pali Canon, and Theravada became part of Vietnamese Buddhist activity in the country. In 1949-1950, Venerable HÙ Tông together with Mr NguyÅn Vãn HiÃu and supporters built a new temple in Saigon (now HÓ Chí Minh City), named Kó Viên Tñ (Jetavana Vihara). This temple became the centre of Theravada activities in Vietnam, which continued to attract increasing interest among the Vietnamese Buddhists.

In 1957, the Vietnamese Theravada Buddhist Sangha Congregation (Giáo HÙi Tãng Già Nguyên Thçy ViÇt Nam) was formally established and recognised by the government, and the Theravada Sangha elected Venerable HÙ Tông as its first President, or Sangharaja. From Saigon, the Theravada movement spread to other provinces, and soon, a number of Theravada temples for ethnic Viet Buddhists were established in many areas in the South and Central parts of Vietnam. As of 1997, there were 64 Theravada temples throughout the country, of which 19 were located in HÓ Chí Minh City and its viccinity. Besides Bíu Quang and Kó Viên temples, other well known temples are Bíu Long, Giác Quang, Tam B£o (Đà Nµng), ThiÁn Lam and HuyÁn Không (Hu¿), and the large Sakyamuni Buddha Monument (Thích Ca Ph-t Đ¡i) in Ving Tàu.

VIETNAMESE BUDDHISM OVERSEAS

After the fall of Southern Vietnam in 1975 (Vietnam War, known as the American War in Vietnam, also the second Indochina War) the first Buddhist community appeared in North America. Since this time the North American Vietnamese Buddhist community has grown to 160 temples and centers, however Vietnamese Buddhism is one of the least popular forms of Buddhism among Buddhists of European descent. Two reasons for this are (1) a lack of meditation within the practice (which is generally favored by Western Buddhists) and (2) not much proselytizing being carried out by the Vietnamese Buddhists.

The most famous practitioner of synchronized ThiÁn Buddhism in the West is Thích Nh¥t H¡nh who has authored dozens of books and founded Dharma center Plum Village in France together with his colleague -Bhiksuni and Zen Master- Chân Không. Thich Nhat Hanh's fame in the Western world as a proponen of engaged Buddhism and a new zen style has "no affinity with or any foundation in traditional Vietnamese Buddhist practices" and his style of Zen Buddhism is not reflective of actual Vietnamese Buddhism. Thich Nhat Hanh's Buddhist teachings have started to return to a Vietnam where the Buddhist landscape is now being shaped by the combined Vietnamese & Westernized Buddhism that is focused more on the meditative practices.

Buddhism came to Vietnam in the first century CE. By the end of the second century, Vietnam developed a major Buddhist centre in the region, commonly known as the Luy-Lau centre, now in the Bac-Ninh province, north of the present day Hanoi city. Luy-Lau was the capital of Giao-Chi, (the former name of Vietnam), and was a popular place visited by many Indian Buddhist missionary monks on their way to China, who were following the sea route from the Indian sub-continent used by Indian traders. A number of Mahayana sutras and the Agamas were translated into Chinese script at that centre, including the sutra of Forty Two Chapters, the Anapanasati, the Vessantara-jataka, the Milinda-panha, etc. In the next 18 centuries, due to geographical proximity with China and to being twice annexed by the Chinese, the two countries shared many common features of cultural, philosophical and religious heritage. Vietnamese Buddhism has been greatly influenced by the development of Mahayana Buddhism in China, with the dominant traditions of Ch'an/Zen, Pure Land, and Tantra.

The southern part of present day Vietnam was originally occupied by the Champa (Cham) and the Cambodian (Khmer) people who followed both a syncretic Saiva-Mahayana Buddhism and Theravada Buddhism, although the Champa probably had a Theravada presence from as early as the 3rd century CE, whilst Cambodia received the Theravada as late as the 12th century. The Vietnamese started to conquer and absorbed the land in the 15th century, and the current shape of the country existed in the 18th century. From that time onward, the dominant Viet followed the Mahayana tradition whilst the ethnic Cambodian practiced the Theravada tradition, and both traditions peacefully co-existed. In the 1920s and 1930s, there were a number of movements in Vietnam for the revival and modernisation of Buddhist activities. Together with the re-organisation of Mahayana establishments, there developed a growing interest in Theravadin meditation and also in Buddhist materials based on the Pali Canon.

These were then available in French. Among the pioneers who brought Theravada Buddhism to the ethnic Viet was a young veterinary doctor named Le Van Giang. He was born in the South, received higher education in Hanoi, and after graduation, was sent to Phnom Penh, Cambodia, to work for the French government. During that time, he developed a growing interest in Buddhism. He started to study and practice the Pure Land and Tantric ways but was not satisfied. By chance, he met the Vice Sangharaja of the Cambodian Sangha and was recommended a book on the Noble Eightfold Path written in French. He was struck by the clear message in the book, and decided to try out the Theravada way. He learnt meditation on the breath (Anapanasati) from a Cambodian monk at the Unalom Temple in Phnom Penh and achieved deep samadhi states. He continued the practice and after a few years, he decided to ordain and took the Dhamma name of Ho-Tong (Vansarakkhita).

In 1940, upon an invitation by a group of lay Buddhists led by Mr Nguyen Van Hieu, a close friend, he went back to Vietnam and helped to establish the first Theravada temple for Vietnamese Buddhists, at Go Dua, Thu Duc (now a district of Saigon). The temple was named Buu-Quang (Ratana Ramsyarama). Later, the Cambodian Sangharaja, Venerable Chuon Nath, together with 30 Cambodian bhikkhus established the Sima boundary at this temple. The temple was destroyed by French troops in 1947, and was rebuilt in 1951. Here at Buu-Quang temple, together with a group of Vietnamese bhikkhus, who had received training in Cambodia, such as Venerables Thien-Luat, Buu-Chon, Kim-Quang, Gioi-Nghiem, Tinh-Su, Toi-Thang, Giac-Quang, An-Lam, Venerable Ho-Tong started teaching the Buddha Dhamma in Vietnamese language. He also translated many Buddhist materials from the Pali Canon, and Theravada became part of Vietnamese Buddhist activity in the country.

In 1949-1950, Venerable Ho-Tong together with Mr Nguyen Van Hieu and supporters built a new temple in Saigon, named Ky-Vien Tu (Jetavana Vihara). This temple became the centre of Theravada activities in Vietnam, which continued to attract increasing interest among the Vietnamese Buddhists. In 1957, the

Vietnamese Theravada Buddhist Sangha Congregation (Giao Hoi Tang Gia Nguyen Thuy Viet Nam) was formally established and recognised by the government, and the Theravada Sangha elected Venerable Ho-Tong as its first President, or Sangharaja. During that time, Dhamma activities were further strengthened by the presence of Venerable Narada from Sri Lanka. Venerable Narada had first came to Vietnam in the 1930s and brought with him Bodhi tree saplings which he planted in many places throughout the country.

During his subsequent visits in the 1950s and 1960s, he attracted a large number of Buddhists to the Theravada tradition, one of whom was the popular translator, Mr Pham Kim Khanh who took the Dhamma name of Sunanda. Mr Khanh translated many books of Venerable Narada, including The Buddha and His Teachings, Buddhism in a Nutshell, Satipatthana Sutta, The Dhammapada, A Manual of Abhidhamma, etc. Mr Khanh, now in his 80s, lives in the USA and is still active in translating Dhamma books of well-known meditation teachers from Thailand, Burma and Sri Lanka. From Saigon, the Theravada movement spread to other provinces, and soon, a number of Theravada temples for ethnic Viet Buddhists were established in many areas in the South and Central parts of Vietnam.

As at 1997, there were 64 Theravada temples throughout the country, of which 19 were located in Saigon and its viccinity. Beside Buu-Quang and Ky-Vien temples, other well known temples are Buu-Long, Giac-Quang, Tam-Bao (Da-Nang), Thien-Lam and Huyen-Khong (Hue), and the large Sakyamuni Buddha Monument (Thich-Ca Phat Dai) in Vung Tau. In the 1960s and 1970s, a number of Vietnamese bhikkhus were sent overseas for further training, mostly in Thailand and some in Sri Lanka and India. Recently, this programme has been resumed and about 20 bhikkhus and nuns are receiving training in Burma. Historically, there has been a close relationship between the Cambodian and the Vietnamese bhikkhus. In fact, in 1979, after the Khmer Rouge were driven out of Phnom Penh, a group of Vietnamese bhikkhus led by Venerables Buu-Chon and Gioi-Nghiem came to that city to re-ordain seven Cambodian monks, and thus re-established the Cambodian Sangha which had been destroyed by the Khmer Rouge when they were in control.

Dhamma literature in the Vietnamese language comes from two main sources: the Pali Canon and the Chinese Agamas, together with a large collection of Mahayana texts. Since the 1980s, there has been an ongoing programme to publish these materials by scholar monks of both Mahayana and Theravada traditions. So far, 27 volumes of the first 4 Nikayas, translated by Venerable Minh-Chau, and the 4 Agamas, translated by Venerables Tri-Tinh, Thien-Sieu and Thanh-Tu, have been produced. Work is under way to translate and publish the 5th Nikaya. In addition, a complete set of the Abhidhamma, translated by Venerable Tinh-Su, has been printed, together with the Dhammapada, the Milinda-Panha, the Visudhi-Magga, the Abhidhammatthasangaha and many other work.

In summary, although Buddhism in Vietnam is predominantly of the Mahayana form, the Theravada tradition is well recognised and is experiencing a growing interest especially in the practice of meditation, in Nikaya-Agama literature and in Abhidhamma studies. India is the historical seat of Buddhism as well as home to both the Theravada and Mahayana sects. As the birthplace of the Buddha and the land where he traveled to spread the word of his teachings, India is considered the center of Buddhist studies. Buddhism is one of the most popular religions in India, and influences the culture in a multitude of ways.

Buddhism's roots are closely related to the Jain and Hindu religions in that its ultimate origin was found in the *Rig Veda* and Brahman tradition. It is possible to see Buddhism as a natural extension of these theologies, building on the foundations of a belief laid a thousand years before. The Jain and Hindu schools both held the idea that life is a series of painful reoccurrence. A person attempts to learn these painful life lessons in order to reincarnate and come back as a more perfect person. Hindu's maintain that one can tell how far an individual has progressed by their position in the caste system.

As a result, the experiences of a person's life are seen as being the result of action taken in previous incarnations. If a person lives in unhappy circumstances that is taken to mean that they made mistakes or acted incorrectly in a past life. This is also true for those who experience great fortune, their happiness is the result of acts of compassion and good works which they engaged in during their last life. In this way, life is a continuous cycle that is improved or harmed by the actions that one commits. In the Buddhist tradition, the mechanism that regulates these occurrences is Karma. The Buddhist centers in India were also responsible for the spread of Buddhism throughout Asia.

During the reign of King Ashoka, missionaries were sent out to Asia, in order to relay the teachings of the Buddha. As a result, the earliest recorded ventures landed in Vietnam through India, then overland from China. When Buddhism was introduced to China, the Chinese civilization was already ancient and had already developed several traditions. Therefore, once the doctrines were introduced, the Chinese quickly translated them. To them, these doctrines were the word of Buddha. The Chinese divided into different sects, Theravada and Mahayana. The Theravada doctrine was canonized first. The Mahayana school composed their text later with a more liberal interpretation.

The Mahayanists said, the Hinayana [Theravada] was not untrue, but was merely a preparatory doctrine, preached by the Buddha to disciples whose minds were not yet receptive to the ultimate truth. When he [the Buddha] had prepared them with the tentative doctrine, he then revealed to them his final truth. Buddhist philosophy first began to flourish in the fourth century CE. It was interpreted and judged in Taoist terms. Altogether, ten schools formed, divided into two categories, schools of Being and schools of Non-being.

The underlying issue which divided the two schools was whether the school affirmed or denied the idea of "self-nature of the dharmas... and the ego." (*The Buddhist Tradition*, 141) Most of these schools did not last long. The schools which are the substance of Chinese Buddhism are the T'ien-t'ai,Hua-yen, Meditation, and Pure Land. All of these schools developed distinct Chinese characteristics. Buddhism began to suffer during the T'ang dynasty, tenth century AD, and continued to do so until the Confucians revived.

The early Vietnamese governed their country in a similar manner as the classical Chinese dynasties, however, their habits and custom differed. The Chinese empires achieved their length of power through their ability to keep track of their family ties. Many Vietnamese families worshipped their ancestors to only the ninth generation. After several wars, the clans have spilt to many families with unknown ties. As a result, the Chinese and Vietnamese governments have never been the same. "The emperors followed the rituals of state... so that time would not flow through the empire, but the 'natural order' of the universe did not hold throughout the society."

The village was the primary community, though. The village was informally a family. "The village was always the efficient unit of local government, but in the fifteenth century, when the court abandoned the village mandarinate and retired the lowest order of its officials from the villages, it became a quasi-autonomous unit." This was demonstrated in the Vietnam War since the government failed continually to satisfy the peasants. In a state of confusion, Vietnam was fighting a civil war between the Confucian government and the Buddhist peasants. The Chinese government ruled with a compassion for all of China, since they kept such close ties amongst their families.

In China, a whole community could be linked together on a line of heritage, whereas the Vietnamese could not. Pure Land is a theology designed to help believers attain Sukhavati (or the Buddha land) in only one lifetime. Sukhavati is Located Billions of Buddha lands away in the western direction from the world. The Buddha who presides over Sukhavati is named Amitabha, meaning immeasurable light. Amitabha created this theology in order to help all mortal beings to Buddha hood. Utilizing meditation and mantras, the faithful will reach a stage of non-retrogression and make the constant cycle of birth and re-birth unnecessary. Upon reaching Sukhavati the newly enlightened soul can choose to return to the world realm and take up the duties of Bodhisattva.

The term Pure Land was first used by T an Lua around 540 CE. Developed in China, there is not any evidence of Pure Land doctrine in India before 700 CE. An important element of Pure Land is the existence of multiple Buddhas. There are indications that this theory was first discussed after the Sakyamuni Buddha's death in 486 CE. This notion is important to the development of Pure Land theology because if Sakyamuni Buddha is not the only Buddha, then others can attain Buddha hood as well. If a believer recites the name of the Buddha, namely the Amitabha incarnation, they will reach enlightenment.

Apparently this form of worship became well liked among the secular population because of its comparative ease to visualization and other meditation techniques. Power is gained by the recitation of the Buddha's name and that will balance against the bad karma from other lives. The sincerity of the chant is an important element of the Pure Land doctrine, mere pronunciation of the name alone will not hasten a follower to enlightenment. Even with these practices, the Pure Land school also emphasizes the importance of the Bodhisattva. No individual can attain Buddha hood without the instruction of an enlightened teacher. The teacher describes the Pure Land as well as the many aspects of the Buddha. The student is expected to receive this instruction and practice singular devotion and contemplation.

CAO DAI

Cao Dai is an attempt to create a perfect synthesis of world religions. It is a combination of Christianity, Buddhism, Islam, Confucianism, Hinduism, Geniism, and Taoism. Established in the Southern regions of Vietnam in the early 1920's, the religion was officially codified in 1926. The functioning center of Cao Daism is located in the Tay Ninh province. Cao Dai literally means high tower or palace, a metaphor for the spender of spiritual growth. The central philosophy of Cao Daism pertains to the duty that the faithful perform for themselves, their family, society and the world at large. Much like Confucianism, this element of the Philosophy pertains to how the individual functions within the context of the community.

Other elements of Cao Dai philosophy are more clearly influenced by Buddhism and Hinduism. The Cao Dai faithful are expected to renounce materialism in order to more fully cultivate their spiritual growth. Similar to the Buddhist concept of Samsara, the material world is seen as a distraction to the greater goal of enlightenment. Also similar to Buddhist belief is the use of the device of Karma. Cao Daism also reflects some of the more ancient belief systems of worship in Vietnam. Believers are expected to worship God, superior spirits, and ancestors. This spiritualism is reminiscent of the Animism philosophy that had been a part of Vietnam during its earliest times.

Cao Dai also utilizes spiritual mediums and channelers. These individuals are an essential part of Cao Dai worship. They offer guidance from superior spirits, departed family members, and other wise individuals. Most of the important cannon of the Cao Dai was gleaned from these spiritual seances. Respected saints of the Cao Dai include: Joan of Arc, Rene Descartes, William Shakespeare, Victor Hugo, Louis Pasteur, and Lenin. The clergy is made up of men and women. The entrances of the temple are divided by gender, men on the right, women on the left. The priests practice spiritual purification including meditation, prayer and vegetarianism. They believe that consuming meat not only pollutes the body, but hinders other life forms during their quest for enlightenment.

CONFUCIANISM

Put simply, Confucianism is the quest for order. Most of the ideology dictates that the primary focus of Confucian doctrine is to balance the relationships of individual family, and society with the Five Agents of the Universe. More a method of management than an actual religion, it became a mode by which rulers and civic leaders could run the bureaucracy of the state. For the most part, Vietnam was considered a Confucian state until the mid nineteenth century. The Confucian state is often stratified into classes, and only the most scholarly elite need conform to Confucian ideals. Leaders were decided by examination over sacred texts.

As a result, the peasant or farmer had little to say over the workings of their government. Confucianism is not an exclusionary doctrine, it works well with other moral codes and can synthesize easily. In Vietnam, Confucianism was used primarily for the running of the state, and Taoism and Buddhism for the morality of its citizens. Most of the issues that the Confucian scholars concerned themselves with, during their tenure in power was the proper regulation of the state from the top down and the division of communal property among the citizenry. The Confucian system of philosophy lost prominence in more recent history, but is still common among government bureaucrats and leaders.

TAOISM

The Tao is the natural order of things. It is a force that flows through every living and sentient object, as well as through the entire universe. When the Tao is in balance it is possible to find perfect happiness. The primary religious figures in Taoism are Lao Tzsu and Chuang Tzu, to scholars who dedicated their lives two balancing their inner spirits. Lao Tzsu claimed that the Tao defines translation that it simply is. Taoism encourages working with natural forces, not against them. Taoism teaches the path of wu-wei - the technique of mastering circumstances, not trying to control them. Teachers of the Tao often use examples of the bending reed or grass blowing in the wind to illustrate this important point. A Taoist would encourage an individual to work with their obstacles and problems instead of fighting adversity at every turn.

The most common graphic representation of Taoist theology is the circular Yin Yang figure. It represents the balance of opposites in the universe. When they are equally present, all is calm. When one is outweighed by the other, there is confusion and disarray. The Yin and Yang are a model that the faithful follow, an aid that allows each person to contemplate the state of their lives. Taoists believe that nature and the earth is constantly in flux. Simply, the only constant in the world is change. When individuals learn that growth and movement are natural and necessary, they can become balanced. Reality is perpetual change.

Another essential element of the Tao is the term P'u or the uncarved block. A person who exemplifies this characteristic is one who is simple and looks at the world without preconceptions. P'u is the student, always held in wonder by the world and its constant change. More a listening technique than an actual theology; Taoism asks that each person focuses on the world around them in order to understand the inner harmonies of the universe. It is a religious system heavily focused on meditation and contemplation. The Tao surrounds everyone and one must listen to find enlightenment.

ANIMISM

The oldest peasant religion in Vietnam was known as Animism or ancestor worship. This system of belief was most common among the peasant or laboring class. It is not a basic theology per se, but more a system of reverence for deceased family members as well as all living things. This respect was manifested in many dramatic rituals, as well as alters and other constructed buildings. It was not uncommon for Vietnamese peasants to dedicate large amounts of time to this form of worship.

It was often believed that the dead would aid in harvest and fertility rites. If there was a famine or flood, it could be interpreted as someone's relative making a commotion in the heavens. Because of the connection between these beliefs and agricultural yield, the family are always incredibly devout. Due to the difficult nature of rice farming, one poor crop could cause a family to starve. The Vietnamese worshipped their ancestors as the source of their lives, their fortunes, and their civilizations.

Many of these rituals were seen as primarily superstitious by nature, and as a result were rebuffed by the intellectuals who preferred Confucianism. The classes were divided in this manner, Animist peasants and Confucian leadership. Animism blended well with Buddhism and added a new dimension onto the belief system. When Buddhism was added to the previous practices of ancestor worship it became an inseparable element of peasant practices. So in effect, the peasants practiced both, not forsaking the old or rejecting the new.

CATHOLICISM

The introduction of Christianity, specifically the Catholic faith, to Vietnam occurred at the same time as the French colonization during the 1850's. During the French reign it came to symbolize both western thought and power. In order for a Vietnamese national to gain employment, or a government position, it was necessary to demonstrate that loyalty was first to France, then Vietnam. Therefore, converting to Catholicism was one of the first important steps to that end. It was a strong sign of loyalty for a Vietnamese citizen to abandon their religious heritage for that of the Catholic tradition.

Because the Catholic faith was more attached to prestige than religious fervor, the demographic breakdown of converts tended to be the upper middle class. Always a minority, Catholics still wielded a significant amount of power in government. During the reign of Diem, being a Catholic was one of the only ways a person could be determined loyal. All non-Catholics were seen as potential traders and communist sympathizers. Today the Catholics are still an affluent, though less powerful, minority. Many of the Vietnamese who left South Vietnam at the end of the American involvement were Catholic. They have had an easier time integrating into western culture and are disproportionately represented in the American Vietnamese community.

ZEN

Possibly the most essential of all Buddhist practices, Zen focuses on the ultimate simplicity of the Buddha mind. Allen Watts writes that "Thus is Zen is to be translated at all, the nearest equivalent is 'Enlightenment', but even so Zen is not only Enlightenment; but the path to its attainment. Zen is a religion without a doctrine, a theology without theologians. Zen stresses the prime importance of the enlightenment experience and the uselessness of ritual. This process stresses the spiritual analysis of doctrine and theology, not the analytical or expressly theological.

Zen Buddhism, which is most commonly practiced in Japan, is the basic practice of meditation in order to reach peace within one's self. Zen is not a belief system ridden by dogma and philosophical intricacies but a belief etched by practice. Zen is more often a monastic practice than one that has a strong ethic of public activism. it is the difference between debate and action, between diatribes about philosophy and turning within one's self and finding the answers that already lie there.

Allan Watts writes in *The Spirit of Zen* that "Enlightenment, however, is living and cannot be fixed down into any form of words; therefore the object of the Zen school of Buddhism is to go beyond words and ideas in order that the original insight of the Buddha may be brought back to life." Watts continues that " It never makes the mistake of confusing teachings with wisdom, for essentially, Zen is that "something" which makes the difference between a Buddha and an ordinary man; it is Enlightenment as distinct from doctrine".

In Vietnam, Thich Nhat Hanh has written many books as guides for Western Buddhists attempting to practice Zen philosophy. His emphasis of ordinary practice as meditation encapsulates an essential ideal of Zen practice, action instead of dogma. Nhat Hanh maintains that "The most precious practice in

Buddhism is meditation, and it is important to practice meditation in a joyful mood. We have to smile a lot in order to be able to meditate, the Bell of Mindfulness helps us do this. One of the poems he includes in his book *Being Peace* discusses the sound of breathing.

THE KINGDOM OF CHAMPA

While probably the strongest single cultural influence in Vietnam was China, the Cham civilization offers a startling contrast to many of Vietnam's Mandarin conventions. The Cham derive their cultural influences almost exclusively from India. Instead of the Confucianism and Taoism of other peoples in Vietnam, the Cham were almost exclusively Hindu. This divergence in religion had substantial impacts in both social organization and world view. The Cham existed from the second to the sixteenth century throughout the central highlands of Vietnam. The strongholds of Cham influence and power were centered in the Dong Nai Basin and Deo Ngang province.

It is generally agreed that the kingdom was separated into five regions: Northern area, Amravati area, Vijaya Area, Kauthara Area, and Panduranga area. Even though this is a considerable portion of Vietnam, the severity of weather and limited area for agriculture limited the size of the population to about two and a half million at its height. The Cham were separated into two clans: Narikel Vamsa (Coconut Clan) and Kramuk Vamsa (Betelnut Clan). The Narikel Vamsa primarily ruled the Northern regions of the kingdom, the Kramuk Vamsa centered in the South.

Much like the Brahman cultures that flourish in India, the Cham culture utilized a caste system. The strict rigor of this system benefited the privileged Brahmans and Kshatriyas, and served to relegate untouchables to the periphery of organized life. Marriages tended to occur within the same caste with little deviation. Bodies were also cremated in a funeral pyre, called a Ghat, instead of being buried in a family grave. A striking difference from some of the older animist beliefs that already existed in Vietnam.

Unlike India, however, the position of women seems to be more central to the government power structure. Chinese historians note that women held considerable power in both matters of family and marriage. At the same time the ritual of Sati was also practiced. The Cham people also adopted the Hindu practice of not eating beef — a practice still observed in some areas of Vietnam today. The Cham worshipped the Trinity of Brahma, Vishnu and Mahesh.

In addition to this powerful trio, the Cham also paid reverence to their consorts and offspring. Shiva is the central figure of worship for most of the civilization of Champa. He is worshipped as both a figure of a man and his symbolic form, the linga. The Linga is often found in the art and architecture of the Cham people. While the majority of the Cham people were Hindu, there is a significant minority of the population that were also Mahayana Buddhist and Islamic.

THIEN MU PAGODA

One of the most important cultural centers in Vietnam, Thien Mu Pagoda represents the finest in Buddhist studies. Long held as the intellectual and political hub of Buddhist activity during the American engagement, the history of Thien Mu stretches back centuries. The Pagoda itself was constructed by Emperor Thieu Tri in 1844. While the structure was completed during the nineteenth century, Thien Mu began as a religious center during the 1600's. Comprised of seven levels, the pagoda is over 20 meters tall. Legend has it that each of the seven levels had solid gold Buddha's that were later stolen under mysterious circumstances. Behind the pagoda itself are the living quarters for the monks and novices.

Often referred to as the command-central for the Buddhist protests during the war, the pagoda was the home of the dissident monk Quang Duc who later became an international symbol of resistance by immolating himself in Saigon. To this day it is possible to see the car that Quang Duc rode to Saigon. The Blue Austin is an important symbol of the politics of the Buddhists at the time. Currently, political involvement is limited for monks not only at Thien Mu, but throughout the country. Lacking any public support, the pagoda's attempt to eke out a living from alms from the faithful, farming and odd tasks.

At this time the leaders of the Thien Mu monastery are incarcerated for their criticism of the current regime in power. This seems to be an ironic counterpoint to burning images of Quang Duc from the War. The classical period of Buddhism in South East Asia was from the 11th to the 15th century. In this period, there were several elements which made it classical. Buddhism, in the classical time period, had homogeneity of form and institutional orthodoxy, as well as helped to formulate kingship.

Buddhism, in this time period, tended to follow the Theravada tradition. Since the 19th century, Buddhism has continued to act as a structure for East Asian societies. Despite the challenges that western science has had on Buddhism, it has provided cultural and ideological support for modern, nationalist movements. Buddhism has also offered solutions to political, economic, and social change. Vietnam, however, is different from the "norm" of the traditional South East Asian period of Classical Buddhism, since it was strongly impacted by the Chinese. With communist revolutions, Buddhism was displaced to as a fundamental mediator of cultural values.

Historically, Buddhism played a significant role in the definition of the classical South East Asian states. With Buddhism, when a country was dominated by a colonial power, nationalist movements grew out of and identified with a religious context. An example of this is the 1960 Buddhist protests, in which the Buddhist monks immolated themselves in fire. After the removal of Deim and his brother Nhu, the United Buddhist Association, which was under the leadership of Thich Tri Quang and Thich Thien Minh, remained politically active? "Vietnamese are Confucians in peacetime, Buddhists in times of trouble."

Confucianism is Vietnam's governing religion. It consists of a hierarchy of relationships which governs day to day life. Husband to Wife, Father to son, Elder brother to younger brother, Emperor to subject, and the relationship amongst friends. Therefore when

Buddhism was introduced to Vietnam, it was introduced to a society which was used to a hierarchical governance. The Buddhist missionaries accepted Confucianism as a political system and social structure. According to a scholar of Asian studies, Paul Mus, "Confucianism was a social order defined by culture and history; Buddhism was a faith relevant to all times and to all men, no matter what their circumstances."

Buddhism was a way to transcend the limitations of society and the self to a higher level. Buddhists were all equal whereas Confucians existed primarily in the five relationships. Buddhism offered the people a Way out of Confucianism are confining restrictions. "In peacetime it offered the Vietnamese an internal life—a soul, a personal identity—outside the conventions of society. In times of tyranny and 'splitting apart,' it indicated a morality that lay beyond loyalty to existing authorities." Buddhism offered a form of brotherhood, where people become equals, rather than a world ruled by a few. Buddhism offered "means of reconciliation and showed the Way back into Confucian society."

Along with this integration with Confucianism, Taoism also played a necessary part in the development of Vietnamese Buddhism. The natural tendency of Taoist philosophy towards meditation and contemplation was a compliment to many of the Buddhist techniques. As a result, many Taoist symbols and meditation tools became mainstreamed into Vietnamese Buddhist thought.

Buddhist entered Vietnam in two significant waves. The first was a missionary wave of scholars from India during the early millennia. These were primarily Mahayana scholars who introduced not only the scholarly elite to Buddhist doctrine, but the peasant class as well. The second wave of Buddhist thought occurred about two hundred years after the Common Era. This was a style of Buddhism filtered first through China, the Theravada school. Both of these schools of Buddhist thought co-existed throughout Vietnam.

The most significant defining features of Buddhist thought in Vietnam is first the integration of Buddhist, Taoist and Confucian traditions. In this respect Vietnam represents almost a unique case. The rituals, beliefs and notions of religion reflect each tradition equally. The second defining feature is the two step development of Mahayana and Theravada schools throughout the country. These two schools not only reflect differences in doctrine and basic theology, but also two different cultural influences: India and China.

Throughout Vietnamese history, these acts of violence towards oneself were considered mysterious and exotic. "To those who knew Vietnamese history, Quang Duc's [the Buddhist who set fire to himself] death recalled the suicide of the great mandarins who could not reconcile their loyalty to the Emperor with their obedience to the will of Heaven." However, even though Quang Duc's suicide recalled part of Vietnam's Buddhist history, the historical deaths were recalled as "quiet, gentlemanly suicides that indicated resignation and inability to resolve a fundamental conflict...." Quang Duc's suicide was considered, "an advertisement of the intolerable gap between morality and the reality of the Diem regime."

The Buddhist civilization in Vietnam, was not apparent to the Americans until the Buddhists began immolating themselves in Saigon's public streets to protest the Diem regime. In Vietnam, both schools of thought, Mahayana and Theravada worked together to end the violence that had separated and devastated Vietnam. The Unified Buddhist Church led historic marches and protests against the violence of the war promoting an "Third Way" of ending the war, a "neutral Vietnam which would cherish its own cultural identity". The first act of fiery protest occurred on May 16, 1967 when a young Buddhist named Nhat Chi Mai made herself "a torch in the dark night" (The Social Face of Buddhism, Jones).

After this first demonstration of protest and passion a rare coordinated efforts between the Buddhist and Catholic community took place to publish her poems and writings. Later, in an even more public demonstration of protest Monk Quang Duc's sacrifice caught many off guard and confused many, it sent a message out to both sides of the war. The image of his immolation is one of the most lasting of the war, and one that symbolizes the intense passion of the Buddhists involved. By taking the pose of Buddha, Quang Duc was indicating to both Vietnamese and Americans a morality and a responsibility for others that lay beyond the divisions of political systems and culture.

To the Vietnamese his self immolation was a call first to reconciliation and then to rebellion. Students of Hue and Saigon, along with many Catholics became Buddhists. "They burst rough the 'net ropes' of Confucian authoritarianism that had paralyzed them with fear and suspicion of one another, and they became for the moment equals." "...Society is breaking out from its untenable pyramid of superiors and inferiors [which is brought on by Confucianism] to become a brotherhood of trust." The city again joined together when Diem and Nhu were assassinated.

Buddhist social activism did not begin with protests against the conflict itself, but also included social organizing that reached out the poor and decimated. "From the two radical Buddhists of Van Hanh University and the School of Youth for Social Service young people went into the country to work alongside the peasants on rural development projects, and a number of unions and other organizations were formed which also embraced urban workers, women, youth, and students. Extensive anti-war literature flourished, of poetry, satire, song and prayer." Thich Nhat Hanh, one of the keyanti-war organizers emphasized that "the struggle of the Vietnamese people is not only for peach and independence. *The struggle of the Vietnamese people is to remain Vietnamese.*"

COMMUNISM IN VIETNAM

Communism and Buddhism in Vietnam had not been much of a concern until the middle of this century. When Ho Chi Minh began to gain popular support during the 1940's and 1950's, the

Buddhists as a whole did not share common interests. It was not until the conflict between the French and Americans escalated that the Buddhists began to make connections with the communist forces. There is very little, if any, place for organized religion in communist ideology. Yet the Buddhist protests against Diem and American involvement in Vietnam was one of the most powerful images of the war. Buddhism began to equate to nationalism, and this notion would be the one that linked communism and religion.

The Buddhists realized, that under American control they would loose many of their freedoms. Since Diem, and his American supporters, were primary Catholic (or at least Christian) the Buddhists began to understand the ramifications of becoming a religious minority. They would loose freedom, political power and in many ways a heritage that spanned thousands of years. It is out of this frustration that the Buddhists became nationalists, and protested American involvement. There is little evidence to suggest that the Buddhists were communist sympathizers, but they preferred national interests to international control.

When examining the world-view of most Buddhist cultures, it becomes difficult to determine how these belief-systems justify the rapid economic growth that many of these countries are experiencing. In many ways the Buddhist ethic rejects materialism as another illusion of Samsara. At the same time the ethic of compassion dictates that if possible all members of a community maintain the same standard of living. According to many social theories many Asian religions are so opposed to materialism that Max Webers refers to them as "world renouncing". Since the world is considered illusionary it is incorrect for devout Buddhists to take a part in the affairs of society. Many Theravada monks reject social activism for that reason.

This approach to worldly affairs is rejected by Mahayana tradition. The ethic of the< Bodhisattva is directly contrary to this notion. The teacher responds to the suffering of the world with compassion and action. This is likely the reason that many look to the Bodhisattva Kuan-Yin for aid through economic and natural disasters. In business matters, Buddhists routinely reject what Petrich refers to as "Big Think" economic matters. Preferring instead business strategies that reflect the cultural integrity, and benefits of economic development. In many ways though, Buddhism outlines the responsibilities of government. It should meet the basic physical needs of its citizens, eliminate violence, and regulate the even distribution of goods. In this manner social order will ensure moral order.

5

BUDDHIST CULTURE IN CHINA

Chinese Buddhism (traditional Chinese: simplified Chinese: Pinyin: fójiào) refers collectively to the various schools of Buddhism that have flourished in China proper since ancient times. Many of these schools integrated the ideas of Confucianism, Taoism and other indigenous philosophical systems so that what was initially a foreign religion (the buddhadharma) came to be a natural part of Chinese civilization, albeit with a unique character. Buddhism has played an enormous role in shaping the mindset of the Chinese people, affecting their aesthetics, politics, literature, philosophy and medicine. At the peak of the Tang Dynasty's vitality, Chinese Buddhism produced numerous spiritual masters.

ARRIVAL ALONG THE SILK ROAD

According to European historians, Mauryan emperor Ashoka the Great sent royal monk Massim Sthavira to Nepal, Bhutan and China to spread Buddhism. An 8th century Chinese mural in Dunhuang describes an Emperor Wu of Han (156–87 BCE) worshiping the Golden Man statues; "golden men brought in 120 BC by a great Han general in his campaigns against the nomads". However, there is no such mention of Emperor Wu of Han worshiping the Buddha in Chinese historical literature. The Hou Hanshu then records the visit of Yuezhi envoys to the Chinese capital in 2 BCE, who gave oral teachings on Buddhist sutras to a student, suggesting that some Yuezhi had already started to disseminate the Buddhist faith in eastern Asia during the 1st century BCE (Baldev Kumar (1973), exact source needed).

The Hou Hanshu describes the enquiry about Buddhism made around 70 CE by the Han Emperor Ming (58–75 CE):

There is a current tradition that Emperor Ming dreamed that he saw a tall golden man the top of whose head was glowing. He questioned his group of advisors and one of them said: "In the West there is a man called Buddha. His body is sixteen chi high (3.7 metres or 12 feet), and is the colour of true gold." The Emperor, to discover the true doctrine, sent an envoy to Tianzhu (Northwestern India) to inquire about the Buddha's doctrine, after which paintings and statues [of the Buddha] appeared in the Middle Kingdom. — *Hou Ḥanshu, trans. John Hill*

This encounter is further described in a 6th-century account by Yang Xuanzhi:

The establishment of the BáimÎ-Sì (White Horse Temple) by Emperor Ming (58–75 CE) of the Han marked the introduction of Buddhism into China. The temple was located on the south side of the Imperial Drive, three leagues (li) outside the Xiyang Gate. The Emperor dreamt of the golden man sixteen Chinese feet tall, with the aureole of sun and moon radiating from his head and his neck. A "golden man", he was known as Buddha. The emperor dispatched envoys to the Western Regions in search of the man, and, as a result, acquired Buddhist scriptures and images. At the time, because the scriptures were carried into China on the backs of white horses, White Horse was adopted as the name of the temple.

These Chinese emissaries are said to have visited the country of the Yuezhi and to have brought back with them two missionaries, named Dharmaraksa and Kasyapa Matanga, together with sutras containing 600,000 Sanskrit words. The two missionaries wrote "The Sutra of forty-two sections spoken by the Buddha" to provide guidance on the ideas of Buddhism and the conduct of monks. It is the first Buddhist text in the Chinese language, although its authenticity is a matter of debate. Their arrival in 67 CE marks Buddhism's official introduction in China. Historians generally agree that by the middle of the 1st century, the religion had penetrated to areas north of the Huai River. Emperor Ming's brother Liu Ying the Prince of Chu was the first high-profile believer of Buddhism, although there is some evidence that Emperor Ming himself might have been as well.

The first documented translation of Buddhist scriptures into Chinese occurs in 148 CE with the arrival of the Parthian missionary An Shih Kao in China, probably on the heels of the Kushan expansion into the Tarim Basin. An Shi Kao established Buddhist temples in Loyang and organized the translation of Buddhist scriptures into Chinese, testifying to the beginning of a wave of Central Asian Buddhist proselytism that was to last several centuries. Traces of Buddhist iconography can also be seen in works of art from this period. Mahayana Buddhism was first propagated into China by Kushan Lokaksema (Ch, Zhi Chen, full name var. Zhi Loujiachen, active ca. 164–186 CE), the first translator of Mahayana sutras into Chinese.

By the end of the second century, a prosperous community had been settled at Pengcheng (modern Xuzhou, Jiangsu). The Silk Road transmission of Buddhism to China started in the 1st century CE with a semi-legendary or quasi-historical account of an embassy sent to the West by the Chinese Emperor Ming (58 – 75 CE). Extensive contacts however started in the 2nd century CE, probably as a consequence of the expansion of the Kushan Empire into the Chinese territory of the Tarim Basin, with the missionary efforts of a great number of Central Asian Buddhist monks to Chinese lands. The first missionaries and translators of Buddhist scriptures into Chinese were either Parthian, Kushan, Sogdian or Kuchean.

From the 4th century onward, Chinese pilgrims also started to travel to India, the origin of Buddhism, by themselves in order to get improved access to the original scriptures, with Fa-hsien's pilgrimage to India (395-414), and later Xuan Zang (629-644). The Silk Road transmission of Buddhism essentially ended around the 7th century with the rise of Islam in Central Asia. The first contacts between China and Central Asia occurred with the opening of the Silk Road in the 2nd century BCE. The 1st century BCE "Records of the Great Historian" (Ch: Shiji) tells of the travels of the Chinese explorer Zhang Qian to Central Asia around 130 BCE, who reports about a country named Shendu (India), whose peaceful Buddhist ways are mentioned in writing in the 1st century CE Han history, the Hanshu.

After 130 BCE, numerous embassies to the West followed Zhang Qian's travels, and there may have been some contacts with Buddhism around that time. Chinese murals in the Tarim Basin city of Dunhuang describe Han Wudi (156-87 BCE) worshiping Buddhist statues, "golden men brought in 120 BCE by a great Han general in his campaigns against the nomads". However, there is no such mention of Han Wudi worshiping the Buddha in Chinese historical literature. The Hou Hanshu also records the visit of Yuezhi envoys to the Chinese capital in 2 BCE, who gave oral teachings on Buddhist sutras to a student, suggesting that some Yuezhi had already started to disseminate the Buddhist faith in eastern Asia during the 1st century BCE (Baldev Kumar (1973)).The Hou Hanshu then describes the enquiry about Buddhism made around 70 CE by Emperor Ming (58-75 CE):

"There is a current tradition that Emperor Ming dreamed that he saw a tall golden man the top of whose head was glowing. He questioned his group of advisors and one of them said: "In the West there is a god called Buddha. His body is sixteen chi high (3.7 metres or 12 feet), and is the colour of true gold." The Emperor, to discover the true doctrine, sent an envoy to Tianzhu (Northwestern India) to inquire about the Buddha's doctrine, after which paintings and statues [of the Buddha] appeared in the Middle Kingdom." (Hou Hanshu, trans. John Hill)

This encounter is further described in a 6th century CE account by Yang Xuanzhi:

"The establishment of the Baima Temple (Temple of the White Horse) by Emperor Ming (58-75 CE) of the Han marked the introduction of Buddhism into China. The temple was located on the south side of the Imperial Drive, three leagues (li) outside the Xiyang Gate. The Emperor dreamt of the golden man sixteen Chinese feet tall, with the aureole of sun and moon radiating from his head and his neck. A "golden god", he was known as Buddha. The emperor dispatched envoys to the Western Regions in search of the god, and, as a result, acquired Buddhist scriptures and images. At the time, because the scriptures were carried into China on the backs of white horses, White Horse was adopted as the name of the temple."

The military expansion of China into Central Asia under the rule of Emperor Ming at that time was very real, in particular with the campaign of the general Ban Chao, who managed to repel the Xiongnu from the Tarim Basin and control most of the area by around 75 CE. These contacts necessarily prompted some level of cultural exchange, and may indeed correspond to the first time Buddhist ideas were transmitted to China. The first documented transmission of Buddhist scriptures to China occurs in 148 CE, with the arrival of the Parthian missionary An Shih Kao in China, probably on the heels of the Kushan expansion into the Tarim Basin.

An Shi Kao established Buddhist temples in Loyang and organized the translation of Buddhist scriptures into Chinese, testifying to the beginning of a wave of Central Asian Buddhist proselytism that was to last several centuries. In the middle of the 2nd century CE, the Kushan empire under king Kanishka expanded into Central Asia and went as far as taking control of Kashgar, Khotan and Yarkand, which were Chinese dependencies in the Tarim Basin, modern Xinjiang. As a consequence, cultural exchanges greatly increased, and Central-Asian Buddhist missionaries became active shortly after in the Chinese capital cities of Loyang and sometimes Nanjing, where they particularly distinguished themselves by their translation work. They promoted both Hinayana and Mahayana scriptures. Thirty-seven of these early tran

- An Shih Kao, a Parthian prince who made the first known translations of Hinayana Buddhist texts into Chinese (148-170).
- Lokaksema, a Kushan and the first to translate Mahayana scriptures into Chinese (167-186).
- An Hsuan, a Parthian merchant who became a monk in China 181
- Zhi Yao (c. 185), a Kushan monk, second generation of translators after Lokaksema.
- Kang Meng-hsiang (194-207), first translator from Kangju.
- Zhi Qian (220-252), a Kushan monk whose grandfather had settled in China during 168-190.
- Zhi Yueh (c.230), a Kushan monk who worked at Nanjing.
- Kang Sengkai (247-280), born in Chiao-chih in the extreme south of the Chinese empire, and son of Sogdian merchant.
- Tan-ti (c.254), a Parthian monk.
- Po Yen (c.259), a Kuchean prince
- Dharmaraksa (265-313), a Kushan whose family had lived for generations at Dunhuang.
- An Fachiin (281-306), a monk of Parthian origins.
- Po Srimitra (317-322), a Kuchean prince.
- Kumarajiva (c. 401), a Kuchean monk, and one of the most important translators.
- Fo T'u-teng (4th century), Central Asian monk who became a counselor to the Chinese court.
- Bodhidharma (440-528), was, according to Yang Xuanzhi, a monk of Central Asian origin whom he met around 520 at Loyang. Bodhidharma was the founder of the Chan (Zen) school of Buddhism.

Five monks from Gandhara traveled in 485 CE to the country of Fusang ("The country of the extreme East" beyond the sea, probably Japan, although some historians suggest the American continent), where they introduced Buddhism:

"In former times, the people of Fusang knew nothing of the Buddhist religion, but in the second year of Da Ming of the Song dynasty (485 CE), five monks from Kipin (Kabul region of Gandhara) traveled by ship to that country. They propagated Buddhist doctrine, circulated scriptures and drawings, and advised the people to relinquish worldly attachments. As a results the customs of Fusang changed".

- Jnanagupta (561-592), a monk and translator from Gandhara.
- Shikshananda (652-710 CE), a monk and translator from Udyana, Gandhara.
- Prajna (c. 810). A monk and translator from Kabul, who educated the Japanese Kûkai in Sanskrit texts.
- Central Asian missionnary efforts along the Silk Road were accompanied by a flux of artistic influences, visible in the development of Serindian art from the 2nd through the 11th century CE in the Tarim Basin, modern Xinjiang.
- Serindian art often derives from the art of the Greco-Buddhist art of the Gandhara district of what is now Pakistan, combining Indian, Greek and Roman influences.
- Highly sinicized forms of this syncretism can also be found on the eastern portions of the Tarim Basin, such as in Dunhuang.
- Silk Road artistic influences can be found as far as Japan to this day, in architectural motifs or representations of Japanese gods.

According to Chinese sources, the first Chinese to be ordained was Zhu Zixing, after he went to Central Asia in 260 to seek out

Buddhism. It is only from the 4th century CE that Chinese Buddhist monks started to travel to India to discover Buddhism first-hand. Fa-hsien's pilgrimage to India (395-414) is said to have been the first significant one. He left along the Silk Road, stayed 6 years in India, and then returned by the sea route. Tens of Chinese monks, possibly hundreds of them, visited India during that period

The most famous of the Chinese pilgrims is Xuan Zang (629-644), whose large and precise translation work defines a "new translation period", in contrast with older Central Asian works. He also left a detailed account of his travels in Central Asia and India. Buddhism in Central Asia began to decline in the 7th century following the incursion of the Muslim Caliphate. The vigorous Chinese culture progressively absorbed Buddhist teachings until a strongly Chinese particularism developed. Central Asian Buddhist monks from the Tarim Basin and East Asian Buddhist monks appear to have maintained strong exchanges until around the 10th century, as shown by frescos from the Tarim Basin.

RELATION TO CONFUCIANISM AND TAOISM

Most of the Chinese gentry were indifferent to the Central Asian travelers and their religion. Not only was their religion unknown, but much of it seemed alien and amoral to Chinese sensibilities. Concepts such as monasticism and individual spiritual enlightenment directly contradicted the core Confucian principles of family and emperor. Confucianism promoted social stability, order, strong families, and practical living. Chinese officials questioned how a monk's personal attainment of nirvana (total state of peace and happiness) benefited the empire. Buddhism was less antithetical to Taoism, the other major religion of China. Indeed, upon first encountering Buddhism, many Chinese scholars regarded it as merely a foreign branch of Taoism.

Kang-nam Oh frames the mutual influential dialogue of Buddhism and Taoism within China and mentions Kumarajiva:

It is a well-known fact that since its introduction into China, Buddhism has had a close relationship with Taoism, more specifically with Neo-Taoism. As a result of this there developed the method of "matching the concepts" of Buddhism and Taoism, which was known as ko-i. By this method of analogy Buddhists adopted many Taoist terms and ideas to explain their concepts. Although this somewhat superficial and arbitrary method of matching was discarded as useless and misleading after the great translator and scholar Kumârajiiva arrived in 401 CE, Taoist influence on Buddhism in general was not, and could not be, totally eliminated.

LOCAL INTERPRETATION OF INDIAN TEXTS

To thrive in China, Buddhism had to transform itself into a system that could exist within the Chinese way of life. Thus highly regarded Indian sutras that advocated filial piety became core texts in China. Buddhism was made compatible with ancestor worship and participation in China's hierarchical system. Works were written arguing that the salvation of an individual was a benefit to that individual's society and family and monks thus contributed to the greater good. It is conjectured that the shocking collapse of the Han Dynasty in 220 and the resulting period of social upheaval and political unrest known as the Three Kingdoms period may have helped the spread of Buddhism. Buddhism was a minor force, however, compared with Taoism which was directly associated with efforts to defy the emperor (cf. Yellow Turban Rebellion).

The Taoist Zhang family self-governed the Hanzhong Commandry for nearly 20 years until invasion by the renowned Chinese warlord Cao Cao. A reason for the lack of interest mostly stemmed from the ruling entity and gentry. All the rulers were Han Chinese and had simply never heard of or knew too little of the religion. The Nine-grade controller system, by which prominent individuals in each local administrative area were given the authority to rank local families and individuals in nine grades according to their potential for government service, further consolidated the importance of Confucianism. Taoism also remained a strong force among the population and philosophers.

BUDDHISM AND SOCIAL CHANGE IN THE NORTH

Subsequent chaotic periods of Sixteen Kingdoms and Southern and Northern Dynasties changed the situation, resulting in state support of Buddhism. Most rulers of the Wu, Hu, and the Northern dynasties originated from more than ten distinct ethnic groups including either non-Han Chinese "barbarians", or Han Chinese after generations of "barbarian" influence. They did not propagate nor trust the combined philosophical concept of Confucianism and Taoism as zealously as their rivals in the south. Official support of Buddhism would eventually mould a new Chinese populace with a common ideology out of the diversely ethnic population, which would in turn consolidate these dynasties. It is instructive that Buddhism propagated faster in northern China than in the south. Social upheaval in northern China worked to break down cultural barriers between the elite ruling families and the general populace, in contrast to the south where elite clans and royal families firmly monopolized politics.

Taoist and Confucian political ideology had long consolidated the political status of elite clans in the south. Support of another religion would have unknown and possibly adverse effects, for which these clans would not risk their privileges. Furthermore pro-Buddhist policy would not be backed by the bureaucracy, which had been staffed by members of the clans. Southern rulers were in weaker positions to strive for their legitimacy - some were even installed by the clans. It was not until the reign of Emperor Wu of the Liang Dynasty that saw the official support of Buddhism. Rebellion of Hou Jing near the end of Emperor Wu's reign wreaked havoc on the political and social privileges of the elite clans, which indirectly assisted the spread of Buddhism. But Buddhism spread pretty well in the peasant populace, both in the north and the south.

The Tang capital of Chang'an (today's Xi'an) became an important center for Buddhist thought. From there Buddhism spread to Korea, and Japanese embassies of Kentoshi helped gain footholds in Japan. The popularization of Buddhism in this period is evident in the many scripture-filled caves and structures surviving from this period. The Mogao Caves near Dunhuang in Gansu province, the Longmen Grottoes near Luoyang in Henan and the Yungang Grottoes near Datong in Shanxi are the most renowned examples from the Northern, Sui and Tang Dynasties. The Leshan Giant Buddha, carved out of a hillside in the 8th century during the Tang Dynasty and looking down on the confluence of three rivers, is still the largest stone Buddha statue in the world.

BUDDHIST SCRIPTURES

During the early Tang dynasty the monk Xuanzang journeyed to Nalanda in India and other important sites to bring back scriptures. He sought to expand influence of Mahayana over Theravada, though the Yogacara school he preferred differs significantly from the later Chinese Mahayana schools that developed such as Pure Land. Making duplications of Buddhist texts was considered to bring meritorious karma. Printing from individually carved wooden blocks and from clay or metal movable type proved much more efficient and eventually eclipsed hand copying. The *Diamond Sutra* of 868 CE, a Buddhist scripture discovered in 1907 inside the Mogao Caves, is the first dated example of block printing. Temple.

NEW AND ESOTERIC TEACHERS

Arrivals of several prestigious monks in the early 5th century also contributed to the propagation of the religion and were welcomed by rulers of the Sixteen Kingdoms and Northern Dynasties. Fo Tu Cheng was entrusted by the tyrant Shi Hu of Later Chao. Kumarajiva was invited by Lü Guang, the founder of Later Liang, and later by Yao Xing, second ruler of Later Qin. Biographies of these monks, among others, were the subject of the *Memoirs of Eminent Monks*. The direct experiential impact of contact with practicing monks should not be underestimated. Confucianism had no equivalent to holy men – the archetypical best and brightest was a wise government minister, not a saint. In this way Buddhism grew to become a major religion in China.

By the beginning of the 6th century, Buddhism had grown in popularity to rival Taoism. We know they were successful because the monks were soon accused of falling into extravagance and their lands and their properties were confiscated by Emperor Wu of the Northern Zhou dynasty and Wuzong of the Tang Dynasty. The Kaiyuan's Three Great Enlightened Masters, Subhakarasimha, Vajrabodhi, and Amoghavajra, established Esoteric Buddhism in China from AD 716 to 720 during the reign of emperor Tang Xuanzong (or Hsuan-Tsung).

They came to Daxing Shansi, Great Propagating Goodness Temple, which was the predecessor of Temple of the Great Enlightener MahaVairocana. Daxing Shansi was established in the ancient capital Chang'an, today's Xi'an, and became one of the four great centers of scripture translation supported by the imperial court. They had translated many Buddhist scriptures, sutra and tantra, from Sanskrit to Chinese. They had also assimilated the prevailing teachings of China, Taoism and Confucianism, with Buddhism, and had further evolved the practice of The Esoteric School. They brought to the Chinese a mysterious, dynamic, and magical teaching, which included mantra formulae and rituals to protect a person or an empire, to affect a person's fate after death, and, particularly popular, to bring rain in times of drought.

It is not surprising, then, that all three masters were well received by the emperor Tang Xuanzong, and their teachings were quickly taken up at the Tang court and among the elite. Mantrayana altars were installed in temples in the capital, and by the time of emperor Tang Taizong (Tai-Tsung, r. 762-779) its influence among the upper classes outstripped that of Taoism. Relations between Amoghavajra and Taizong were especially good. In life the emperor favored Amoghavajra with titles and gifts, and when the master died in 774, he honored his memory with a stupa, or funeral monument.

SUBHAKARASIMHA

Subhakarasimha (637-735), an eminent Indian Tantric master, arrived in the capital Chang'an in 716 and translated the

Vairocanabhi-Sambodhi-Tantra, better known as the MahaVairocana-Sutra, or Great Sun Buddha Scripture. Four years later another master, Vajrabodhi (670-741), and his pupil Amoghavajra (705-775), arrived, and proceeded to translate other scriptures, thus establishing a second, though not rival, Mantrayana (Chen-Yen, or Zhen-Yan) lineage.

VAJRABODHI

Vajrabodhi (671-732), an Indian Buddhist master, and a graduate of the Nâlandâ Monastery, received complete empowerment and transmission from Nagabodhi, who in turn received from Nagarjuna. He was born of a South Indian Brahmin family, and his father was a priest for the royal house. Vajrabodhi probably converted to Buddhism at the age of sixteen, although some accounts place him at Nâlaṇdâ at the age of ten. He studied all varieties of Buḍdhism and was said to have studied for a time under the famous Buddhist logician Dharmakîrti. Uṇder Santijnana, Vajrabodhi studied Vajrayâna teachings and was duly initiated into yoga.

Leaving India, Vajrabodhi traveled to Sri Lanka and Srivijaya (present-day Sumatra), where he apparently was taught a Vajrayâna tradition distinct from that taught at Nâlandâ. From Srivijaya he sailed to China via the escort of thirty-five Persian merchant-vessels and by AD 720 was ensconced in the Jian'fu Temple at the Chinese capital, Chang'an (present-day Xi'an). Accompanying him was his soon-to-be-famous disciple, Amoghavajra. When Vajrabodhi arrived in Chang'an, Subhakarasimha had already been there for four years. Subhakarasimha was eighty some years old. Vajrabodhi was about thirty something, and Amoghavajra a teenager. Subhakarasimha and Vajrabodhi met and debated. Afterward, they bowed to each other as each other's teacher.

Like Subhakarasimha, who preceded him by four years, Vajrabodhi spent most of his time in ritual activity, in translating texts from Sanskrit to Chinese, and in the production of Esoteric art. Particularly important was hiṣ partial translation of the Sarva-

Tathâgata-Tattva-Samgraha between the years 723 and 724. This Yoga Tantra, along with the Mahâvairocana Sutra translated by Subhakarasimha the same year, provides the foundation of the Chen-Yen school in China and the Shingon and Esoteric branch of the Tendai schools in Japan. Like Subhakarasinha, Vajrabodhi had ties to high court circles and enjoyed the patronage of imperial princesses. He also taught Korean monk Hyecho, who went on to travel India. Vajrabodhi died in 732 and was buried south of the Longmen Grottoes. He was posthumously awarded the title Guoshi, 'National Master'.

AMOGHAVAJRA

Amoghavajra (705-774), a Singhalese, was the most famous Yogacharya of his time. He was a prolific translator who became one of the most politically powerful Buddhist monks in Chinese history, acknowledged as one of the eight patriarchs of the doctrine in Shingon lineage. Born in Samarkand of an Indian father and Sogdian mother, he went to China at age 10 after his father's death. In 719, he was ordained into the Sangha by Vajrabodhi and became his disciple. He also became Subhakarasimha's disciple a few years later. Both Subhakarasimha, the holder of the Garbhadhatu Womb Realm teachings, and Vajrabodhi, the holder of the Vajradhatu Thunderbolt Realm teachings transmitted the Dharma Lineage to Amoghavajra, who began the Not-Two Dharma Teachings of Garbhadhatu and Vajradhatu.

The Tang emperor granted Dharma instruments to Amoghavajra to setup the first Abhiseka-Bodhi-Mandala at Daxing Shansi, thus began the Chinese Esoteric School. After Vajrabodhi's death in 732, and at his wish, Amoghavajra went on a pilgrimage in search of esoteric or tantric writings, visiting Ceylon, Southeast Asia and India. During this voyage, he apparently met Nagabodhi, master of Vajrabodhi, and studied the Tattvasamgraha system at length. He returned to China in 746 with some five hundred volumes, and baptized the Emperor Tang Xuanzong. He was especially noted for rainmaking and stilling storms. In 749 he received permission to return home, but was stopped by imperial orders when in the south of China.

In 750, he left the court to join the military governorship of Geshu Han, for whom he conducted large-scale tantric initiations at field headquarters. In 754, he translated the first portion of the Tattvasamgraha, the central text of Esoteric Buddhism, which became one of his most significant accomplishments. He regarded its teachings as the most effective method for attaining enlightenment yet devised, and incorporated its basic schema in a number of writings. In 756, under emperor Suzong, Amoghavajra was recalled to the capital. He was captured in general An Lushan's rebellion but in 757 was freed by loyalist forces, whereupon he performed rites to purify the capital and consolidate the security of the Tang state. Two years later, he initiated the emperor Suzong as a cakravartin.

In 765, Amoghavajra used his new rendition of the Scripture for Humane Kings in an elaborate ritual to counter the advance of a 200,000-strong army of Tibetans and Uyghurs, which was poised to invade Chang'an. Its leader, Pugu Huaien, dropped dead in camp and his forces dispersed. The opulent Jin'ge Temple on Mt. Wutai was completed in 767, a pet project of Amoghavajra's, and one of his many efforts to promote the Bodhisattva Mañjuúrî as the protector of China. Amoghavajra continued to perform rites to avert disaster at the request of the emperor Tang Taizong. His time until 771 was spent translating and editing tantric books in 120 volumes, and the Yogachara rose to its peak of prosperity.

He died greatly honored at 70 years of age, in 774, the twelfth year of Taizong, the third emperor under whom he had served. On his death, three days of mourning were officially declared, and he posthumously received various exalted titles. He was given the title of the Thesaurus of Wisdom, Amogha Tripikata and the posthumous rank and title of a Minister of State. The Chinese monks Huilang, Huiguo and Huilin were among his most prominent successors. Seventy-seven texts were translated by Amoghavajra according to his own account, though many more, including original compositions, are ascribed to him in the Chinese canons. Huiguo was the most well-known disciple of Amoghavajra. Both Amoghavajra and Huiguo were emperors' guru, in other words, they were National Masters. Huiguo's main residence was the Qinglong. Tang Emperor Wuzong, distrusting its popularity and magical claims, prohibited these new practices.

TANG STATE REPRESSION OF 845

There were several components that lead to opposition of Buddhism. One factor is the foreign origins of Buddhism, unlike Taoism and Confucianism. Han Yu wrote, "Buddha was a man of the barbarians who did not speak the language of China and wore clothes of a different fashion. His sayings did not concern the ways of our ancient kings, nor did his manner of dress conform to their laws. He understood neither the duties that bind sovereign and subject, nor the affections of father and son." Other components included the Buddhists' withdrawal from society, since the Chinese believed that Chinese people should be involved with family life. Wealth and power of the Buddhist temples and monasteries also annoyed many critics.

As mentioned earlier, persecution came during the reign of Emperor Wuzong in the Tang Dynasty. Wuzong was said to hate the sight of Buddhist monks. In 845, he ordered the destruction of 4,600 Buddhist monasteries and 40,000 temples. Another 250,000 Buddhist monks and nuns had to give up their Buddhist lives. Wuzong cited that Buddhism was an alien religion, which is the reason he also persecuted the Christians in China. Ancient Chinese Buddhism never fully recovered from the persecution.

BUDDHISM AFTER FORFEITURE OF 845

SONG DYNASTY

Buddhist ideology began to merge with Confucianism and Taoism, due in part to the use of existing Chinese philosophical terms in the translation of Buddhist scriptures. Various Confucian scholars of the Song dynasty, including Zhu Xi (wg: Chu Hsi), sought to redefine Confucianism as Neo-Confucianism.

MING DYNASTY

"By the Ming period (1368–1644) the preeminence of Chan had been so firmly established that almost the entire Buddhist clergy were affiliated with either its Lin-chi or Ts'ao-tung lineages, both of which claimed descent from Bodhidharma."

QING DYNASTY

The official religion of the Qing court was the Gelukpa School of Tibetan Buddhism. Early in the Taiping rebellion, the Taiping rebels targeted Buddhism. In the Battle of Nanjing (1853), the Taiping army butchered thousands of monks in Nanjing. But from the middle of the Taiping rebellion, Taiping took a more moderate approach, demanding that monks should have licences.

MODERN CHINESE BUDDHISM

Today the most popular form of Buddhism in both mainland China and Taiwan is a mix of the Pure Land and Chán schools. More recent surveys put the total number of Chinese Buddhists between 660 million (50%) and over 1 billion (80%), thus making China the country with the most Buddhist adherents in the world, followed by Japan. However, it was difficult to estimate accurately the number of Buddhists because they did not have congregational memberships and often did not participate in public ceremonies. Many lay people practice Buddhism and Taoism at the same time.

Buddhism is tacitly supported by the government. The 108-metre-high statue is the world's tallest of Guanyin Statue of Hainan was enshrined on April 24, 2005 with the participation of 108 eminent monks from various Buddhist groups in Taiwan, Hong Kong, Macao and Mainland China, and tens of thousands of pilgrims. The delegation also included monks from the Theravada and Vajrayana traditions. China belongs to those countries that own most of the world's highest Buddhist statues. In April 2006 China organized the World Buddhist Forum and in March 2007 the government banned mining on Buddhist sacred mountains.

In May of the same year, in Changzhou, world's tallest pagoda was built and opened. In March 2008 the Taiwan-based Tzu Chi Foundation was approved to open a branch in mainland China. The central scripture of Pure Land Buddhism, the Amitabha Sutra was first brought to China by An Shigao, circa 147 CE; however, the school did not become popular until later. The Platform Sutra is the most important sutra for Chán Buddhism, and is considered to be the only scripture written by an ethnic Han Chinese which is called a sutra. Theravada Buddhism and Vajrayana Buddhism exist mainly among ethnic minorities in the southwest and the north.

SPREAD OF BUDDHISM AMONG THE CHINESE

During the third century B.C., Emperor Asoka sent missionaries to the northwest of India, that is, present-day Pakistan and Afghanistan. The mission achieved great successes as the region soon became a centre of Buddhist learning with many distinguish monks and scholars. When the merchants of Central Asia came into this region for trade, they learnt about Buddhism and accepted it as their religion. By the second century B.C., some central Asian cities like Kotan, has already become important centres for Buddhism. The Chinese people had their first contact with Buddhism through Central Asians who were already Buddhists. When the Han Dynasty of China extended its power to Central Asia in the first century B.C., trade and cultural ties between China and Central Asia also increased. In this way, the Chinese people learnt about Buddhism so that by the middle of the first century C.E., a community of Chinese Buddhists was already in existence.

As interest in Buddhism grew, there was a great demand for Buddhist texts to be translated from Indian languages into Chinese. This led to the arrival of translators from Central Asia and India.

The first notable one was Anshigao from Central Asia who came to China in the middle of the second century. With a growing collection of Chinese translations of Buddhist texts, Buddhism became more widely known and a Chinese monastic order was also formed. The first known Chinese monk was said to be Anshigao's disciple. The early translators had some difficulty in finding the exact words to explain Buddhist concepts in Chinese, so they often used Taoist terms in their translations. As a result, people began to relate Buddhism with the existing Taoist tradition. It was only later on that the Chinese came to fully understand the teachings of the Buddha.

After the fall of the Han Dynasty in the early part of the third century, China faced a period of political disunity. Despise the war and unrest, the translations of the Buddhist texts continued. During this time, both foreign and Chinese monks were actively involved in establishing monasteries and lecturing on the Buddhist teachings. Among the Chinese monks, Dao-an who lived in the fourth century, was the most outstanding. Though he had to move from place to place because of the political strife, he not only wrote and lectured extensively, but prepared the first catalogues of them. He invited the famous translator, Kumarajiva, from Kucha. With the help of of Do-an's disciples, Kumarjiva translated a large number of important texts and revised the earlier Chinese translations. His fine translations are still in use to this day. Because of political unrest, Kumarkiva's disciples were later dispersed and this helped to spread Buddhism to other parts of China.

The Establishment of Buddhism in China: From the beginning of the fifth century to around the end of the sixth century, northern and southern China came under separate rule. The south remained under native dynasties while the north was controlled by non-Chinese rulers. The Buddhist in southern China continued to translate Buddhist texts and to lecture and write commentaries on the major texts. Their rulers were devout Buddhists who saw to the construction of numerous temples, participated in Buddhist ceremonies and organised public talks on Buddhism. In northern

China, except for two short periods of persecution, Buddhism flourished under the lavish royal patronage of rulers who favoured the religion. By the latter half of the sixth century, monks were employed in government posts. During this period, Buddhist art flourished, especially in the caves at Dun-huang, Yun-gang and Long-men. In the thousand caves at Dun-huang, Buddhist paintings covered the walls and there were thousands of Buddha statues in these caves. At Yun-gan and Long-men, many Buddha images of varying sizes were carved out of the rocks. All these activities were a sign of the firm establishment of Buddhism in China by the end of this period.

The Development of Chinese Schools of Buddhism: With the rise of the Tang Dynasty at the beginning of the seventh century, Buddhism reached out to more and more people. It soon became an important part of Chinese culture and had great influence on Chinese Art, Literature, Sculpture, Architecture and the Philosophy of that time. By then the number of Chinese translations of Buddhist texts had increased tremendously. The Buddhist were now faced with the problem of how to put their teachings into practice. As a result, a number of schools of Buddhism arose, with each school concentrating on certain texts for their study and practice. The Tian-tai school, for instance, developed a system of teaching and practice based on the *Lotus Sutra*. It also arranged all the Buddhist texts into graded categories to suit the varying aptitude of the followers. Other schools arose which focused on different areas of the Buddha's teachings.

The two most prominent schools were the Ch'an and the Pure Land schools. The Ch'an school emphasized the practice of meditation as the direct way of gaining insight and experiencing Enlightenment in this very life. The Pure Land school centres its practices on the recitation of the name of Amitabha Buddha. The practice is based on the sermon which teaches that people could be reborn in the Western Paradise (Pure Land) of Amitabha Buddha if they recite his name and have sincere faith in him. Once in the Pure Land, the devotees are said to be able to achieve

Enlightenment more easily. Because of the simplicity of its practice, this school became popular especially among the masses throughout China.

Further Development of Buddhism in China: In the middle of the ninth century, Buddhism faced persecution by a Taoist emperor. He decreed the demolition of monasteries, confiscation of temple land, return of monks and nuns to secular life and the destruction of Buddha images. Although the persecution lasted only a short time, it marked the end of an era for Buddhism in China. Following the demolition of monasteries and the dispersal of scholarly monks, a number of Chinese schools of Buddhism ceased to exist as separate movements. They were absorbed into the Ch'an and Pure Land schools which survived. The eventual result was the emergence of a new form of Chinese Buddhist practice in the monastery.

Besides practicing Ch'an meditation, Buddhist also recited the name of Amitabha Buddha and studied Buddhist texts. It is this form of Buddhism which survives to the present time. Just as all the Buddhist teachings and practices were combined under the one roof in the monasteries, Buddhist lay followers also began to practice Buddhism, Taoism and Confucianism simultaneously. Gradually, however, Confucian teachings became dominant in the court and among the officials who were not in favour of Buddhism.

Buddhism generally, continues to be a major influence in Chinese religious life. In the early twentieth century, there was an attempt to modernize and reform the tradition in order to attract wider support. One of the most well-known reformist was Tai-xu, a monk noted for his scholarship. Besides introducing many reforms in the monastic community, he also introduced Western-style education which included the study of secular subjects and foreign languages for Buddhist. In the nineteen-sixites, under the People's Republic, Buddhism was suppressed. Many monasteries were closed and monks and nuns returned to lay life. In recent years, a more liberal policy regarding religion has led to a growth of interest in the practice of Buddhism.

BUDDHIST CUISINE

Buddhist cuisine is an East Asian cuisine which is followed by some believers of Buddhism. It is primarily vegetarian, in order to keep with the general Buddhist precept of ahimsa (non-violence). Vegetarian cuisine is known as *zhâicài* ("(Buddhist) vegetarian food") in China, Hong Kong, Singapore and Taiwan; *shôjin ryôri* ("devotion cuisine") in Japan; *sachal eumsik* ("temple food") in Korea and by other names in many countries. Buddhism, along with Jainism, recognizes that even eating vegetables could contribute to the indirect killing of living beings because animal life is destroyed by tilling the soil or the use of pesticides.

Jainism consequently considers death by starvation as the ultimate practice of non-violence, while Buddhism considers extreme self-mortification to be undesirable for attaining enlightenment. Both Mahayana and Theravada thinking is that eating meat in and of itself does not constitute a violation of the Five Precepts which prohibit one from directly harming life. However, when monks and nuns who follow the Theravadan way feed themselves by alms, they must eat whatever leftover foods which are given to them, including meat. (The Pali/Sanskrit term for monks and nuns means one who seek alms.) The exception to this alms rule is when monks and nuns have seen, heard or known that animal(s) have been specifically killed to feed the alm seeker, in which case, consumption of such meat would be karmically negative. This is also followed by lay Buddhists; and is known as the consumption of the 'triply-clean meat'.

On the other hand, when lay communities specifically purchase meat for consumption of monks and nuns, the permissibility of meat eating differ among Buddhist sects. The Theravada Pali Canon records instances of Buddha eating meat which were specifically purchased for Buddha. This act was deliberately performed by the Buddha to demonstrate that if need be, a Buddhist can bend the rules in times of emergency or inconvenience. Obstinately observing vegetarianism or Buddhist rules in times when you cannot, conflicts with Mahayana philosophy because obstinacy or attachment for anything, is considered to be 'stubbornness' which will become an obstacle to nirvana or enlightenment. However even then, if one undertakes a vow to be a Buddhist vegetarian, one is expected to follow this vow until it is humanly impossible to continue one's vegetarian diet.

Acceptance of authenticity of the Pali Sutras differ within Mahayana sects and Mahayana sutras do not record Buddha eating meat. While no Mahayana sects consider Pali sutras to be inauthentic, Chinese Buddhist sects tend to consider this particular part of writing in Pali sutras to be false. Japanese Buddhist sects generally accept that Buddha ate meat. Still, both Mahayana and Theravada Buddhists consider that one may practice vegetarianism as part of cultivating Bodhisattvas's paramita.

Since Mahayana Buddhists recognise the consumption of meat to be cruel and devoid of compassion, some Mahayana Buddhists are vegetarians. Numbers of Mahayana sutra record Buddha praising the virtue of avoiding meat. However, Tibetan Buddhism believes that tantric practice makes vegetarianism unnecessary. All Japanese Kamakura sects of Buddhism (Zen, Nichiren, Jodo) have relaxed Mahayana vinaya, and as a consequence, do not practice vegetarianism but rather pescetarianism. Chinese Buddhism and part of Korean Buddhism strictly adhere to vegetarianism.

BUDDHISM AND OTHER FOOD CONSIDERATIONS

East Asian "Buddhist" cuisine differs from Western vegetarian cuisine in one aspect, that is avoidance of killing plant life. Buddhist vinaya for monks and nuns prohibit harming of plant. Therefore, strictly speaking, no root vegetables (such as potatoes, carrots or onion) are to be used as this will result in death of vegetables. Instead, vegetables such as beans or fruits are used. However, this stricter version of diet is often practiced only on special occasion. Some Mahayana Buddhists in China and Vietnam specifically avoid eating strong-smelling plants, traditionally garlic, *Allium chinense*, asafoetida, shallot, and *Allium victorialis* (victory onion or mountain leek), and refer to these as 'Five Acrid And Strong Smelling Vegetables' or 'Five Spices' as they tend to excite senses.

This is based on teachings found in the Brahma Net Sutra, the Surangama Sutra and the Lankavatara Sutra. In modern times this rule is often interpreted to include other vegetables of the onion genus, as well as coriander. The food that a strict Buddhist takes, even if he/she is not a vegetarian, is also specific. For many Chinese Buddhists, beef and the consumption of large animals and exotic species is avoided. Then there would be the aforementioned sanjingrou rule. One restriction on food that is not known to many is the abstinence from eating animal innards and organs. This is known as *xia shui*, and is not to be confused with the term for sewage.

Alcohol and/or other drugs are also avoided by many Buddhists because of their effects on the mind and "mindfulness". It is part of the Five Precepts which dictate that one is not to consume "addictive materials". The definition of "addictive" depends on each individual but most Buddhists consider alcohol,tobacco and contraband drugs to be addictive.

COMMON SOURCES FOR BUDDHIST FOODS

Buddhist vegetarian chefs have become extremely creative in imitating meat using prepared wheat gluten, also known as "seitan" or "wheat meat", soy (such as tofu or tempeh), agar, and other plant products. Some of their recipes are the oldest and most-refined meat analogues in the world. Soy and wheat gluten are very versatile materials, because they can be manufactured into various shapes and textures, and they absorb flavourings (including, but not limited to, meat-like flavourings), whilst having very little flavour of their own. With the proper seasonings, they can mimic various kinds of meat quite closely. Some of these Buddhist vegetarian chefs are in the many monasteries which serve *wu hun* and mock-meat (also known as 'meat analogues') dishes to the monks and visitors (including non-Buddhists who often stay for a few hours or days, to Buddhists who are not monks, but staying overnight for anywhere up to weeks or months).

Many Buddhist restaurants also serve vegetarian, vegan, non-alcoholic, and/or *wu hun* dishes. Some Buddhists eat vegetarian only once per week or month, or on special occasions such as annual visits to an ancestor's grave. To cater to this type of customer, as well as full-time vegetarians, the menu of a Buddhist vegetarian restaurant usually shows no difference from a typical Chinese or far-Eastern restaurant, except that in recipes originally made to contain meat, a chicken flavoured soy or wheat gluten might be served instead.

6

BUDDHIST CULTURE IN INDIA

Initially, Buddhism remained one of the many small sects in India. The main breakthrough came when King Asoka (ca. 270-232 BCE) converted to Buddhism. He did not make it a state religion, but supported all ethical religions. He organised the spreading of Buddhism throughout India, but also beyond; most importantly to Shri Lanka. This occurred after the Third Council.

THE BUDDHIST COUNCILS

THE FIRST COUNCIL

Three months after the Buddha's Mahaparinirvana (passing away), his immediate disciples convened a council at Rajagaha. Maha Kassapa, the most respected and senior monk, presided at the Council. Two very important personalities who specialised in the two areas of the teachings:

- The Dharma: Ananda, the closest constant companion and disciple of the Buddha for 25 years. Endowed with a remarkable memory, Ananda was able to recite what was spoken by the Buddha.
- The Vinaya: Upali remembered all the Vinaya rules.

Only these two sections - the Dharma and the Vinaya - were recited at the First Council (no mention was made of the Abhidharma yet). Though there were no differences of opinion on the Dharma there was some discussion about the Vinaya rules. Before the Buddha's Parinirvanana, he had told Ananda that if the Sangha wished to amend or modify some minor rules, they could do so. But Ananda forgot to ask the Buddha what the minor rules were.

As the members of the Council were unable to agree as to what constituted the minor rules, Maha Kassapa finally ruled that no disciplinary rule laid down by the Buddha should be changed, and no new ones should be introduced. No intrinsic reason was given. Maha Kassapa did say one thing, however: "If we changed the rules, people will say that Ven. Gautama's disciples changed the rules even before his funeral fire has ceased burning." At the Council, the Dharma was divided into various parts and each part was assigned to an Elder and his pupils to commit to memory. The Dharma was then passed on from teacher to pupil orally. The Dharma was recited daily by groups of people who regularly cross-checked with each other to ensure that no omissions or additions were made.

THE SECOND COUNCIL

According to the Theravadin school (Rahula), about one hundred years after the Buddha's passing away, the Second Council was held to discuss some Vinaya rules, and no controversy about the Dharma was reported. The orthodox monks (Sthavarivada) said that nothing should be changed, while the others insisted on modifying some rules. Finally, a group of monks left the Council and formed the Mahasanghika - the Great Community. (The Mahasanghika should not to be confused with Mahayana.)

According to another version (Skilton), the Second Council may have had two parts: initially in Vaisali, some 60 years after the Buddha, and 40 years after that, a meeting in Pataliputra, where Mahadeva maintained five theses on the Arhat. The actual split may have occurred at Pataliputra, not Vaisali over details of the Vinaya. In the non-Theravadin version of events, the Mahasangha followed the original vinaya and the Sthaviravada (the Elders) wanted changes. What exactly happened is unlikely to be ever revealed, but the first split in the Sangha was a fact.

THE THIRD COUNCIL

During the reign of Emperor Aśoka in the 3rd Century BCE, the Third Council was held to discuss the differences of opinion among the bhikkhus of different sects. At this Council differences of opinion were not confined to the Vinaya, but also concerned the Dharma. The President of the Council, Moggaliputta Tissa, compiled a book called the Kathavatthu which refuted the heretical, false views and theories held by some sects occurring at the time. The teaching approved and accepted by this Council became known as Sthaviras or Theravada, "Teaching of the Elders". The Abhidhamma Pitaka was included at this Council.

After the Third Council, King Asoka sent missionaries to Sri Lanka, Kanara, Karnataka, Kashmir, Himalaya region, Burma, even nowadays Afghanistan. Asoka's son, Ven. Mahinda, brought the Tripitaka to Sri Lanka, along with the commentaries that were recited at the Third Council. These teachings later became known as the "Pali-canon".

THE FOURTH COUNCIL

The Fourth Buddhist Council was held under the auspices of King Kaniska at Jalandhar or in Kashmir around 100 CE, where 499 monks of the Sarvastivadin school compiled a new canon. This council was never recognised by the Theravada school.

THE FIFTH COUNCIL (BURMA)

The 5th Buddhist Council was held from 1868 to 1871 in Mandalay, Burma where the text of the Pali Canon was revised and inscribed on 729 marble slabs.

THE SIXTH COUNCIL (BURMA)

The 6th Buddhist Council was held at Rangoon, Burma in 1954-1956.

FROM 200 BCE TO THE PRESENT

Prior to the Third Council, several schools developed from the Sthavarivadin: Vasiputriya/Pudgalavadin/Sammitiya (three names for the same school), Sarvastivadin and Vibajyavadin. Later on, the Vibhajyavadin school was divided into the Mahisasika and the Theravada. The Sarvastivadin developed later sub-schools known as Vaibasika and Sautrantika. The Sarvastivadin school is important in that it formed the basis for the later development of Mahayana. With the conversion of King Asoka, Buddhism suddenly became a main religion in India; it had been just one of the many sects before him.

After the death of Asoka, there followed a period of persecution under Pusyamitra Sunga (183-147 BCE). The second royal patron for Buddhism was Kaniska (1st to 2nd century). Under his auspices, the Fourth Council was held. Legend reports that Nagarjuna (ca.150-250 CE) was the person preordained by Buddha to recover and explicate the Perfection of Wisdom texts. The first of these texts was the 'Perfection of Wisdom in 8,000 Lines'. After one of his lectures, some nagas approached him and told him of the texts hidden in their kingdom, and so Nagarjuna traveled there and returned with the sutras to India. He is credited with founding the Madhyamaka (Middle Way) school of Buddhist philosophy, which emphasized the centrality of the doctrine of emptiness.

Nagarjuna's philosophy is usually connected to the emergence of Mahayana around this time, which meant a clear distinction into the two main schools of Buddhism. Approximately two centuries after Nagarjuna, a new Mahayana school arose in India, which is commonly known as the Yogachara (Yogic Practice School). The main scriptural source for this school is the Sutra Explaining the Thought (Samdhinirmochana-sutra), which consists of a series of questions put to the Buddha by a group of bodhisattvas. The name "Yogic Practice School" may have been derived from an important treatise by Asanga (ca. 310-390) entitled the Levels of Yogic Practice (Yogachara-bhumi).

Along with his brother Vasubandhu (ca. 320-400), Asanga is credited with founding this school and developing its central doctrines. Yogachara emphasizes the importance of meditative practice, and several passages in Yogachara texts indicate that the founders of the school perceived other Mahayana Buddhists as being overly concerned with dialectical debate while neglecting meditation. The Yogachara school is commonly referred to in Tibet as "Mind Only" (sems tsam; Sanskrit: chitta-matra) because of an idea found in some Yogachara texts that all the phenomena of the world are "cognition-only" (vijnapti-matra), implying that everything we perceive is conditioned by consciousness.

From around the 4th cent CE, Vajrayana (Tantrayana) Buddhism started to develop in India as part of the Mahayana tradition. In addition to the developments in philosophy, a new trend in practice developed in India, which was written down in texts called tantras. These texts purported to have been spoken by the historical Buddha (or sometimes by other Buddhas), and while they incorporated the traditional Mahayana ideal of the bodhisattva who seeks Buddhahood for the benefit of all beings, they also proposed some radically new practices and paradigms.

The central practices of tantra include visualizations intended to foster cognitive reorientation, the use of prayers (mantra) to Buddhas that are intended to facilitate the transformation of the meditator into a fully enlightened Buddha, and often elaborate rituals. In the 5th cent CE, a Buddhist monastic university was founded at Nalanda, India. This university would become the largest and most influential Buddhist center for many centuries to come.

Chandrakirti (ca. 550-600) was one of the most influential commentators of Nagarjuna. In the following centuries, a number of syncretic schools developed. They tended to mingle Madhyamaka and Yogachara doctrines. The greatest examples of this syncretic period are the philosophers Shantarakshita (ca. 680-740) and Kamalashila (ca. 740-790), who are among the last significant Buddhist philosophers in India.

Following this last flowering of Buddhist thought in India, Buddhism began to decline. It became increasingly a tradition of elite scholar-monks who studied in great monastic universities like Nalanda and Vikramashila in Northern India. Buddhism failed to adapt to changing social and political circumstances, and apparently lacked a wide base of support.

When a series of invasions by Turkish Muslims descended on India in the ninth through twelfth centuries, after the invaders had sacked the great north Indian monastic universities and killed many prominent monks, Buddhism was dealt a death blow from which it never recovered. In 1193 the Moslems attacked and conquered Magadha, the heartland of Buddhism in India, and with the destruction of the Buddhist Monasteries, like Nalanda (1200) in that area Buddhism was wiped out. Only some small remnants of Buddhist communities, like in the Himalayan areas, Buddhism remained alive. Apart from the Moslims, most Indians are Hindu, and to them Buddhism is a old, dead branch of Hinduism, not a seperate, independent religion.

During the English Colonial Rule, there was a small resurgence of Buddhism in India. In the 1890's, for example, Dammapara of Sri Lanka founded the Mahaboddhi Society, and Ayoti Daas founded the Buddhist Society of South India, as well as other unrelated Buddhist activities in Bengal and other places in India. The effects of these activites where localized, never spreading widely. In 1956 in the state of Maharashutra, in the city of Nagpur, Dr. Ambedkar held a conversion ceremony, and converted 500,000 untouchables to Buddhism. One of the underlying thoughts of this re-introduction was to reduce the influence of the Hindu caste system in India and its detrimental influence on people of the lower castes.

The number of Buddhists in India in 1981 (according to India Govt. estimates) was 4.65 million people, and in 1991, became 6.32 million people. About 80% of this population live in the state of Maharashutra, and in the city of Nagpur; mainly connected to Dr.

Ambedkar's efforts. In the last few years, the counciousness of human rights has increased in India, and the number of Untouchables converting to Buddhism is increasing. The decline of Buddhism in India, the land of its birth, occurred for a variety of reasons, and happened even as it continued to flourish beyond the frontiers of India. Buddhism was established in the area of ancient Magadha and Kosala by Gautama Buddha in the 6th century BCE, in what is now modern Uttar Pradesh and Bihar. Buddhism, over the next 1500 years became the region's dominant belief system, spreading across the Indian sub-continent.

After the death of Gautama Buddha, Buddhism saw rapid expansion in its first century, especially in northern and central India. The Mauryan Emperor Ashoka (304-232 BCE) and later monarchs encouraged the expansion of Buddhism into Asia through religious ambassadors. Chinese scholars traveling through the region between the 5th and 8th centuries CE, such as Faxian, Xuanzang, I-ching, Hui-sheng, and Sung-Yun, began to speak of a decline of the Buddhist *sangha*, especially in the wake of the White Hun invasion. A continuing decline occurred after the fall of the Pala dynasty in the 12th century CE, continuing with the later destruction of monasteries by Muslim conquerors.

Buddhism was virtually extinct by the end of the 19th century. In recent times, Buddhism has seen a revival in India from the influence of Anagarika Dharmapala, Kripasaran Mahasthavir, Dr. B. R. Ambedkar and Tenzin Gyatso, the 14th Dalai Lama.

THE RISE AND DECLINE OF BUDDHISM'S INDIAN SOCIAL BASE

The Buddha's period saw not only urbanization, but also the beginnings of centralized states. While the Brahmin law-givers of this time were explicitly hostile to towns, there is evidence that the Buddha's message appealed especially to town-dwellers and the new social classes. Buddhism became successful by filling the moral vacuum in the new social world of commerce and city life with a universalistic social morality which was lacking in both the Brahmanical and shramana religions. In turn, the successful expansion of the Buddhist movement, with its surge of monasteries and monuments, depended on the growing economy of the time, together with increased centralized political organization capable of extracting and channeling surplus.

Regardless of the religious beliefs of their kings, states usually patronized all the important sects relatively even-handedly. This consisted of building monasteries and religious monuments, donating property such as the income of villages for the support of monks, and protecting previously donated property by leaving them exempt from taxation. Donations were most often made by private persons such as wealthy merchants and female relatives of the royal family, but this correlated with periods in which the state also gave its support and protection. In the case of Buddhism, this support was particularly important because of its high level of institutional organization and the dependence of monks on donations from the laity. State patronage of Buddhism took the form of massive propertied foundations.

Buddhism flourished in the strongest states, and was welcomed by rulers in India and later throughout Asia who were centralizing power in areas previously organized on the basis of clans. Although the Buddhist monks deliberately kept themselves uninvolved in affairs of state, they were useful for rulers as they promoted peaceful societies with their moral preaching and provided institutions for literate education. During the Maurya Empire, in which period Ashoka banned Vedic sacrifices as contrary to Buddhist benevolence, Buddhism began its spread outside of its Magadha homeland. The successor Shungas reinstated the sacrifices and persecuted Buddhism, but without much success. The overall trend of Buddhism's spread across India and state support by various regional regimes continued.

The consolidation of monastic organization made Buddhism the center of religious and intellectual life in India. The Gupta

Empire period was a time of great development of Hindu culture, but even then in the Ganges Plain half of the population supported Buddhism, and the five precepts were widely observed. The Hindu rulers and wealthy laity gave lavish material support to Buddhist monasteries. After the Guptas, the Shaivite kings of Gujarat also patronized Buddhist monasteries, building a great center of Buddhist learning at Valabhi. The Buddhist emperor Harsha and the later Buddhist Pala dynasty were great patrons of Buddhism, but Buddhism had already begun to lose its political and social base.

The gradual expansion in the scope and authority of caste regulations shifted political and economic power to the local arena, reversing the trend of centralization. The caste system gradually expanded into secular life as a regulative code of social and economic transactions. In ancient times, the four varnas were primarily a categorization scheme; the Vedas contained no prohibitions regarding intermarriage. There were, however, large numbers of jatis, probably originally tribal lineage groups. Brahman legists organized these groups into castes. The law books of Manu and Yajnavalkya, which were attributed to legendary figures, reached their canonical forms around 200 CE. These lay out caste duties, prohibitions, and penalties for violating their regulations.

Brahmans developed a new relationship with the state. It became the duty of political officials to enforce the caste regulations written by Brahmans. Caste regulations grew over a long period of time. As they did, states gradually lost control of landed revenue. A key transition was the downfall of the Guptas. Indian social structure developed in a manner opposite to that of China or Rome, where administration of law was dominated by government officials. Instead, Brahmans became hereditary monopolists of the law in a series of weak, ephemeral states. Brahmans came to regulate more and more aspects of public life, and collected fees for the performance of their rituals. Eventually, caste laws controlled everything from guilds and interest rates to criminal penalties.

Caste law, administered by Brahmans, was built up to control all local economic production and much of its distribution. The transformation of Brahman priests to linchpins of the caste system transformed the functioning property system. The political ascendancy of Hinduism and its displacement of Buddhism's political and social base came by this indirect route. Orthodox Brahmins were now capable of cutting off the flow of material resources upon which institutional Buddhism depended. Parallel developments that led to the decrease in the influence of Buddhism were the institution of rival Hindu temples, which were an innovation of the bhakti movement, and eventually orders of Hindu monks. These undercut Buddhist patronage and popular support.

DECLINE OF BUDDHISM UNDER VARIOUS GOVERNMENTS

THE SUNGAS

Following the Mauryans, Pusyamitra Sunga is linked in legend with the persecution of Buddhists and a resurgence of a form of Hinduism (Brahmanism) that forced Buddhism outwards to Kashmir, Gandhara and Bactria. There is some doubt as to whether he did or did not persecute Buddhists actively. A Buddhist tradition holds him as having taken steps to check the spread of Buddhism as "the number one enemy of the sons of the Sakyas and a most cruel persecutor of the religion". The *Divyavadana* ascribes to him the razing of *stupas* and *viharas* built by Ashoka, the placing of a bounty of 100 dinaras upon the heads of Buddhist monks (*bhiksus*) and describes him as one who wanted to undo the work of Ashoka.

This account has however been described as "exaggerated". Historian Romila Thapar writes that the Asokavadana legend is, in all probability, a "Buddhist version of Pusyamitra's attack of the Mauryas", and reflects the fact that, with the declining influence of Buddhism in the Imperial court, Buddhist monuments and institutions would receive less attention. The accuracy of the Buddhist texts that record Pushyamitra's persecution of Buddhists has been debated by historians. The first accounts appear two centuries after Pushyamitra's reign in *Asokâvadâna* and the *Divyâvadâna.* Sir John Marshall states that it is possible that the original brick stupa built by Ashoka was destroyed by Pusyamitra and then restored by his successor Agnimitra.

Archaeological evidence is scarce and uncertain.Following Ashoka's sponsorship of Buddhism, it is possible that Buddhist institutions fell on harder times under the Sungas but no evidence of active persecution has been noted. The Sungas were patrons of Hinduism and their lack of royal patronage was also a setback to Buddhism, resulting in the splintering of Buddhism into many forces. Some of them were: the *Saravastivadins*, *Mahasargikas*, *Sthaviravadha*, and *Yogacara*. This resulted in a diversity of opinions and interpretations that led to a conflict between different schools shortly after the fall of the Mauryans. Traditional Hinduism is said by some writers to have competed in political and spiritual realm with Buddhism in the gangetic plains while Buddhism flourished in the realms of the Bactrian kings.

CONTRIBUTION TO BUDDHISM

However to many scholars, Sunga kings were seen as more amenable to Buddhism and as having contributed to the building of the stupa at Bharhut. An inscription at Bodh Gaya at the Mahabodhi Temple records the construction of the temple as follows: "The gift of Nagadevi the wife of King Brahmamitra" So then this further means that the Sungas were in support of Buddhism. Another inscription reads: "The gift of Kurangi, the mother of living sons and the wife of King Indragnimitra, son of Kosiki. The gift also of Srima of the royal palace shrine."

Guptas

Buddhism saw a brief revival under the Guptas. By the 4th to 5th century Buddhism was already in decline in northern India, even as it was achieving multiple successes in Central Asia and along the Silk Road as far as China. It continued to prosper in Gandhara under the Shahi kingdom.

White Huns

Central Asian and North Western Indian Buddhism weakened in the 6th century following the White Hun invasion, who followed their own religions such as Tengri, Nestorian Christianity, and Manichean. Their Saivite King, Mihirakula (who ruled from 515 CE), suppressed Buddhism as well. He did this by destroying monasteries as far away as modern-day Allahabad, before his son reversed the policy.

Harsha

In the North and west the collapse of Harshavardana's kingdom gave rise to many smaller kingdoms. This led to the rise of the martial Rajputs clans across the gangetic plains. It also marked the end of Buddhist ruling clans, along with a sharp decline in royal patronage. This carried on until a revival under the Pala Empire in the Bengal region.

BUDDHISM IN SOUTHERN INDIA

In the south of India while there was no overt persecution of Buddhists at least two Pallava rulers Simhavarma and Trilochana are known to have destroyed Buddhist stupas and have had Hindu temples built over them. Bodhidharma, a patriarch of Zen Buddhism was of the original Kshatriya caste. (Reference: The Story Of Karate, by Luana Metil and Jace Townsend, Lerner Publications Company, Minneapolis, USA, Page Number: 11, ISBN Number: 0-8225-9770-5)

Nagarjuna, the founder of Mahayana Buddhism, was a Brahmin from southern India. The Satavahanas were worshipers of Buddha as well as other Hindu gods such as Krishna, Shiva, Gauri, Indra, Surya, and Chandra. Under their reign Amaravati, the historian Durga Prasad notices that Buddha had been worshiped as a form of Vishnu. Furthermore a vigorous Hindu revival of Vaishnavite Hinduism in the region led to a sharp decline of Buddhism.

Muhammad bin Qasim

In AD 711, Muhammad bin Qasim conquered the Sindh bringing Indian societies into contact with Islam. Nicholas Gier notes the opinion that he succeeded partly because Dahir was an unpopular Hindu king that ruled over a Buddhist majority and that Chach of Alor and his kin were regarded as usurpers of the earlier Buddhist Rai Dynasty. Some others, however doubt this, noting that the diffuse and blurred nature of Hindu and Buddhist practices in the region, especially that of the royalty to be patrons of both leading them to believe that Chach himself may have been a Buddhist. The forces of Muhammad bin Qasim defeated Raja Dahir in alliance with the Jats and other regional governors.

The Chach Nama records a couple of instances of conversion of stupas to mosques such as at Nerun as well as the incorporation of the religious elite into the ruling administration such as the allocation of 3% of the government revenue was allocated to the Brahmins. As a whole, the non-Muslim populations of conquered territories were treated as People of the Book and granted Hindu and Buddhist religions the freedom to practice their faith in return for payment of the poll tax (jizya). They were then excused from military service or payment of the tax paid by Muslim subjects - Zakat. The jizya enforced was a graded tax, being heaviest on the elite and lightest on the poor. While proslytization occurred, the social dynamics of Sind were no different from other regions newly conquered by Muslim forces such as Egypt, where conversion to Islam was slow and took centuries.

Mahmud of Ghazni

By the 10th century Mahmud of Ghazni defeated the Hindu-Shahis, effectively removing Hindu influence and ending Buddhist self-governance across Central Asia, as well as the Punjab region. He demolished both stupas and temples during his numerous campaigns across North-Western India, but left those within his domains and Afghanistan alone, even as al-Biruni recorded Buddha as the prophet "Burxan". Mahmud of Ghazni is said to have been an iconoclast. Hindu and Buddhist statues, shrines and temples were looted and destroyed, and many Buddhists had to take refuge in Tibet.

Palas

In the East under the Palas in Bengal, Mahayana Buddhism flourished and spread to Bhutan and Sikkim. The Palas created many temples and a distinctive school of Buddhist art. Mahayana Buddhism flourished under the Palas between the 8th and the 12th century, before it collapsed at the hands of the attacking Sena dynasty.

However some scholars believe that they were also Shaivaite judging by the image of Shiva and His ox on their coins and the etymology of their names. Art of Shiva also exists in temples such as the Melakadambur in Bengal where Nataraja and his bull are found. They had also dedicated shrines to Vishnu. Figures of Vishnu were substantial in number in the Pala Era. Other than figures of Buddha, Vishnu and Shiva there were also those of Sarasvati.

Muhammad of Ghor

Muhammad attacked the North-Western regions of the Indian subcontinent many times. Gujarat later fell to Muhammad of Ghor's armies in 1197. Muhammad of Ghor's armies destroyed many Buddhist structures, including the great Buddhist university of Nalanda. In 1200 Muhammad Khilji, one of Qutb-ud-Din's generals destroyed monasteries fortified by the Sena armies, such as the one at Vikramshila. Many monuments of ancient Indian civilization were destroyed by the invading armies, including Buddhist sanctuaries near Benares. Buddhist monks who escaped the massacre fled to Nepal, Tibet and South India.

The Mongols

In 1215, Genghis Khan conquered Afghanistan and devastated the Muslim world. In 1227, after his death, his conquest was divided. Chagatai then established the Chagatai Khanate, where his son Arghun made Buddhism the state religion. At the same time, he came down harshly on Islam and demolished mosques to build many stupas. He was succeeded by his brother, and then his son Ghazan who converted to Islam and in 1295 changed the state religion. After his reign, and the splitting of the Chagatai Khanate, little mention of Buddhism or the stupas built by the Mongols can be found in Afghanistan and Central Asia.

Timur (Tamarlane)

Timur was a 14th-century warlord of Turco-Mongol descent, conqueror of much of Western and central Asia, and founder of the Timurid Empire. Timur destroyed Buddhist establishments and raided areas in which Buddhism had flourished.

Mughals

Mughal rule also contributed to the decline of Buddhism. They are reported to have destroyed many Hindu temples and Buddhist shrines alike or converted many sacred Hindu places into Muslim shrines and mosques. Mughal rulers like Aurangzeb not only destroyed Buddhist temples and monasteries but also destroyed Hindu temples and replaced them with Islamic mosques.

IDEOLOGICAL AND FINANCIAL CAUSES

The period between the 400 BCE and 1000 CE saw gains by Hinduism at the expense of Buddhism. Some Hindu rulers resorted to military means in an effort to suppress Buddhism. However it is seen that the evolution of Hindu ideology influenced by Buddhism was more important factor for the growth of Hinduism. Hinduism became a more "intelligible and satisfying road to faith for many ordinary worshippers" than it had been because it now included not only an appeal to a personal god, but had also seen the development of an emotional facet with the composition of devotional hymns.

Xuanzang's Report

Much of what we know about the state of Buddhism in the second half of the first millennium CE comes from the 7th century

Chinese pilgrim Xuanzang, who traveled widely and documented his journey. Although he found many regions where Buddhism was still flourishing, he also found many where it had sharply and startlingly declined, giving way to Jainism and a Brahmanical order. Xuanzang compliments the patronage of Harshavardana. He reported that Buddhism was popular in Kanyakubja (modern day Uttar Pradesh), where he noted "an equal number of Buddhists and heretics" and the presence of 100 monasteries and 10,000 bhikshus along with 200 "Deva" (Hindu) temples.. He found a similarly flourishing population in Udra (modern Orissa).

He found a mixed population in Kosala, homeland of Nagarjuna, and in Andhra, and Dravida which today roughly correspond to the modern day Indian states of Andhra Pradesh and Tamil Nadu. In a region he calls Konkanapura, which may be Kolhapur in southern Maharashtra, he found great numbers of Buddhists coexisting with a similar number of non-Buddhists, and a similar situation in Northern Maharashtra. In Sindh he finds a large Theravada population. He reports a fair number of Buddhists in what is now Pakistan. In Dhanyakataka (today's Vijayawada), he found a striking decline, with Jainism and Shaivism ascendant. In Bihar, site of a number of important landmarks, he also found a striking decline and relatively few followers, with Hinduism and Jainism predominating.

He also found relatively few Buddhists in Bengal, Kamarupa (modern Assam). He reported no Buddhist presence in Konyodha, few in Chulya (in the Tamil region), and few in Gujarat and Rajasthan, except in Valabhi, where he found a large Theravada population. During the reign of the Chalukya dynasty, Xuanzang reported that numerous Buddhist stupas in regions previously ruled by Buddhist-sympathetic Andhras and Pallavas were "ruined" and "deserted". These regions came under the control of the Vaishnavite Eastern Chalukyas, who were not favorable to Buddhism and did not support the religion.

Xuanzang's report also mentions that, in the 7th Century, Shashanka of the Kingdom of Gouda (Bengal), was expanding his influence in the region in the aftermath of the fall of the Gupta Empire. He is blamed by Xuanzhang and other Buddhist sources for the murder of Rajyavardhana, a Buddhist king of Thanesar. Xuanzang writes that Shashanka destroyed the Bodhi tree of enlightenment at Bodh Gaya and replaced Buddha statues with Shiva Lingams. However, it has been claimed that Xuanzhang had a Buddhist bias in favor of the Buddhist rulers such as Harshavardhana and that his account may therefore be slanted.

Philosophical convergence

Literary evidences point towards an absorption of Buddhist elements by Hindu culture over a period of centuries. Anti-Buddhist propaganda was also reaching its peak during the 8th century when Shankara modeled his monastic order after the Buddhist Sangha. An upsurge of Hinduism had taken place in North India by the early eleventh century as illustrated by the influential Sanskrit drama *Prabodhacandrodaya* in the Chandela court; a devotion to Vishnu and an allegory to the defeat of Buddhism and Jainism.

The population of North India had become predominantly Shaiva, Vaishnava or Shakta. By the 12th century a lay population of Buddhist hardly existed outside the monastic institutions and when it did penetrate the Indian peasant population it was hardly discernible as a distinct community. Buddhist monasteries were well-funded and life within was relatively easy. To avoid unwanted members, many monasteries became selective about whom they admitted, in some cases based on social class.

Islam

By the time of the Muslim conquests in India, there were only glimpses of Buddhism nor any evidence of a provincial government in control of the Buddhists. During the seventh to thirteenth centuries when Islam arrived it replaced Buddhism as the great cosmopolitan trading religion in many places accompanied by a consolidation of the communal peasant religions of Hinduism. The Tibetan scholar of the seventeenth century Taranatha writes that during the time of the Sena king *Stag-gzigs* (Turks) had begun to appear on horses and that monasteries had been fortified with troops stationed in them; however, they were overrun and monks at Uddandapura were massacred, the monastery razed and replaced by a new fort and further north-east Vikramshila was destroyed as well.

Hardly a contemporary evidence however exists on the destruction of Buddhist monasteries. Brief Muslim accounts and the one eye witness account of Dharmasmavim in wake of the conquest during the 1230s talks about abandoned viharas being used as camps by the Turukshahs. Later historical traditions such as Taranathas are mixed with legendary materials and summarized as "the Turukshah conquered the whole of Magadha and destroyed many monasteries and did much damage at Nalanda, such that many monks fled abroad" thereby bringing about a sudden demise of Buddhism with their destruction of the Viharas.

Buddhism lingered longer in Iran than South Asia and was officially professed under fifty years of Mongol conquest. With the conversion of Ghazan to Islam in 1295, the backlash resulted in the destruction of many Buddhist places of worship and the further migration of monks into Kashmir. Many places were destroyed and renamed. For example, Udantpur's monasteries were destroyed by in 1197 Mohammed-bin-Bakhtiyar and the town was renamed. Taranatha in his *History of Buddhism in India* (dpal dus kyi 'khor lo'i chos bskor gyi byung khungs nyer mkho) of 1608 C.E., gives an account of the last few centuries of Buddhism, mainly in Eastern India. His account suggests aconsiderable decline but not an extinction of Buddhism in India in his time.

Sufis and the Bhakti movement

When Islam arrived in India, it sought conversion from, not assimilation to or integration with, the already present religions. Under Sufi influence, the pressures of caste, and with no political support structure left in place to resist social mores, many converted to Islam in the Bengal region. After the Mongol invasions of Islamic lands across Central Asia, many Sufis also found themselves fleeing towards India and around the environs of Bengal. In Bengal, their influence, caste attitudes towards Buddhists, previous familiarity with converting Buddhists, a lack of Buddhist political power, Hinduism's resurgence through movements such as the Advaita and the bhakti movement, all contributed to a significant realignment of beliefs that relegated Buddhism in India to the peripheries.

SURVIVAL OF BUDDHISM IN INDIA

At the beginning of the modern era, Buddhism was very nearly extinct in mainstream Indian society. Some tribal peoples living in the territory of modern India did continue to practice Buddhism. In Bengal, the Bauls still practice a syncretic form of Hinduism that was strongly influenced by Buddhism. There is also evidence of small communities of Indian Theravada Buddhists existing continuously in Bengal in the area of Chittagong hill tracts among the indigenous Chakma people up to the present. Though they are under increasing pressure from mostly Muslim Bengali settlers. There was genocide of the Chakma and Buddhists by Islamists in East Pakistan. The Chakma spiritual practices are a blend of Buddhism/Vaishnavism.

Buddhist institutions flourished in eastern India right until the Islamic invasion. Buddhism still survives among the Barua (though practicing Vaishnava/Hindu elements), a community of Bengali/ Magadh descent that migrated to Chittagong region. Indian Buddhism also survives among Newars of Nepal. Buddhism survived in Gilgit and Baltistan until 13-14th century, perhaps slightly longer in the nearby Swat Valley. In Ladakh region, adjacent to Kashmir valley, Tibetan Buddhism survives to this day.

The historic prevalence and history of Tibetan Buddhism in the above mentioned Northern regions of Jammu and Kashmir is reported in the Rajatarangini of Kalhana written sometime during 1147–1149 CE. In Tamilnadu and Kerala, Buddhism survived until 15-16th century. At Nagapattinam, in Tamil Nadu, Buddhist icons were cast and inscribed until this time, and the ruins of the Chudamani Vihara stood until they were destroyed by the Jesuits in 1867. In the South in some pockets, it may have survived even longer.

Revival

On pilgrimage to Bodh Gaya in 1891, the Sri Lankan Buddhist leader Anagarika Dharmapala was shocked to find the temple in the hands of a Saivite priest, the Buddha image transformed into a Hindu icon and Buddhists barred from worship. The Buddhist revival then began in India, when he founded the Maha Bodhi Society. The organization's initial efforts were for the purpose of resuscitation of Buddhism in India and of restoring the ancient Buddhist shrines at Bodh Gaya, Sarnath and Kushinara. The Buddhist renaissance inaugurated by Anagarika Dharmapala through his Mahabodhi Movement is also described as "conservative" for it held the Muslim Rule in India responsible for the decay of Buddhism in India in the then current mood of Hindu-Buddhist brotherhood. The organization's initial efforts were to restore various Buddhist shrines that had been neglected under Hindu administration, and to open to the public various Buddhist sites and temples that had been destroyed in various periods of Muslim invasion.

Later in the 1950s Bhimrao Ramji Ambedkar pioneered the Dalit Buddhist movement in India. Dr. Ambedekar saw conversion to Islam and to Christianity as a factor contributing to the "denationalisation" of India. The revival movement of Buddhism in India underwent a major change when after publishing a series of books and articles arguing that Buddhism was the only way for the untouchables to gain equality, Ambedkar publicly converted on October 14, 1956 in Nagpur and then in turn led a mass-conversion ceremony for over 380,000 dalits. Many other such mass-conversion ceremonies organized since and has become a politically charged issue. Since Ambedkar's conversion, many more people from different castes have converted to Buddhism. Many Dalits employ the term "Ambedkar(ite) Buddhism" to designate the Buddhist movement, which started with Ambedkar's conversion.

in 1959 Tenzin Gyatso, the 14th Dalai Lama transitioned from Tibet to India and set up the government of Tibet in Exile in Dharamsala, India, which is often referred to as "Little Lhasa." Tibetan exiles numbering several thousand have since settled in the town. Most of these exiles live in Upper Dharamsala, or McLeod Ganj, where they established monasteries, temples and schools. The town is sometimes known as "Little Lhasa", after the Tibetan capital city, and has become one of the centres of Buddhism in the world. Kashmir has been one of the most important centres for the spread and development of Buddhism. Buddhism was an important part of the classical Kashmiri culture, as is reflected in the Nilamata Purana and the Kalhana's Rajatarangini.

Buddhism is generally believed to have become dominant in Kashmir in the time of Emperor Ashoka, although it was widespread there long before his time. It enjoyed the patronage not only of the Buddhist rulers but of Hindu and early Muslim rulers too. From Kashmir, it spread to the neighbouring Ladakh. The first known ruler of Kashmir, Gonanda (mentioned by Kalhana in his Rajatarangini), was related to Jarasandha, who ruled Magadha during the time of the Kurukshetra war. Surrendra is perhaps the first Buddhist ruler of Kashmir. He erected the first viharas in Kashmir. One of these, known as Narendrabhavana, was in the city of Sauraka (Suru, beyond the Zoji La.) The other vihara was at Saurasa, corresponding to the village Sowur on the shore of Anchar Lake to the north of Srinagar.

MAURYAN PERIOD

Ashoka

Kalhana claims that though it was situated far from the Mauryan capital (Pataliputra), Kashmir enjoyed all the benefits of Ashoka's benign rule. The provincial capital Shrinagari (Srinagar) was 'resplendent with prosperity and wealth.' According to some

Buddhist writers including Taranatha, the Buddhist preacher Madhyantika introduced saffron cultivation into Kashmir. Buddhism and Shaivism flourished side by side in Kashmir during Ashoka's time and received the Emperor's patronage in equal measure. Kalhana notes that Ashoka built two Shiva temples at Vijayeshvara (Bijbihara), and ordered several others renovated. In Vitastatra (Vethavutur) and at Shuskaletra (Hukhalitar) he built a number of viharas and stupas. He deputed Madhyantika for the propagation of Buddhism in Kashmir and Gandhara.

Ashoka's successors

Buddhism suffered a temporary eclipse during the reign of Ashoka's successors Jalauka and Damodara. Kalhana, a Hindu historian, asserted that large number of Buddhist scholars was vanquished in debates with Jalauka's guru Avadhuta, and hence traditional observances were slowly revived. Later, however, Jalauka created a big vihara, the Krityashramavihara, in the vicinity of Varahamula (Baramulla), which still existed as late as the 11th century. The history of Kashmir after Damodara is not certain until the time of the Kushanas.

Kushana period

The Kushana period saw a great resurgence of Buddhism in Kashmir, especially during the reign of Kanishka. The fourth Buddhist Council was held in Kashmir, under the presidency of Katyayaniputra, in Kanishka's time. The south Indian Buddhist philosopher Nagarjuna lived in Kashmir during the Kushana period.

Post-Kushana reaction

During the reign of Abhimanyu, which in Kalhana's chronicle follows that of Kanishka, Buddhist scholars under the guidance of Nagarjuna defeated the Shaivite clergy in debates, encouraging people to choose Buddhism. However, during the time of Chandradeva, revival of knowledge of the works of Patanjali, like the Mahabhashya which had become rare, led to a resurgence of Shaivism.

By the time of Gonanda, the old philosophy was completely revived. Nothing is known about the religious affiliations of Pratapaditya, a scion of the Gupta dynasty and his successors, except that they are stated to have ruled well, and fullest liberty of faith was accorded. Buddhism is stated by Kalhana and Hiuen Tsang to have suffered severe setbacks under the Huns, especially under Mihirakula, whom Hiuen Tsang describes as a great persecutor of the Buddhists.

Meghavahana

Upon Mihirakula's death, Kashmir was ruled by Meghavahana, who belonged to the old ruling dynasty of Kashmir. Meghavahana was a staunch Buddhist, who issued a proclamation against killing of all animals at the very time of his coronation, and built numerous stupas.

BUDDHIST INFLUENCE IN KASHMIR

In Kalhana's time, and before, there was apparently no distinction between "Hindus" and Buddhists in Kashmir. Kalhana himself used Buddhist terms and expressions as a Buddhist would. Nilamata Purana was the text of the worshippers of Nila Naga, the Naga worship was common in Kashmir. It mentions the prevalence of Buddhist worship as a common practice in Kashmir.

Here are some quotes from Nilamat Purana from Kashmir (trans. by Dr. Ved Kumari). It correctly represents the religious spirit of ancient India.

709-710a. O Brahman, the god Visnu, the lord of the world, shall be (born as) the preceptor of the world, Buddha by name, at the time when the Pusya is joined with the moon, in the month of Vaisaksha, in twenty eighth Kali Age.

710b-12. Listen from as to how his worship should be performed in the bright-half, from that period onwards, in future. The image of Buddha should be bathed (with water rendered holy) with all medicinal herbs, all jewels and all scents, in accordance with the sayings of the Sakyas. The dwellings of the Sakyas (i.e. Viharas) should be whitewashed with care.

713. Here and there, the Caityas - the abodes of the god - should be provided with paintings. The festival, swarming with the actors and the dancers, should be celebrated.

714. The Sakyas should be honoured with Civara (the dress of a Buddhist mendicant), food and books. All this should be done till the advent of Magha.

715. O twice-born, eatable offerings should be made for three days. Worship with flowers, clothes etc. and charity for the poor (should continue for three days).

Kalhana's Ṛajatarangini mentions that a monumental metallic image of Buddha once stood in Srinagar, which was eventually destroyed by Sikandar Butshikan. A significant number of beautifully crafted Buddhist bronzes have survived. In Kashmir valley, a Buddhist Bhikshu was present in Baramula in the 13th century. The Kashmiri Pandits still worship the triratna symbol.

BODH GAYA

Bodh Gaya or Bodhgaya is a city in Gaya district in the Indian state of Bihar. It is famous for being the place of Gautama Buddha's attainment of nirvana (Enlightenment). Historically, it was known as the Bodhimanda (ground around the Bodhi-tree), Uruvela, Sambodhi, Vajrasana and Mahabodhi. The name Bodh Gaya did not come into use until the 18th century. The main monastery of Bodhgaya used to be called the Bodhimanda-vihâra (Pali). Now it is called the Mahabodhi Temple.

For Buddhists, Bodh Gaya is the most important of the main four pilgrimage sites related to the life of Gautama Buddha, the other three being Kushinagar, Lumbini, and Sarnath. In 2002, Mahabodhi Temple, located in Bodh Gaya, became a UNESCO World Heritage Site. The surrounding town, by contrast, is dusty, noisy and somewhat polluted, due in large part to the large numbers of pilgrims and tourists who visit there. A new development plan has been proposed to "ensure a sustainable and prosperous future" for Bodh Gaya, but has become controversial because such a plan may require the relocation of whole neighborhoods.

According to Buddhist traditions, circa 500 BC Prince Gautama Siddhartha, wandering as an ascetic, reached the sylvan banks of Falgu River, near the city of Gaya. There he sat in meditation under a bodhi tree (*Ficus religiosa*). After three days and three nights of meditation, Siddharta attained enlightenment and insight, and the answers that he had sought. He then spent seven weeks at seven different spots in the vicinity meditating and considering his experience. After seven weeks, he travelled to Sarnath, where he began teaching Buddhism.

Disciples of Gautama Siddhartha began to visit the place where he had gained enlightenment during the full moon in the month of Vaisakh (April-May), as per the Hindu calendar. Over time, the place became known as Bodh Gaya, the day of enlightenment as Buddha Purnima, and the tree as the Bodhi Tree. The history of Bodh Gaya is documented by many inscriptions and pilgrimage accounts. Foremost among these are the accounts of the Chinese pilgrims Faxian in the 5th century and Xuanzang in the 7th century. The area was at the heart of a Buddhist civilization for centuries, until it was conquered by Turkish armies in the 13th century.

The complex, located about 96 kilometers from Patna, contains the Mahabodhi Temple with the diamond throne (called the *Vajrasana*) and the holy Bodhi tree. This tree was originally a sapling of the Sri Maha Bodhi tree in Sri Lanka, itself grown from a sapling of the original Bodhi tree. It is believed that 250 years after the Enlightenment of the Buddha, Emperor Asoka visited Bodh Gaya. He is considered to be the founder of the original Mahabodhi temple. It consisted of an elongated spire crowned by a miniature stupa and a *chhatravali* on a platform.

A double flight of steps led up to the platform and the upper sanctum. The mouldings on the spire contained Buddha images in niches. Some historians believe that the temple was constructed or renovated in the 1st century during the Kushan period. With the decline of Buddhism in India, the temple was abandoned and forgotten, buried under layers of soil and sand. The temple was later restored by Sir Alexander Cunningham as part of his work for the British Archaeological Society in the late 19th century. In 1883, Cunningham along with J. D. Beglar and Dr Rajendralal Miitra painstakingly excavated the site. Extensive renovation work was carried out to restore Bodh Gaya to its former glory.

Kittisirimegha of Sri Lanka, contemporary of Samudragupta, erected with the permission of Samudragupta, a Sanghârâma near the Mahâbodhi-vihâra, chiefly for the use of the Singhalese monks who went to worship the Bodhi tree. The circumstances in connection with the Sanghârâma are given by Hiouen Thsang (Beal, op. cit., 133ff) who gives a description of it as seen by himself. It was probably here that Buddhaghosa met the Elder Revata who persuaded him to come to Ceylon. Presently, several Buddhist temples and monasteries have been built by the people of Bhutan, China, Japan, Myanmar, Nepal, Sikkim, Sri Lanka, Thailand, Tibet and Vietnam in a wide area around the temple.

These buildings reflect the architectural style, exterior and interior decoration of their respective countries. The statue of Buddha in the Chinese Temple is 200 years old and was brought from China. Japan's Nippon Temple is shaped like a pagoda. The Myanmar (Burmese) Temple is also pagoda shaped and is reminiscent of Bagan. The Thai Temple has a typical sloping, curved roof covered with golden tiles. Inside, the temple holds a massive and spectacular bronze statue of Buddha. Next to the Thai temple there is a recent 25 meter statue of Buddha located within a garden which has existed there for over 100 years. For Tibetan Buddhism there are two temples.

Demographics

As of 2001, India census, Bodh Gaya had a population of 30,883. Males constitute 54% of the population and females 46%.

Bodh Gaya has an average literacy rate of 51%, lower than the national average of 59.5%; with male literacy of 63% and female literacy of 38%. 18% of the population is under 6 years of age.

BODHI TREE

The Bodhi Tree, also known as Bo (from the Sinhalese Bo), was a large and very old Sacred Fig tree (*Ficus religiosa*) located in Bodh Gaya (about 100 km/62 mi from Patna in the Indian state of Bihar), under which Siddhartha Gautama, the spiritual teacher and founder of Buddhism later known as Gautama Buddha, achieved enlightenment, or *Bodhi*. In religious iconography, the Bodhi tree is recognizable by its heart-shaped leaves, which are usually prominently displayed. The term "Bodhi tree" is also widely applied to currently existing trees, particularly the Sacred Fig growing at the Mahabodhi Temple, which is allegedly a direct descendant of the original specimen.

This tree is a frequent destination for pilgrims, being the most important of the four holy sites for Buddhists. Other holy Bodhi trees which have a great significance in the history of Buddhism are the Anandabodhi tree in Sravasti and the Bodhi tree in Anuradhapura. Both are believed to have been propagated from the original Bodhi tree. The Bodhi tree at the Mahabodhi Temple is called the Sri Maha Bodhi. According to Buddhist texts the Buddha, after his Enlightenment, spent a whole week in front of the tree, standing with unblinking eyes, gazing at it with gratitude. A shrine was later erected on the spot where he stood, and was called the Animisalocana cetiya.

The spot was used as a shrine even in the lifetime of the Buddha. King Asoka was most diligent in paying homage to the Bodhi tree, and held a festival every year in its honour in the month of Kattika. His queen, Tissarakkhâ was jealous of the Tree, and three years after she became queen (i.e., in the nineteenth year of Asoka's reign), she caused the tree to be killed by means of mandu thorns. The tree, however, grew again, and a great monastery was attached to the Bodhimanda called the Bodhimanda Vihara. Among those present at the foundation of the Mahâ Thûpa are mentioned thirty thousand monks from the Bodhimanda Vihara, led by Cittagutta.

To Jetavana, Sravasti

Buddhist tradition recounts that while the Buddha was yet alive, in order that people might make their offerings in the name of the Buddha when he was away on pilgrimage, he sanctioned the planting of a seed from the Bodhi tree in Bodhgaya in front of the gateway of Jetavana Monastery near Sravasti. For this purpose Moggallana took a fruit from the tree as it dropped from its stalk, before it reached the ground. It was planted in a golden jar by Anathapindika with great pomp and ceremony. A sapling immediately sprouted forth, fifty cubits high, and in order to consecrate it the Buddha spent one night under it, rapt in meditation. This tree, because it was planted under the direction of Ananda, came to be known as the Ananda Bodhi.

TO ANURADHAPURA, SRI LANKA

According to the Mahavamsa, the Sri Maha Bodhi in Sri Lanka was planted in 288 BC, making it the oldest verified specimen of any angiosperm. In this year (the twelfth year of King Asoka's reign) the right branch of the Bodhi tree was brought by Sanghamittâ to Anurâdhapura and placed by Devânâmpiyatissa in the Mahâmeghavana.

The Buddha, on his death bed, had resolved five things, one being that the branch which should be taken to Ceylon should detach itself. From Gayâ, the branch was taken to Pâtaliputta, thence to Tâmalittî, where it was placed in a ship and taken to Jambukola, across the sea; finally it arrived at Anuradhapura, staying on the way at Tivakka. Those who assisted the king at the ceremony of the planting of the Tree were the nobles of Kâjaragâma and of Candanagâma and of Tivakka.

The Trees of Previous Buddhas

According to the Mahavamsa, branches from the Bodhi trees of all the Buddhas born during this kalpa were planted in Ceylon on the spot where the sacred Bodhi tree stands today in Anurâdhapura. The branch of Kakusandha's tree was brought by a nun called Rucânandâ, Konagamana's by Kantakânandâ (or Kanakadattâ), and Kassapa's by Sudhammâ.

Modern Plantings

A Sri Maha Bodhi sapling was planted in the Buddha Jayanti Park in New Delhi, India in 1993. Another sapling exists in the botanical garden of Uppsala, Sweden. Buddhism arose in India during a period of intense intellectual and social ferment. It was a period during which the authority of the Vedas had been placed in doubt, the concept of god as a Supreme Being and creator was in question, the hereditary restrictions on caste mobility were under attack, and the efficacy of Brahminical rituals was being challenged. The authors of the *Upanishads* had opened the door for various heterodox currents to emerge in society, and amongst the most significant of these were the *Lokayatas* who polemicized against religious charlatans, and the *Nyayavadis* whose rational epistemology created the foundation for intense philosophical debate and encouraged the investigation of the real world based on reason and logic, freed from the burden of superstition and irrational adherence to burdensome rituals.

Various ideological sects competed for the attention and acceptance of the ruling elites and the public. The most important amongst these were the Jains and the Buddhists. Although each of the various sects made original and interesting contributions to philosophy, it was the early Buddhists who attempted to provide a unified philosophical system where ethical conduct and social criticism lay at the very core of their ideological system. Although today, Buddhism is viewed as a religion by many of its followers, the early Buddhists sects were either strongly atheistic or agnostic.

The atheists believed that rather than "God having created man in his own image" it was man who had created "God" in his image. In their view, the liberation of humanity was contingent upon humanity shedding the delusion that "God" existed. Other parables from surviving Buddhist texts indicate agnosticism. For instance, there is a suggestion that Buddhist followers ought not to waste their time on unsolvable metaphysical questions such as "does god exist". The search to identify the "one true god" or to speculate on the nature of god was seen as an exercise in futility. But the most frequently cited argument against god by the Buddhists was that if an omnipotent and omniscient being such as "God" truly existed, and who was also all good, there could not be the kind of *dukkha* (suffering) that was so widespread in the real world.

These *shlokas* (verses) from the *Bhûridatta Jataka* illustrates this point

If the creator of the entire world they call "God" be the lord of every being, why does he order such misfortune, and not create concord?

If the creator of the entire world they call "God" be the lord of every being; why let prevail deceit, lies and ignorance, why create such inequity and injustice?

If the creator of the entire world they call "God" be the lord of every being, then an evil master is he, knowing what's right did let wrong prevail!

Unlike religions that ascribed earthly miseries to human sinfulness that brought upon the wrath of a vengeful god who needed to be feared, Buddhism saw the root of human suffering in ignorance that could only be ended through the acquisition of wisdom. Rather than expect some supernatural entity to end human suffering, the Buddhists argued that it was in human hands to end their sorrows through conduct and action driven by knowledge and correct understanding of human nature and the physical world. Hence, the aspiration for knowledge *(jigyasa)* was seen as the answer to blind faith. Although the Buddhists were not alone in developing this view, the elaboration of this point of view became pivotal to early Buddhist philosophy.

Central to Buddhist philosophy was an understanding of human nature and what caused *dukkha* - i.e. human suffering. They saw human personality as constituting five attributes, i.e. body, feeling, perception, disposition and consciousness, and used this framework to develop their understanding of human suffering. Citing examples of conditions that led to human suffering, such as aging, sickness and death, or association with the unpleasant, (or separation from the pleasant), or the inability to get what one wished - they concluded that suffering was a condition of stress and conflict inherent within human existence and interaction with the world.

They also connected suffering to the very impermanence of things. They observed how people lamented over the loss of a loved one, or experienced sorrow when something or someone that had once given them happiness became separated from them. They noted that even human pleasures were not immune from suffering because they didn't last forever, and the loss of pleasure inevitably left people feeling deprived. Seeing as how clinging to things (that were necessarily impermanent) was one of the primary causes of *dukkha,* they cautioned against excessive attachment. At the same time, they recognized a recurring and more general type of existential unease and anxiety *(aniccha)* that arises from the very transience of life, and our inability to control or comprehend all worldly phenomenon, which they characterized as *viparinama-dukkha.*

But the Buddhists did not see *dukkha* only emanating from the difficulties of an individual. They also saw suffering emerge on a much larger scale from hostile social conditions such as poverty, war, and social oppression which they described as *dukkha-dukkha.* As a formula (*char-mulya*) for addressing these different types of suffering, the Buddhists advocated a four-fold scheme of a) recognizing the problem i.e. suffering *(dukkha)*; b) identifying the cause of the suffering - such as craving stemming from ignorance *(samudaya)* ; c) establishing the goal of ending the problem *(nirodha)* - i.e. the cessation of suffering *(nirvana);* d) conducting life in a manner that was consistent with the cessation of suffering - following the right path or engaging in the right practice (*marga*).

Followers were thus goaded into developing both a sense of personal ethics and a social conscience:

"He who has understanding and great wisdom does not think of harming himself or another, nor of harming both alike. He rather thinks of his own welfare, of that of others, of that of both, and of the welfare of the whole world. In that way one shows understanding and great wisdom." *Anguttara Nikaya* - (Gradual Sayings)

"By protecting oneself (e.g., morally), one protects others; by protecting others, one protects oneself." *Samyukta Nikaya* (Kindred Sayings)

Human actions (*kamma, kaama*, or *karma*) in the Buddhist framework were to be judged based on both the intention or motive (*chetanaa*) and the consequences (*vipaaka*) of the action. Altruistic actions which helped in the establishment and promotion of a just society were encouraged in the *dharmaniyama* (moral duty code). {The discourses, or *suttas* in the *Digha Nikaya*, illustrate how there was deep concern with the creation of social conditions favorable to the cultivation of Buddhist values and the expansion of social equity and justice. These views undoubtedly influenced the creation of a "welfare state" during the reign of emperor, Ashoka (B.C. 274-236)}

In their theories of causality Buddhists challenged the view that human destiny was unaffected by the ethics or morality of human actions. They countered the doctrine of amoral causation (*akriyavaada)* whose adherents argued that there was no merit in doing good and no demerit for doing evil. (An extreme expression of such thinking was seen in philosophers who denied all morality and saw no crime in the killing of any person.)

Realizing that such a world-view could lead to the rejection of moral distinctions and personal responsibility for ones actions, they argued strenuously against such beliefs. They also argued against the theory of Makkali Ghosha (or Ghoshala) who believed that human fate was predetermined, and therefore denied that human actions had any bearing on the results of things *(ahetuvaada)* and maintained that human intention and effort were essentially powerless in changing human destiny, and therefore advocated fatalism (*niyati*). They also countered philosophers from the school of "absolute skepticism" who doubted everything and never committed themselves to any specific position in doctrinal debates. Philosophers from this school such as *Sanjaya Belarthaputra (*who was known as a theorist of endless equivocation or an equivocationist (*amraavikkhepavaadin*)) were criticized in the *Brahmajaala Sutta* (or *Sutra*) as "eel-wrigglers" who were incapable of taking a definitive stance on the vital philosophical questions of the day.

Such skepticism was seen as emanating from both the fear of being in error and the lack of knowledge (or inability) to provide reasonable answers to question put forward for discussion. Such all-pervading doubt coupled with a cynical skepticism (*vichikicchaa*) was viewed as a serious mental hindrance, a fetter in the path to wisdom. Other theories that contradicted the notion that human actions mattered were theories of accidentalism (*ahetu-apachayavaada*), theistic determinism (*ishvaranimmaanavaada*) and past-action determinism (*purvaketavaada* or *purvekatahetu*). All of these were were opposed by the Buddhists. Accidentalism was an indeterminist theory which held that whatever was experienced was uncaused and unconditioned by human intervention.

Theistic determinism was a determinist theory, which held that whatever was experienced was due to God's will or by plan of a "Supreme-Being". Past-action determinism was also a determinist theory, but it held the belief that whatever was experienced, whether pleasurable or painful or indifferent was entirely due to ones past actions (from a previous life), and ones present actions had no relevance. The danger in each of these theories was highlighted in these words: "Thus for those who fall back on these three erroneous views as essential dogma, there is neither the will to do what is ought to be done, or not to do what is ought not to be done, nor necessity to do this deed or abstain from that deed. No moral improvement or intellectual culture can be expected from them."

Some of the theories in circulation at that time built on a germ of truth but generalized to the point of absurdity. For instance the accidentalists were correct only to the extent that certain things did indeed appear to happen by random chance or accident. But they failed to recognize that sometimes what may have seemed to be accidental was more due to inadequate understanding or improper or incomplete perception, and that other activities had a clearly discernible cause. To deal with the extreme generalizations of such theorists, they introduced a middle standpoint for their epistemology and ethics.

They thus rejected the theory admitting that everything exists (*sabba atthii ti*) and in permanence - i.e. the extreme of eternalism (*sassatavaada*), and its opposite which advocated that nothing actually exists (*sabba natthii ti*) i.e. nihilism (the denial of all reality in real-world phenomenon) or the extreme of annihilationalism (*ucchedavaada*). Related to their critique of the eternalist and nihilist philosophies was their rejection of both hedonism and self-mortification (*attakilamathaanuyoga*) which they viewed as painful, fruitless, unprofitable and ignoble. Buddhist texts also expressed suspicion about claims by heretical teachers of being constantly "all-knowing" and "all-seeing" and in possession of "all-embracing knowledge-and-vision."

Such claims were countered with arguments relating to the actual behaviour of such charlatans in different situations. For instance, they wondered why such "all-knowing" and "all-seeing" spiritual teachers lost their way in an unfamiliar place or why they were unable to escape from trouble while countering a fierce animal such as dog, elephant, horse or bull. Moreover, if they were really omniscient, they wouldn't need to ask for people's names, clans, or the name of a village or market town or make enquiries about anything. That they did such things indicated that their knowledge was evidently limited just like that of any average worldly person (*puthujjana*).

Unlike religions that were based on revealed truth or the sanctity of every word in a holy textbook, the Buddhist belief system prescribed reasoning based on investigation as the means of determining ones *dhamma,* (or *dharma* as in Hindu practise). In a parable in the *Kaalaama Sutta*, followers of Budhism are advised not to accept any moral codes on the following ten grounds: (1) Vedic authority (*anussava*), (2) tradition (*paramparaa*), (3) hearsay or report (*itikiraa*), (4) textual authority (*pittakasampadaa*), (5) apparent agreebility of the view (*sama o no garu*), (6) authority of the holder of the view (*takkahetu*), (7) apparent logicality of the view (*nayahetu*), (8) the fact that the view is an accepted standpoint (*aakaaraparivitakka*), (9) inadequate reflection on reasons (*bhabbaruupataa*), or (10) the fact that the view agrees with one's own (*ditthinijjhaanakkhanti*).

In this manner, the Buddhism developed a very sophisticated philosophical system in which social ethics were integrated with rational investigation of human nature, social organization and the physical world. Buddhist ideas and concepts left a powerful impression on other Indian philosophical and religious belief systems, and over time, many commonalities developed amongst the competing ideologies. However, there were also certain problems with the Buddhist world view which prevented its complete acceptance by intellectuals committed to the scientific method. For instance, although the Buddhists rejected the theory of past action determinism, they did posit the existence of a soul which survived a person's death and carried with it the merits and demerits of a person's past lives.

Presumably this concept was essential to the Buddhist goal of encouraging right conduct but it was rejected by those who considered the soul as inseparable from the body and did not believe that the soul survived death. Those who rejected the concept of transmigration of the soul naturally couldn't accept the idea that human destiny had anything to do with merits and demerits accumulated in previous incarnations of the "soul". In their view, morality and ethics were entirely social constructs and had to be dealt with accordingly. The realists (such as the Nyayavadis) who shared the Buddhist concern for morals and ethics in society argued that while morals and ethics ought to be encouraged, they could only be enforced through societal laws and judicial codes. Another problem facing the Buddhists was that in many ways, their views were too advanced for their times.

Society had not yet developed to the point where education was universal, and knowledge of the real world sufficient to prevent superstitions and irrational beliefs from being completely abandoned by the masses. In an era where society had only limited control over nature, it was inevitable that sections of society would continue with beliefs in deities and supernatural phenomenon in the hope that they may be spared from natural disasters or that their crops might withstand attacks from pests and disease. Thus although the Buddhists had a very important and salutatory effect on Indian society, the most advanced Buddhist concepts could be understood and practised by only a minority in society. Over time, the spirit of inquiry and rational investigation that had spurred the early Buddhist scholars towards dialectical thinking and critical social analysis became more and more replaced by narrow and literalist interpretations of the earlier texts.

For instance, advice against accepting something that appeared "logical" without personal verification was taken to mean that logic could be rejected. Advice against wasting ones time on unsolvable metaphysical questions was also taken too literally and many Buddhist scholars remained aloof from the metaphysical debates pursued by other philosophical schools such as those of the Jains and the Nyaya Vaisheshikas. What they didn't anticipate was that some of these debates might lead to useful advances in mathematics or deeper understanding of human thought processes and new insights on human memory and psychology. These led to valuable advances in the interpretation of moods and emotions - thus benefiting Indian art, literature and music. In addition, later Buddhist monks lapsed into some of the very things that had been attacked by the early Buddhists such as indulgence in unnecessary and elaborate rituals, belief in supra-natural phenomenon, and alienation of the priests from the masses.

Activities such as meditation which were encouraged as a means to gaining wisdom became ends in themselves, and were turned into idealistic fetishes. Although Buddhist monks dutifully delivered sermons on right conduct and right action, they often failed to engage in relevant and timely social criticism - and did not always connect the textual suggestions to concrete practice. Intra-Buddhist disputes developed around less significant details, even as some of the most important ideas that had initially shaped the philosophy were pushed into the background. As a result Buddhism as it was practised came to be associated with idealism and inaction. Whereas the early Buddhists saw no merit in worshipping god or its images, later Buddhism developed a pantheon of deities not very different from other Indian religions.

Thus even as Buddhism had spread almost throughout Asia by the 5th-6th C AD, it gradually began to lose its distinct edge and liberating influence on much of Indian society. Within the Indian subcontinent, strains of Buddhism survived in Sri Lanka, Bengal, Bhutan, Sikkim, parts of Bihar and Nepal, and parts of Sindh, Punjab, Kashmir and Afghanistan. In parts of Orissa and adjoining regions (such as Chhattisgarh and Telengana), Tantric (and other) influences reshaped the practice of Buddhism. Yet, Buddhism continued to have an impact outside India and developed pockets of influence as far West as Syria, as well as in much of Central Asia (including what is now Uzbekistan, Tajikistan, Kyrgyzia, Kazakhstan) and Tibet. In the East, its influence was felt on virtually every nation including Burma, Thailand, Malaya and Indonesia, Laos, Cambodia, Vietnam, China, Korea and Japan.

As noted earlier, the vast literature of Buddhism (like much of Hindu or Jain literature) was not a literature of revelation and authority. Its essays on social ethics and moral responsibilities, its treatises on philosophy and science, its art and poetry were but pointers to a path to wisdom. This gave Buddhism both flexibility and adaptability. Owing to its non-hegemonic character and humanist appeal, Buddhism was adopted without coercion or force. It was also successfully fused with Hinduism in many parts of South East Asia just as elements of it had been integrated into Hindu practices in India. In China, it was integrated with Taoism and Confucian principles; in Japan with Shinto beliefs. For several centuries, within India and outside, several people followed multiple faiths and identified as both Buddhists and Hindus, or as both Buddhists and Tantrics, (or Buddhists and Taoists) and so on.

During the Gupta period (and in other reigns), philosophers from various schools of thought received royal patronage and temple grants were conferred for the construction of Buddhist and Hindu monuments alike. It is also important to recognize that the form of Buddhism that was embraced in each nation was often quite different. For instance, in Western and Central Asia, it was not the philosophical or intellectual aspects of Buddhism that were popularized, but rather, its personal moral codes. Buddhist prosletysers imbued their stories of the Buddha with examples of miraculous healing and super-natural compassion so as to win more followers. While such tendencies were also to be seen as Buddhism travelled within India or outwards, in Burma, Sri Lanka and Thailand, Buddhism developed organizational structures that appear to have been much more resilient. It was perhaps realized that the development of Buddhist virtue would require leadership and constant interaction with the community.

In these nations, Buddhism did not degenerate into the extremes of mysticism or retreatism that became commonplace in certain parts of India (such as in the foothills of the Western Himalayas). Burmese and Thai monks maintained a practical and benevolent connection with the community, and thus retained a measure of respect within the community. This also appears to be the case in Japan. In Korea, the emphasis on gaining wisdom was taken very seriously, and Buddhist monks took the lead in promoting mass literacy. This propelled the growth of technologies associated with the production of paper, writing instruments, inks, and furniture. And unlike in India, (where due to Upanishadic influences, "inner" wisdom came to be favored over outer wisdom), Buddhist concern for disseminating the writings of the Buddha had significant positive secular impact.

In Korean (and other Eastern) Buddhism, there was the correct realization that a Buddhist mindset, or that a Buddhist society could not be constructed overnight. There was thus the emphasis on the (helical) upgradation of individuals and society towards greater "Buddhahood". This philosophical element was perhaps signficant in that it prevented the sort of philosophical stagnation that occurred in India, where followers too often sought immediate succuor, and thus not only became divorced from reality, but also lost sight of the strategic potential of the philosophy. In addition, it ought to be noted that Buddhism in India also had to contend with strongly anarchic and ultra-democratic tendencies. Precisely because its philosophical structure emphasized the relative and changing nature of truth, different tendencies under the Buddhist mantle competed for leadership through argument and debate.

Initially, this led to important advances in democratic practices within the Sanghas. But over time, it also led to clashes of egoes, hair-splitting and deadlock. While some Buddhist sects compromised and fused with other tendencies (even alien tendencies), others remained fiercely autonomous. To survive, Buddhism had to confront both the tendency to be co-opted, as well as the tendency to atomize. However, the catastrophic demise of Buddhism in India was triggered by the onslaught of Islam which first obliterated the remnants of Buddhism in Central Asia, and then later in Afghanistan and India. By and large, Buddhism survived only in those countries that escaped invasions by Islamic conquerors.

As a gentle faith that encouraged its followers to abjure violence, it was perhaps unable to protect itself from iconoclasts and proselytizers who intended to enforce a new religio-political order. Accustomed to centuries of peaceful co-existence, India's Buddhists had not anticipated the need to develop viable strategies for self-defence that could have combated the violence of India's Islamic conquerors who virtually obliterated Buddhism from the land of its birth. Yet, it also appears that (in large part) later Buddhism had deviated considerably from the rational principles outlined in the early texts.

Monasteries often became isolated from mainstream society, and monks who focused exclusively on meditative practices and idealistic or esoteric philosophical speculation contributed little to social progress. Some have even argued that the monastic orders had degenerated into sheer parasitism and were becoming a heavy social drain. Consequently, value judgements on the demise of Buddhism and the rise of Islam in India need to be made with a measure of caution. Nevertheless, it must be acknowledged that the ascent of Islam was concomitant with the eclipse of Buddhism, and since the influence of Buddhism was greatly dependant on the existence of the monastic orders, the destruction of monasteries and their conversion to mosques and institutions of Quranic learning simply lead to mass conversions to Islam.

In the long term, this could have had the effect of stunting India's future intellectual development, since the destruction of important institutions of Buddhist learning also led to a notable decline in the opportunity (and social sanction) to study secular subjects such as logic and epistemology (which were also taught at Buddhist universities - such as Bhagalpur). It might also be observed that the destruction of Buddhist centers of learning coincided with the destruction of extremely valuable textual materials - which could have been potentially rediscovered, and revived or reinterpreted by future generations of Indians so as to achieve a society that was more thoughtful and learned.

Islamic texts did not offer anything comparable in terms of causality or epistemology. Nor did they offer the psychological, sociological, or moral insights that had been developed under the ambit of Buddhism. Nor was there any comparable stress on seeking knowledge or constantly updating ones understanding of nature and human society. One can, therefore, only speculate as to the full consequences of this profound sociolgical and cultural loss (and discontinuity). But East of India, Buddhism did survive, and in countries such Korea, Thailand and Burma, it continued to enjoy a loyal popular following. Philosophical innovations also took place, and as noted earlier, Buddhist scholars in China, Korea and Japan offered their own commentaries and somewhat individual interpretations of Buddhist concepts and formulations outlined in later (5-7th C.) Indian texts.

And although the sacking of monasteries and centers of learning (such as Nalanda and Vikramshila in Bihar) led to records of the original Buddhist texts being permanently destroyed, it has been possible to reconstruct some of them from translations that survived outside India such as in Thailand and Tibet. Notwithstanding the virtual erasure of Buddhism in India, it is possible to infer from these reconstructed texts and other archaeological records (and surviving monuments and artifacts) that Buddhism had a very powerful impact in shaping the destiny of India, and in triggering a social and cultural renaissance that would take Indian and other Asian civilizations to a higher level of social, cultural and material development.

India saw wave after wave of outsiders and invaders rather from beginning of history. Only those who are known as adivasis or aboriginals and Dravidians are known to be original inhabitants of India. The Dravidian culture may not have had composite character as also the aboriginal one which was essentially a folk culture. The Aryan culture that begins with Aryan invasion, is the dawn of composite culture in India. I know a section of scholars, especially those affiliated with Sangh Parivar, maintain that Aryans were original inhabitants and never came from outside. However, most noted historians and scholars do not subscribe to this view and maintain that Aryans came from outside.

I propose in this chapter to deal with composite culture which came into existence with the invasion of various Muslim dynasties in Sultanate as well as Mughal period. Preceding these Muslim dynasties were many others like Sakias, Huns and Greeks and all of them left their deep imprints on our culture. It is more difficult and challenging to trace their influences now as they constitute remotest past. However, influences of Turks, Tughlaks, Khaljis, Lodis and especially Moghuls have been very well recorded and continue to be part of our culture. But in our mutual animosities we deliberately ignore these influences or even try to reduce our culture to a monolithic one or pure one. It is well known that all communal as well as bigoted elements try to project a 'pure' culture. They try to emphasise a pure Hindu or pure Islamic culture. In other words we communalise our culture as we communalize our politics.

When we say pure Hindu or Islamic culture we imply that culture is product of religion and nothing else. This is not true. Religion undoubtedly is an important influence but not the only one. Religion is, among others, one of the factors in giving birth to a culture. Culture, in fact, is product of several factors like customs, traditions, whether, locally available materials, geographical conditions and so on. A religion may appear within the frame of a pre-existent culture. And then religious teachings may deeply influence that pre-existent culture and re-fashion it in its own way. For example, Islam appeared within the frame of pre-existing Arab culture and subsequently remoulded that culture in its own way. But what we call 'Islamic culture' cannot be thought of without Arab culture of its time.

Similarly what we call 'Hindu' culture or Buddhist culture came into existence within the framework of pre-existent Dravidian and Aryan cultures and the Hindu or Buddhist cultures cannot be imagined without their pre-existent cultures. Also, when these religions spread to areas other than that of their origin, they imbibed, assimilated and integrated elements of cultures already existing in those areas. Buddhism spread to various countries like Sri Lanka, China, Thailand, Tibet, Cambodia, Vietnam and Japan and so on. This gave rise to syncretic cultures in Thailand, Sri Lanka, China, Cambodia and Tibet. The Buddhist culture in India cannot be same as say Buddhist culture of Tibet or Buddhist culture of Japan. All these cultures are radically different though Buddhism is a common factor among them.

Similarly Islam also spread to many areas far away from Arabia, the land of its origin. It spread from Indonesia in South East Asia to Algeria in North Africa. Though Islam is a common factor and yet indigenous cultures of Indonesia, Malaysia, Thailand, Sri Lanka, India, Iran, Central Asia, Egypt, Sudan, Morocco, Tunisia and Algeria, china, Turkey and Eastern Europe gave rise to numerous cultures different from each other. If religion were the only factor all these cultures would not differ. In India its existence for almost thousand years gave rise to Indo-Islamic culture which in northern India is also called by various names like Ganga-Jamni tehzib (culture of the region between the rivers Ganga and Jamuna or Mili-juli tahzib(syncretic culture) or Sanjhi virasat (composite heritage). Though these terms mainly refer to north Indian culture.

Composite culture is not essential restricted to north India. India is land of many cultures and all regional cultures from north to south and east to western parts of India. When we refer to culture it includes art and architecture, language, poetry, music, paintings, dances, draperies, food habits, customs, traditions and some religious, especially spiritual practices. After years of composite traditions coming into existence it becomes so assimilated that we consider it part of our original culture. Only scholars know its composite nature. The discourse about Composite culture is also deeply influenced by political needs. The communal forces, as pointed out before, want to deny existence of syncretism or composite nature of culture and those who promote national integration and communal harmony try to develop a composite discourse for our culture as it helps bringing communities together.

This composite discourse becomes a great political need in a society like India which is so diverse and in the process of nation building fusion of various communities and harmony among them becomes very necessary. The British rulers were busy dividing us and our liberation from British rule would not have been possible without bringing various communities, especially Hindus and Muslims together. Thus even during our freedom struggle communal forces were emphasizing our separate communal identities. The theories of Hindu Rashtra and Islamic nation were result of such attempts by communal forces. Ultimately these communal forces on both sides succeeded in dividing our nation despite such composite nature of our cultural and some religious practices.

The national discourse, of course, emphasized composite nature of our culture but for various reasons, not to be discussed here, this discourse was drowned in the separatist cacophony and more than half a million human beings lost their lives. Today in contemporary India communal forces are no less active. These forces still talk of Hindu Rashtra and have coined slogan of 'one nation, one culture and one language. Such an approach denies the rich diversity of India and our composite heritage. Thus it is in the interest of our unity to emphasize and re-emphasize the syncretic nature of our heritage to draw people together.

It is true that this is our political need but one should not emphasize syncretic nature of our heritage such for the sake of political need but also in the interest of our authentic history. History should not be distorted either way - to divide people as also to unite people. Distortion of history, even for positive purpose, is a dangerous thing. History should be written rising above all religious, political or cultural needs. Those who temper with their past would temper with their future as well.

FUSION OF RELIGIOUS AND SPIRITUAL PRACTICES

Islamic ritual practices influenced indigenous Hindu practices and vice versa. Many scholars have pointed out that Satya Narayan Katha which is widely prevalent in northern India today came into existence by imitating Muslim practice of public narration of Prophet's life story especially in Bengal and subsequently it spread to other parts of north India. Common Hindus are hardly aware of origin of practice of Satya Narayan Katha. Similarly several Sufi rituals, practices and beliefs, have deep imprint of indigenous practices. The noted German scholar Gruhnbalm thinks that the Sufi doctrine of fana' fi Allah (annihilation in Allah) is result of Hindu doctrine of smadhi in which a person annihilates himself in Ishwara, the ultimate being.

It is also important to note that many great Sufi saints like Baba Farid of Punjab, Sheikh Mohammad of Maharashtra and others wrote in local languages like Punjabi or Marathi. This made them much more acceptable among the local populace. Baba Farid is highly respected by Sikhs as his Punjabi verses have been included in the Adi Granth sahib. The Punjab University has established Baba Farid Chair and lot of work on Sufism is done through this department. Sikh Gurus had great regard for Sufi saints. When the foundation stone for Har Mandir was being laid the Sikh Guru Arjan Dev insisted that Mian Mir, the Sufi saint of Lahore would be the one to lay the foundation stone. He was requested and he came and laid the foundation stone of Har Mandir.

Sufis showed respect for Hindu religion and indigenous practices. Many rituals during the urs (death anniversary) of a Sufi saint have been borrowed by local Hindu customs around a temple. Khwaja Hasan Nizami in his book Fatimi D'awat-e-Islam have described in detail some of these rituals. According to him the annual day rituals of Hindu temple were adopted for urs rituals like taking out sandal paste in procession and chador in a palkhi (palanquin) and washing the grave of the Sufi and offering chador is adoption of temple rituals. Only difference is that idol is replaced by grave. In annual day ritual idol is washed with sandal paste and on urs Sufi saint's grave is washed with the paste after bringing it in a procession along with a chador. It is interesting to note that in Mahim, Mumbai, the police inspector (generally a Hindu) carries the chador in a thali (large dish) on his head and offers on the grave of Sufi saint Makhdum Mahimi.

7

Cultural Elements of Buddhism

BUDDHIST ART

Buddhist art originated in the Indian subcontinent in the centuries following the life of the historical Gautama Buddha in the 6th to 5th century BCE, before evolving through its contact with other cultures and its diffusion through the rest of Asia and the world. A first, essentially Indian, *aniconic phase* (avoiding direct representations of the Buddha), was followed from around the 1st century CE by an *iconic phase* (with direct representations of the Buddha). From that time, Buddhist art diversified and evolved as it adapted to the new countries where the faith was expanding. It developed to the north through Central Asia and into Eastern Asia to form the Northern branch of Buddhist art, and to the east as far as Southeast Asia to form the Southern branch of Buddhist art. In India, Buddhist art flourished and even influenced the development of Hindu art, until Buddhism almost disappeared around the 10th century with the expansion of Hinduism and Islam.

Buddhist art originated on the Indian subcontinent following the historical life of Siddhartha Gautama, 6th to 5th century BCE, and thereafter evolved by contact with other cultures as it spread throughout Asia and the world. Early Buddhist art followed one Indian aniconic tradition, which avoids direct representation of the human figure. Around the 1st century CE an iconic period emerged lasting to this day which represents the Buddha in human form.

Buddhist art followed believers as the dharma spread, adapted, and evolved in each new host country. It developed to the north through Central Asia and into Eastern Asia to form the Northern branch of Buddhist art, and to the east as far as Southeast Asia to form the Southern branch of Buddhist art. In India, Buddhist art flourished and even influenced the development of Hindu art, until Buddhism nearly disappeared in India around the 10th century due in part to the vigorous expansion of Islam alongside Hinduism.

ANICONIC PHASE (5TH CENTURY - 1ST CENTURY BCE)

During the 2nd to 1st century BCE, sculptures became more explicit, representing episodes of the Buddha's life and teachings. These took the form of votive tablets or friezes, usually in relation to the decoration of stupas. Although India had a long sculptural tradition and a mastery of rich iconography, the Buddha was never represented in human form, but only through some of his symbols.

This reluctance towards anthropomorphic representations of the Buddha, and the sophisticated development of aniconic symbols to avoid it (even in narrative scene where other human figures would appear), seems to be connected to 70 of the Buddha's sayings, reported in the Dighanikaya, that disfavored representations of himself after the extinction of his body. This tendency remained as late as the 2nd century CE in the southern parts of India, in the art of the Amaravati school. It has been argued that earlier anthropomorphic representations of the Buddha may have been made of wood and may have perished since then. However, no related archaeological evidence has been found.

ICONIC PHASE (1ST CENTURY CE – PRESENT)

Anthropomorphic representations of the Buddha started to emerge from the 1st century CE in northern India. The two main centers of creation have been identified as Gandhara in today's North West Frontier Province, in Pakistan, and the region of Mathura, in central northern India. The art of Gandhara benefited from centuries of interaction with Greek culture since the conquests of Alexander the Great in 332 BCE and the subsequent establishment of the Greco-Bactrian and Indo-Greek Kingdoms, leading to the development of Greco-Buddhist art. Gandharan Buddhist sculpture displays Greek artistic influence, and it has been suggested that the concept of the "man-god" was essentially inspired by Greek mythological culture. Artistically, the Gandharan school of sculpture is said to have contributed wavy hair, drapery covering both shoulders, shoes and sandals, acanthus leaf decorations, etc.

The art of Mathura tends to be based on a strong Indian tradition, exemplified by the anthropomorphic representation of divinities such as the Yaksas, although in a style rather archaic compared to the later representations of the Buddha. The Mathuran school contributed clothes covering the left shoulder of thin muslin, the wheel on the palm, the lotus seat, etc. Mathura and Gandhara also strongly influenced each other. During their artistic florescence, the two regions were even united politically under the Kushans, both being capitals of the empire. It is still a matter of debate whether the anthropomorphic representations of Buddha was essentially a result of a local evolution of Buddhist art at Mathura, or a consequence of Greek cultural influence in Gandhara through the Greco-Buddhist syncretism.

This iconic art was characterized from the start by a realistic idealism, combining realistic human features, proportions, attitudes and attributes, together with a sense of perfection and serenity reaching to the divine. This expression of the Buddha as a both a man and a god became the iconographic canon for subsequent Buddhist art. Buddhist art continued to develop in India for a few more centuries. The pink sandstone sculptures of Mathura evolved during the Gupta period (4th to 6th century) to reach a very high fineness of execution and delicacy in the modeling. The art of the Gupta school was extremely influential almost everywhere in the rest of Asia. By the 10th century, Buddhist art creation was dying out in India, as Hinduism and Islam ultimately prevailed.

As Buddhism expanded outside of India from the 1st century CE, its original artistic package blended with other artistic influences, leading to a progressive differentiation among the countries adopting the faith.

- A Northern route was established from the 1st century CE through Central Asia, Tibet, Bhutan, China, Korea, Japan and Vietnam, in which Mahayana Buddhism prevailed.
- A Southern route, where Theravada Buddhism dominated, went through Myanmar, Thailand, and Cambodia.

NORTHERN BUDDHIST ART

The Silk Road transinission of Buddhism to Central Asia, China and ultimately Korea and Japan started in the 1st century CE with a semi-legendary account of an embassy sent to the West by the Chinese Emperor Ming (58-75 CE). However, extensive contacts started in the 2nd century CE, probably as a consequence of the expansion of the Kushan Empire into the Chinese territory of the Tarim Basin, with the missionary efforts of a great number of Central Asian Buddhist monks to Chinese lands. The first missionaries and translators of Buddhists scriptures into Chinese, such as Lokaksema, were either Parthian, Kushan, Sogdian or Kuchean.

Central Asian missionary efforts along the Silk Road were accompanied by a flux of artistic influences, visible in the development of Serindian art from the 2nd through the 11th century CE in the Tarim Basin, modern Xinjiang. Serindian art often derives from the Greco-Buddhist art of the Gandhara district of what is now Pakistan, combining Indian, Greek and Roman influences. Silk Road Greco-Buddhist artistic influences can be found as far as Japan to this day, in architectural motifs, Buddhist imagery, and a select few representations of Japanese gods.

The art of the northern route was also highly influenced by the development of Mahayana Buddhism, an inclusive faith characterized by the adoption of new texts, in addition to the traditional Pali canon, and a shift in the understanding of Buddhism. Mahayana goes beyond the traditional Theravada ideal of the release from suffering (dukkha) and personal enlightenment of the arhats, to elevate the Buddha to a god-like status, and to create a pantheon of quasi-divine Bodhisattvas devoting themselves to personal excellence, ultimate knowledge and the salvation of humanity. Northern Buddhist art thus tends to be characterized by a very rich and syncretic Buddhist pantheon, with a multitude of images of the various Buddhas, Bodhisattvas and lesser deities.

Afghanistan

Buddhist art in Afghanistan (old Bactria) persisted for several centuries until the spread of Islam in the 7th century. It is exemplified by the Buddhas of Bamyan. Other sculptures, in stucco, schist or clay, display very strong blending of Indian post-Gupta mannerism and Classical influence, Hellenistic or possibly even Greco-Roman.

Although Islamic rule was rather tolerant of other religions "of the Book", it showed little tolerance for Buddhism, which was perceived as a religion depending on idolatry. Human figurative art forms also being prohibited under Islam, Buddhist art suffered numerous attacks, which culminated with the systematic destructions by the Taliban regime. The Buddhas of Bamyan, the sculptures of Hadda, and many of the remaining artifacts at the Afghanistan museum have been destroyed. The multiple conflicts since the 1980s also have led to a systematic pillage of archaeological sites apparently in the hope of reselling in the international market what artifacts could be found.

Central Asia

Central Asia long played the role of a meeting place between China, India and Persia. During the 2nd century BCE, the expansion of the Former Han to the West led to increased contact with the Hellenistic civilizations of Asia, especially the Greco-Bactrian Kingdom. Thereafter, the expansion of Buddhism to the North led to the formation of Buddhist communities and even Buddhist kingdoms in the oases of Central Asia. Some Silk Road cities consisted almost entirely of Buddhist stupas and monasteries, and it seems that one of their main objectives was to welcome and service travelers between East and West.

The eastern part of Central Asia (Chinese Turkestan (Tarim Basin, Xinjiang) in particular has revealed an extremely rich Serindian art (wall paintings and reliefs in numerous caves, portable paintings on canvas, sculpture, ritual objects), displaying multiple influences from Indian and Hellenistic cultures. Works of art reminiscent of the Gandharan style, as well as scriptures in the Gandhari script Kharoshti have been found. These influences were rapidly absorbed however by the vigorous Chinese culture, and a strongly Chinese particularism develops from that point.

China

Buddhism arrived in China around the 1st century CE, and introduced new types of art into China, particularly in the area of statuary. Receiving this distant religion, strong Chinese traits were incorporated into Buddhist art.

Northern Dynasties

In the 5th to 6th centuries, the Northern Dynasties, developed rather symbolic and abstract modes of representation, with schematic lines. Their style is also said to be solemn and majestic. The lack of corporeality of this art, and its distance from the original Buddhist objective of expressing the pure ideal of enlightenment in an accessible and realistic manner, progressively led to a change towards more naturalism and realism, leading to the expression of Tang Buddhist art.

Sites preserving Northern Wei Dynasty Buddhist sculpture:

- Longmen Grottoes, Henan
- Bingling Temple, Gansu

Tang Dynasty

Following a transition under the Sui Dynasty, Buddhist sculpture of the Tang evolved towards a markedly life-like expression. Because of the dynasty's openness to foreign influences, and renewed exchanges with Indian culture due to the numerous travels of Chinese Buddhist monks to India, Tang dynasty Buddhist sculpture assumed a rather classical form, inspired by the Indian art of the Gupta period. During that time, the Tang capital of Chang'an (today's Xi'an) became an important center for Buddhism. From there Buddhism spread to Korea, and Japanese embassies of Kentoshi helped it gain a foothold in Japan.

However, foreign influences came to be negatively perceived in China towards the end of the Tang dynasty. In the year 845, the Tang emperor Wuzong outlawed all "foreign" religions (including Christian Nestorianism, Zoroastrianism and Buddhism) in order to support the indigenous religion, Taoism. He confiscated Buddhist possessions, and forced the faith to go underground, therefore affecting the development of the religion and its arts in China. Chán Buddhism however, at the origin of Japanese Zen, continued to prosper for some centuries, especially under the Song Dynasty (960-1279), when Chan monasteries were great centers of culture and learning.

The popularization of Buddhism in China has made the country home to one of the richest collections of Buddhist arts in the world. The Mogao Caves near Dunhuang and the Bingling Temple caves near Yongjing in Gansu province, the Longmen Grottoes near Luoyang in Henan province, the Yungang Grottoes near Datong in Shanxi province, and the Dazu Rock Carvings near Chongqing municipality are among the most important and renowned Buddhist sculptural sites. The Leshan Giant Buddha, carved out of a hillside in the 8th century during the Tang Dynasty and looking down on the confluence of three rivers, is still the largest stone Buddha statue in the world.

Korea

Korean Buddhist art generally reflects an interaction between Chinese Buddhist influence and a strongly original Korean culture. Additionally, the art of the steppes, particularly Siberian and Scythian influences, are evident in early Korean Buddhist art based on the excavation of artifacts and burial goods such as Silla royal crowns, belt buckles, daggers, and comma-shaped gogok. The style of this indigenous art was geometric, abstract and richly adorned with a characteristic "barbarian" luxury. Although Chinese influence was strong, Korean Buddhist art "bespeaks a sobriety, taste for the right tone, a sense of abstraction but also of colours that curiously enough are in line with contemporary taste" (Pierre Cambon, *Arts asiatiques- Guimet'*).

The first of the Three Kingdoms of Korea to officially receive Buddhism was Goguryeo in 372. However, Chinese records and the use of Buddhist motifs in Goguryeo murals indicate the introduction of Buddhism earlier than the official date. The Baekje Kingdom officially recognized Buddhism in 384. The Silla Kingdom, isolated and with no easy sea or land access to China, officially adopted Buddhism in 535 although the foreign religion was known in the kingdom due to the work of Goguryeo monks since the early fifth century. The introduction of Buddhism stimulated the need for artisans to create images for veneration, architects for temples, and the literate for the Buddhist sutras and transformed Korean civilization.

Particularly important in the transmission of sophisticated art styles to the Korean kingdoms was the art of the "barbarian" Tuoba, a clan of non-Han Chinese Xianbei people who established the Northern Wei Dynasty in China in 386. The Northern Wei style was particularly influential in the art of the Goguryeo and Baekje. Baekje artisans later transmitted this style along with Southern Dynasty elements and distinct Korean elements to Japan. Korean artisans were highly selective of the styles they incorporated and combined different regional styles together to create a specific Korean Buddhist art style.

While Goguryeo Buddhist art exhibited vitality and mobility akin with Northern Wei prototypes, the Baekje Kingdom was also in close contact with the Southern Dynasties of China and this close diplomatic contact is exemplified in the gentle and proportional sculpture of the Baekje, epitomized by Baekje sculpture exhibiting the fathomless smile known to art historians as the Baekje smile. The Silla Kingdom also developed a distinctive Buddhist art tradition epitomized by the Bangasayusang, a half-seated contemplative maitreya whose Korean-made twin, the Miroku Bosatsu, was sent to Japan as a proselytizing gift and now resides in the Koryu-ji Temple in Japan.

Buddhism in the Three Kingdoms period stimulated massive temple-building projects, such as the Mireuksa Temple in the Baekje Kingdom and the Hwangnyongsa Temple in Silla. Baekje architects were famed for their skill and were instrumental in building the massive nine-story pagoda at Hwangnyongsa and early Buddhist temples in Yamato Japan such as Hoko-ji (Asuka-dera) and Hôryû-ji. Sixth century Korean Buddhist art exhibited the cultural influences of China and India but began to show distinctive indigenous characteristics.

These indigenous characteristics can be seen in early Buddhist art in Japan and some early Japanese Buddhist sculpture is now believed to have originated in Korea, particularly from Baekje, or Korean artisans who immigrated to Yamato Japan. Particularly, the semi-seated Maitreya form was adapted into a highly developed Korean style which was transmitted to Japan as evidenced by the Koryu-ji Miroku Bosatsu and the Chugu-ji Siddhartha statues. Although many historians portray Korea as a mere transmitter of Buddhism, the Three Kingdoms, and particularly Baekje, were instrumental as active agents in the introduction and formation of a Buddhist tradition in Japan in 538 or 552.

During the Unified Silla period, East Asia was particularly stable with China and Korea both enjoying unified governments. Early Unified Silla art combined Silla styles and Baekje styles.

Korean Buddhist art was also influenced by new Tang Dynasty styles as evidenced by a new popular Buddhist motif with full-faced Buddha sculptures. Tang China was the cross roads of East, Central, and South Asia and so the Buddhist art of this time period exhibit the so-called international style. State-sponsored Buddhist art flourished during this period, the epitome of which is the Seokguram Grotto.

The fall of the Unified Silla Dynasty and the establishment of the Goryeo Dynasty in 918 indicates a new period of Korean Buddhist art. The Goryeo kings also lavishly sponsored Buddhism and Buddhist art flourished, especially Buddhist paintings and illuminated sutras written in gold and silver ink. The crowning achievement of this period is the carving of approximately 80,000 woodblocks of the Tripitaka Koreana which was done twice. The Joseon Dynasty actively suppressed Buddhism beginning in 1406 and Buddhist temples and art production subsequently decline in quality in quantity although beginning in 1549, Buddhist art does continue to be produced.

Japan

Before the introduction of Buddhism, Japan had already been the seat of various cultural (and artistic) influences, from the abstract linear decorative art of the indigenous Neolithic Jômon from around 10500 BCE to 300 BCE, to the art during the Yayoi and Kofun periods, with developments such as Haniwa art. Japan, the largest Buddhist country today, discovered Buddhism in the 6th century when missionary monks travelled to the islands together with numerous scriptures and works of art. The Buddhist religion was adopted by the state in the following century. Being geographically at the end of the Silk Road, Japan was able to preserve many aspects of Buddhism at the very time it was disappearing in India, and being suppressed in Central Asia and China.

From 711, numerous temples and monasteries were built in the capital city of Nara, including a five-story pagoda, the Golden

Hall of the Horyuji, and the Kôfuku-ji temple. Countless paintings and sculptures were made, often under governmental sponsorship. Indian, Hellenistic, Chinese and Korean artistic influences blended into an original style characterized by realism and gracefulness. The creation of Japanese Buddhist art was especially rich between the 8th and 13th centuries during the periods of Nara, Heian and Kamakura. Japan developed an extremely rich figurative art for the pantheon of Buddhist deities, sometimes combined with Hindu and Shinto influences. This art can be very varied, creative and bold. From the 12th and 13th, a further development was Zen art, following the introduction of the faith by Dogen and Eisai upon their return from China. Zen art is mainly characterized by original paintings (such as sumi-e) and poetry (especially haikus), striving to express the true essence of the world through impressionistic and unadorned "non-dualistic" representations.

The search for enlightenment "in the moment" also led to the development of other important derivative arts such as the Chanoyu tea ceremony or the Ikebana art of flower arrangement. This evolution went as far as considering almost any human activity as an art with a strong spiritual and aesthetic content, first and foremost in those activities related to combat techniques (martial arts). Buddhism remains very active in Japan to this day. Still around 80,000 Buddhist temples are preserved. Many of them are in wood and are regularly restored.

Tibet and Bhutan

Tantric Buddhism started as a movement in eastern India around the 5th or the 6th century. Many of the practices of Tantric Buddhism are derived from Brahmanism (the usage of mantras, yoga, or the burning of sacrificial offerings). Tantrism became the dominant form of Buddhism in Tibet from the 8th century. Due to its geographical centrality in Asia, Tibetan Buddhist art received influence from Indian, Nepali, Greco-Buddhist and Chinese art.

One of the most characteristic creations of Tibetan Buddhist art are the mandalas, diagrams of a "divine temple" made of a circle enclosing a square, the purpose of which is to help Buddhist devotees focus their attention through meditation and follow the path to the central image of the Buddha. Artistically, Buddhist Gupta art and Hindu art tend to be the two strongest inspirations of Tibetan art.

Vietnam

Chinese influence was predominant in the north of Vietnam (Tonkin) between the 1st and 9th centuries, and Confucianism and Mahayana Buddhism were prevalent. Overall, the art of Vietnam has been strongly influenced by Chinese Buddhist art. In the south thrived the former kingdom of Champa (before it was later overtaken by the Vietnamese from the north). Champa had a strongly Indianized art, just as neighboring Cambodia. Many of its statues were characterized by rich body adornments. The capital of the kingdom of Champa was annexed by Vietnam in 1471, and it totally collapsed in the 1720s, while Cham people remain an abundant minority across Southeast Asia.

SOUTHERN BUDDHIST ART

During the 1st century CE, the trade on the overland Silk Road tended to be restricted by the rise of the Parthian empire in the Middle East, an unvanquished enemy of Rome, just as Romans were becoming extremely wealthy and their demand for Asian luxury was rising. This demand revived the sea connections between the Mediterranean Sea and China, with India as the intermediary of choice. From that time, through trade connections, commercial settlements, and even political interventions, India started to strongly influence Southeast Asian countries. Trade routes linked India with southern Burma, central and southern Siam, lower Cambodia and southern Vietnam, and numerous urbanized coastal settlements were established there.

For more than a thousand years, Indian influence was therefore the major factor that brought a certain level of cultural unity to the various countries of the region. The Pali and Sanskrit languages and the Indian script, together with Mahayana and Theravada Buddhism, Brahmanism and Hinduism, were transmitted from direct contact and through sacred texts and Indian literature such as the Ramayana and the Mahabharata. This expansion provided the artistic context for the development of Buddhist art in these countries, which then developed characteristics of their own. Between the 1st and 8th centuries, several kingdoms competed for influence in the region (particularly the Cambodian Funan then the Burmese Mon kingdoms) contributing various artistic characteristics, mainly derived from the Indian Gupta style. Combined with a pervading Hindu influence, Buddhist images, votive tablets and Sanskrit inscriptions are found throughout the area.

From the 9th to the 13th centuries, Southeast Asia had very powerful empires and became extremely active in Buddhist architectural and artistic creation. The Sri Vijaya Empire to the south and the Khmer Empire to the north competed for influence, but both were adherents of Mahayana Buddhism, and their art expressed the rich Mahayana pantheon of the Bodhisattvas. The Theravada Buddhism of the Pali canon was introduced to the region around the 13th century from Sri Lanka, and was adopted by the newly founded ethnic Thai kingdom of Sukhothai.

Since in Theravada Buddhism only monks can reach Nirvana, the construction of temple complexes plays a particularly important role in the artistic expression of Southeast Asia from that time. From the 14th century, the main factor was the spread of Islam to the maritime areas of Southeast Asia, overrunning Malaysia, Indonesia, and most of the islands as far as the Philippines. In the continental areas, Theravada Buddhism continued to expand into Burma, Laos and Cambodia.

Myanmar

A neighbor of India, Myanmar was naturally strongly influenced by the eastern part of Indian Territory. The Mon of southern Burma are said to have been converted to Buddhism around 200 BCE under the proselytizing of the Indian king Ashoka, before the schism between Mahayana and Hinayana Buddhism. Early Buddhist temples are found, such as Beikthano in central Myanmar, with dates between the 1st and the 5th centuries.

The Buddhist art of the Mons was especially influenced by the Indian art of the Gupta and post-Gupta periods, and their mannerist style spread widely in Southeast Asia following the expansion of the Mon Empire between the 5th and 8th centuries. Later, thousands of Buddhist temples were built at Bagan, the capital, between the 11th and 13th centuries, and around 2,000 of them are still standing. Beautiful jeweled statues of the Buddha are remaining from that period. Creation managed to continue despite the seizure of the city by the Mongols in 1287.

Cambodia

Cambodia was the center of the Funan kingdom, which expanded into Burma and as far south as Malaysia between the 3rd and 6th centuries CE. Its influence seems to have been essentially political, most of the cultural influence coming directly from India. Later, from the 9th to 13th centuries, the Mahayana Buddhist and Hindu Khmer Empire dominated vast parts of the Southeast Asian peninsula, and its influence was foremost in the development of Buddhist art in the region. Under the Khmer, more than 900 temples were built in Cambodia and in neighboring Thailand.

Angkor was at the center of this development, with a Buddhist temple complex and urban organization able to support around 1 million urban dwellers. A great deal of Cambodian Buddhist sculpture is preserved at Angkor; however, organized looting has had a heavy impact on many sites around the country. Often, Khmer art manages to express intense spirituality through divinely beaming expressions, in spite of spare features and slender lines.

Thailand

From the 1st to the 7th centuries, Buddhist art in Thailand was first influenced by direct contact with Indian traders and the expansion of the Mon kingdom, leading to the creation of Hindu and Buddhist art inspired from the Gupta tradition, with numerous monumental statues of great virtuosity. From the 9th century, the various schools of Thai art then became strongly influenced by Cambodian Khmer art in the north and Sri Vijaya art in the south, both of Mahayana faith. Up to the end of that period, Buddhist art is characterized by a clear fluidness in the expression, and the subject matter is characteristic of the Mahayana pantheon with multiple creations of Bodhisattvas.

From the 13th century, Theravada Buddhism was introduced from Sri Lanka around the same time as the ethnic Thai kingdom of Sukhothai was established. The new faith inspired highly stylized images in Thai Buddhism, with sometimes very geometrical and almost abstract figures. During the Ayutthaya period (14th-18th centuries), the Buddha came to be represented in a more stylistic manner with sumptuous garments and jeweled ornamentations. Many Thai sculptures or temples tended to be gilded, and on occasion enriched with inlays.

Indonesia

Like the rest of Southeast Asia, Indonesia seems to have been most strongly influenced by India from the 1st century CE. The islands of Sumatra and Java in western Indonesia were the seat of the empire of Sri Vijaya (8th-13th century CE), which came to dominate most of the area around the Southeast Asian peninsula through maritime power. The Sri Vijayan Empire had adopted Mahayana and Vajrayana Buddhism, under a line of rulers named the Sailendra. Sri Vijaya spread Mahayana Buddhist art during its expansion into the Southeast Asian peninsula. Numerous statues of Mahayana Bodhisattvas from this period are characterized by a very strong refinement and technical sophistication, and are found throughout the region.

Extremely rich and refined architectural remains are found in Java and Sumatra. The most magnificent is the temple of Borobudur (the largest Buddhist structure in the world, built around 780-850 AD). This temple is modelled after the Buddhist concept of universe, the Mandala which counts 505 images of the seated Buddha and unique bell-shaped stupa that contains the statue of Buddha. Borobudur is adorned with long series of bas-reliefs narrated the holy Buddhist scriptures. The oldest Buddhist structure in Indonesia probably is the Batujaya stupas at Karawang, West Java, dated from around 4th century AD. This temple is some plastered brick stupas.

However, Buddhist art in Indonesia reach the golden era during the Sailendra dynasty rule in Java. The bas-reliefs and statues of Boddhisatva, Tara, and Kinnara found in Kalasan, Sewu, Sari, and Plaosan temple is very graceful with serene expression, While Mendut temple near Borobudur, houses the giant statue of Vairocana, Avalokitesvara, and Vajrapani. In Sumatra Sri Vijaya probably built the temple of Muara Takus, and Muaro Jambi. The the most beautiful example pf classical Javanese Buddhist art is the serene and delicate statue of Prajnaparamita (the collection of National Museum Jakarta) the goddess of transcendental wisdom from Singhasari kingdom. The Indonesian Buddhist Empire of Sri Vijaya declined due to conflicts with the Chola rulers of India, then followed by Majapahit empire, before being destabilized by the Islamic expansion from the 13th century.

BUDDHIST ARCHITECTURE

Buddhist religious architecture most notably developed in the South Asia in the third century BCE. Two types of structures are associated with early Buddhism: stupas and viharas. The initial function of a stupa was the veneration and safe-guarding of the relics of the Buddha. The earliest existing example of a stupa is in Sanchi (Madhya Pradesh). In accordance with changes in religious practice, stupas were gradually incorporated into chaitya-grihas (stupa halls). These reached their highpoint in the first century BCE, exemplified by the cave complexes of Ajanta and Ellora

(Maharashtra). Viharas were developed to accommodate the growing and increasingly formalised Buddhist monasticism. An existing example is at Nâlandâ, (Bihar).

Buddhist temples were developed rather later and outside South Asia, where Buddhism gradually declined from the early centuries CE onwards, though an early example is that of the Mahabodhi temple at Bodh Gaya in Bihar. Buddhist religious architecture developed in the South Asia in the third century BC.

Three types of structures are associated with the religious architecture of early Buddhism: monasteries (viharas), stupas, and temples (chaitya grihas). Viharas initially were only temporary shelters used by wandering monks during the rainy season, but later were developed to accommodate the growing and increasingly formalised Buddhist monasticism. An existing example is at Nalanda (Bihar). A distinctive type of fortress architecture found in the former and present Buddhist kingdoms of the Himalayas are dzongs

The initial function of a stupa was the veneration and safe-guarding of the relics of the Buddha. The earliest surviving example of a stupa is in Sanchi (Madhya Pradesh). In accordance with changes in religious practice, stupas were gradually incorporated into chaitya-grihas (temple halls). These reached their highpoint in the first century BC, exemplified by the cave complexes of Ajanta and Ellora (Maharashtra). The Mahabodhi Temple at Bodh Gaya in Bihar is another well known example. The Pagoda is an evolution of the Indian stupa.

Buddhist architecture emerged slowly in the period following the Buddha's life, building on Brahmanical Vedic models, but incorporating a specifically Buddhist symbols. Brahmanical temples at this time followed a simple plan – a square inner space, the sacrificial arena, often with a surrounding ambulatory route separated by lines of columns, with a conical or rectangular sloping roof, behind a porch or entrance area, generally framed by freestanding columns or a colonnade. The external profile represents Mount Meru, the abode of the gods and centre of the universe. The dimensions and proportions were dictated by sacred mathematical formulae. This simple plan was adopted by early Buddhists, sometimes adapted with additional cells for monks at the periphery (especially in the early cave temples such as at Ajanta, India).

In essence the basic plan survives to this day in Buddhist temples throughout the world. The profile became elaborated and the characteristic mountain shape seen today in many Hindu temples was used in early Buddhist sites and continued in similar fashion in some cultures (such as the Khmer). In others, such as Japan and Thailand, local influences and differing religious practices led to different architecture. Early temples were often timber, and little trace remains, although stone was increasingly used. Cave temples such as those at Ajanta have survived better and preserve the plan form, porch and interior arrangements from this early period. As the functions of the monastery-temple expanded, the plan form started to diverge from the Brahmanical tradition and became more elaborate, providing sleeping, eating and study accommodation.

A characteristic new development at religious sites was the stupa. Stupas were originally more sculpture than building, essentially markers of some holy site or commemorating a holy man who lived there. Later forms are more elaborate and also in many cases refer back to the Mount Meru model. The layered, multi-roofed 'pagoda' form emerged in Nepal, and spread east to Japan and China. One of the earliest Buddhist sites still in existence is at Sanchi, India, and this is centred on a stupa said to have been built by Ashoka the Great (273-236 BCE). The original simple structure is encased in a later, more decorative one, and over two centuries the whole site was elaborated upon. The four cardinal points are marked by elaborate stone gateways.

As with Buddhist art, architecture followed the spread of Buddhism throughout south and East Asia and it was the early Indian models that served as a first reference point, even though Buddhism virtually disappeared from India itself in the 10th century. Decoration of Buddhist sites became steadily more elaborate through the last two centuries BCE, with the introduction of tablets and friezes, including human figures, particularly on stupas. However, the Buddha was not represented in human form until the first century CE. Instead, aniconic symbols were used.

This is treated in more detail in Buddhist art, Aniconic phase. It influenced the development of temples, which eventually became a backdrop for Buddha images in most cases. As Buddhism spread, Buddhist architecture diverged in style, reflecting the similar trends in Buddhist art. Building form was also influenced to some extent by the different forms of Buddhism in the northern countries, practising Mahayana Buddhism in the main and in the south where Theravada Buddhism prevailed.

BUDDHIST MUSIC

Buddhist music prominently includes Honkyoku, Buddhist chant, and Shomyo. Honkyoku are the pieces of shakuhachiyoku for enlightenment and alms as early as the 13th century. Buddhist chant is the chant used in or inspired by Buddhism, including many genres in many cultures. It includes:

- Repetition of the name of Amitâbha in Pure Land Buddhism.
- Shomyo in Japanese Tendai and Shingon Buddhism.
- Throat singing in Tibetan Buddhist chant.

Musical chanting, most often in Tibetan or Sanskrit, is an integral part of the religion. These chants are complex, often recitations of sacred texts or in celebration of various festivals. Yang chanting, performed without metrical timing, is accompanied by resonant drums and low, sustained syllables. Shomyo is a style of Japanese Buddhist chant; mainly in the Tendai and Shingon sects. There are two styles: ryokyoku and rikkyoku, described as difficult and easy to remember, respectively. Many ritual musical instruments are used in association with Buddhist practice including singing bowls, bells, tingsha, drums, cymbals, wind instruments and others.

HONKYOKU

Honkyoku are the pieces of shakuhachi or hocchiku music played by wandering Japanese Zen monks called Komuso. Komuso played honkyoku for enlightenment and alms as early as the 13th century. In the 18th century, a Komuso named Kinko Kurosawa of the Fuke sect of Zen Buddhism was commissioned to travel throughout Japan and collect these musical pieces. The results of several years of travel and compilation were thirty-six pieces known as the Kinko-Ryu Honkyoku.

BUDDHIST CHANT

Buddhist chant is chant used in or inspired by Buddhism, including many genres in many cultures:

- Repetition of the name of Amitabha in Pure Land Buddhism.
- Shomyo in Japanese Tendai and Shingon Buddhism.
- Throat singing in Tibetan Buddhist chant

Tibetan Buddhism is the most widespread religion in Tibet. Musical chanting, most often in Tibetan or Sanskrit, is an integral part of the religion. These chants are complex, often recitations of sacred texts or in celebration of various festivals. Yang chanting, performed without metrical timing, is accompanied by resonant drums and low, sustained syllables. Other styles include those unique to Tantric Buddhism, the classical, popular Gelugpa school, the romantic Nyingmapa and Sakyapa and Kagyupa.

A Buddhist chant is a form of musical verse or incantation, in some ways analogous to Hindu or Christian religious recitations. They exist in just about every part of the Buddhist world, from the Wats in Thailand to the Tibetan Buddhist temples of India (re: Tibetan Government in Exile). Almost every Buddhist school has some tradition of chanting associated with it, regardless of being Theravada or Mahayana. In Buddhism, chanting is the traditional means of preparing the mind for meditation; especially as part of formal practice (in either a lay or monastic context). Some forms of Buddhism also use chanting for ritualistic purposes.

While the basis for most Theravada chants is the Pali Canon, Mahayana and Vajrayana chants draw from a wider range of sources.

In the Theravada tradition, chanting is usually done in Pali, sometimes with vernacular translations interspersed. Among the most popular Theravada chants are:

- Buddhabhivadana (Preliminary Reverence for the Buddha)
- Tisarana (The Three Refuges)
- Pancasila (The Five Precepts)
- Buddha Vandana (Salutation to the Buddha)
- Dhamma Vandana (Salutation to his Teaching)
- Sangha Vandana (Salutation to his Community of Noble Disciples)
- Upajjhatthana (The Five Remembrances)
- Metta Sutta (Discourse on Loving Kindness)
- Reflection on the Body (recitation of the 32 parts of the body).

In the *Ghitassara Sutta*, the Buddha teaches:

Bhikkhus, there are five dangers of reciting the Dhamma with a musical intonation. What five?

Oneself gets attached to the sound, others get attached to the sound, householders are annoyed, saying, "Just as we sing, these sons of the Sakyan sing", the concentration of those who do not like the sound is destroyed, and later generations copy it.

These, monks, are the five dangers of reciting the Dhamma with a musical intonation.

In the Mahayana tradition, different schools are known for different chants, often accompanied by melodious chanting, elaborate rituals and utiilization of musical instruments (either of which are not used by its Theravadin counterpart):

- Central to daily Nichiren practice is the chanting of the phrase Nam Myoho Renge Kyo (Homage to the Lotus

Sutra). Nichiren practitioners will sometimes chant certain chapters from the Lotus Sutra, in particular the 2nd and 16th chapters.

- Pure Land Buddhists chant nianfo, *Namu Amida Butsu* or *Namo Amituofo* (Homage to Amitabha Buddha). In more formal services, practitioners will also chant excerpts from the Larger Sutra of Immeasurable Life or occasionally the entire Smaller Sutra of Immeasurable Life.
- Popular with Zen, Shingon or other Mahayana practitioners is chanting the Prajñâpâramitâ Hridaya Sûtra (Heart Sutra). In more formal settings, larger discourses of the Buddha (such as the Diamond Sutra) may be chanted as well. Particularly in the Chinese and the Japanese traditions, repentance ceremonies involving paying deep reverence to the Buddhas and bodhisattvas, as well as executing rituals to rescue and feed hungry ghosts are also occasionally practiced.

In the Vajrayana tradition, chanting is also used as an invocative ritual in order to set one's mind on a deity, Tantric ceremony, mandala, or particular concept one wishes to further in themselves. For Vajrayana practitioners, the chant Om Mani Padme Hum is very popular around the world as both a praise of peace and the primary mantra of Avalokitesvara. Other popular chants include those of Tara, Bhaisajyaguru, and Amitabha. Tibetan monks are noted for their skill at throat-singing, a specialized form of chanting in which, by amplifying the voice's upper partials, the chanter can produce multiple distinct pitches simultaneously.

There are also a number of New Age and experimental schools related to Buddhist thought which practise chanting, some with understanding of the words, others merely based on repetition. A large number of these schools tend to be syncretic and incorporate Hindu japa and other such traditions alongside the Buddhist influences. While not strictly a variation of Buddhist chanting in itself, Japanese *Shigin* is a form of chanted poetry that reflects several principles of Zen Buddhism. It is sung in the *seiza* position, and participants are encouraged to sing from the gut - the Zen locus of power. *Shigin* and related practices are often sung at Buddhist ceremonies and quasi-religious gatherings in Japan.

Shomyo

Shomyo is a style of Japanese Buddhist chant; mainly in the Tendai and Shingon sects. There are two styles: ryokyoku and rikkyoku, described as difficult and easy to remember, respectively.

Influence of Buddhism on music

United States composer and practicing Buddhist Philip Glass claims his religion does not influence his music directly: "The real impact of Buddhist practice affects how you live your life on a daily basis, not how you do your art."

BUDDHIST FESTIVALS

ASALHA PUJA

Asalha Puja (known as Asanha Puja in Thailand) is a Theravada Buddhist festival which typically takes place in July, on the fifteenth day of the waxing moon of the eighth lunar month. It commemorates the Buddha's first sermon in the Deer Park in Benares and the founding of the Buddhist *sangha*. In Thailand, Asalha Puja is a government holiday. The day is observed by donating offerings to temples and listening to sermons. The following day is known in Thailand as *Wan Kao Pansa*; it is the first day of vassa, the Theravada rains retreat.

VESAK

Vesak is an annual holiday observed traditionally by practicing Buddhists in South Asian & South East Asian countries like Nepal, Singapore, Vietnam, Thailand, Cambodia, Malaysia, Sri Lanka, Myanmar, Indonesia, Pakistan and India. Sometimes informally called "Buddha's birthday," it actually encompasses the birth, enlightenment Nirvana, and passing (Parinirvana) of Gautama Buddha. In Mahayana Buddhist traditions, the holiday is known by its Sanskrit name, *Vaiúâkha*, and derived variants of it. The word *Vesak* itself is the Sinhalese language word for the Pali variation, *Vesâkha*. Vesak is also known as *Buddha Jayanti* in India, Bangladesh and Nepal, (*Hanamatsuri*) in Japan, *Seokka Tanshin-il* in Korean, (Mandarin: *Fódàn*, Cantonese: *Fâtdàahn*) in Chinese-speaking communities, *Ph-t Đ£n* in Vietnamese, *Saga Dawa* (*sa ga zla ba*) in Tibetan, *Visak Bochéa* in Khmer, *Visakah Puja* (or *Visakha Bucha*) in Thai, *Waisak* in Indonesia, *Vesak* (*Wesak*) in Sri Lanka and Malaysia. The equivalent festival in Laos is called *Vixakha Bouxa* and in Myanmar is called *Ka-sone-la-pyae* meaning "Fullmoon Day of Kasone" which is also the second month of the Myanmar Calendar.

The exact date of Vesak varies according to the various lunar calendars used in different traditions. In Theravada countries following the Buddhist calendar, it falls on the full moon Uposatha day (typically the 5th or 6th lunar month). While the Vesak Day in China, it is on the eighth of the fourth month in the Chinese lunar calendar. The date varies from year to year in the Western Gregorian calendar but falls in April or May. The 2009 date for Vesak as observed by the Dhammayutika and Mahânikâya sects of Thai Buddhism was 8 May; 8 May 2009 was also Vesak in Sri Lanka. The 2009 date for Vesak as observed in Singapore is 9 May.

The decision to agree to celebrate Vesak as the Buddha's birthday was formalized at the first Conference of the World Fellowship of Buddhists held in Sri Lanka in 1950, although festivals at this time in the Buddhist world are a centuries-old tradition. The Resolution that was adopted at the World Conference reads as follows:

"That this Conference of the World Fellowship of Buddhists, while recording its appreciation of the gracious act of His Majesty, the Maharaja of Nepal in making the full-moon day of Vesak a Public Holiday in Nepal, earnestly requests the Heads of

Governments of all countries in which large or small number of Buddhists are to be found, to take steps to make the full-moon day in the month of May a Public Holiday in honour of the Buddha, who is universally acclaimed as one of the greatest benefactors of Humanity."

On Vesak Day, Buddhists all over the world commemorate events of significance to Buddhists of all traditions: The birth, enlightenment and the passing away of Gautama Buddha. As Buddhism spread from India it was assimilated into many foreign cultures, and consequently Vesak is celebrated in many different ways all over the world.

The Celebration of Vesak

May 2007 had two full moon days, the 1st and the 31st. Some countries (including Sri Lanka, Cambodia and Malaysia) celebrated Vesak on the 1st, while others (Thailand, Singapore) celebrated the holiday on the 31st due to different local lunar observance. This difference also manifests in the observance of other Buddhist holidays, which are traditionally observed at the local full moon. On Vesak day, devout Buddhists and followers alike are expected and requested to assemble in their various temples before dawn for the ceremonial, and honorable, hoisting of the Buddhist flag and the singing of hymns in praise of the holy triple gem: The Buddha, The Dharma (his teachings), and The Sangha (his disciples).

Devotees may bring simple offerings of flowers, candles and joss-sticks to lay at the feet of their teacher. These symbolic offerings are to remind followers that just as the beautiful flowers would wither away after a short while and the candles and joss-sticks would soon burn out, so too is life subject to decay and destruction. Devotees are enjoined to make a special effort to refrain from killing of any kind. They are encouraged to partake of vegetarian food for the day. In some countries, notably Sri Lanka, two days are set aside for the celebration of Vesak and all liquor shops and slaughter houses are closed by government decree during the two days. Also birds, insects and animals are released by the thousands in what is known as a 'symbolic act to liberation'; of giving freedom to those who are in captivity, imprisoned, or tortured against their will. Some devout Buddhists will wear a simple white dress and spend the whole day in temples with renewed determination to observe the Ten Precepts.

Devout Buddhists undertake to lead a noble life according to the teaching by making daily affirmations to observe the Five Precepts. However, on special days, notably new moon and full moon days, they observe the Ten Percepts to train themselves to practice morality, simplicity and humility. Some temples also display a small image of the baby Buddha in front of the altar in a small basin filled with water and decorated with flowers, allowing devotees to pour water over the statue; it is symbolic of the cleansing of a practitioners bad karma, and to reenact the events following the Buddha's birth, when devas and spirits made heavenly offerings to him.

Devotees are expected to listen to talks given by monks. On this day monks will recite verses uttered by the Buddha twenty-five centuries ago, to invoke peace and happiness for the Government and the people. Buddhists are reminded to live in harmony with people of other faiths and to respect the beliefs of other people as the Buddha had taught.

Bringing happiness to others

Celebrating Vesak also means making special efforts to bring happiness to the unfortunate like the aged, the handicapped and the sick. To this day, Buddhists will distribute gifts in cash and kind to various charitable homes throughout the country. Vesak is also a time for great joy and happiness, expressed not by pandering to one's appetites but by concentrating on useful activities such as decorating and illuminating temples, painting and creating exquisite scenes from the life of the Buddha for public dissemination. Devout Buddhists also vie with one another to provide refreshments and vegetarian food to followers who visit the temple to pay homage to the Enlightened One.

Paying homage to the Buddha

Tradition ascribes to the Buddha himself instruction on how to pay him homage. Just before he died, he saw his faithful attendant

Ananda, weeping. The Buddha advised him not to weep, but to understand the universal law that all compounded things (including even his own body) must disintegrate. He advised everyone not to cry over the disintegration of the physical body but to regard his teachings (The Dhamma) as their teacher from then on, because only the Dhamma truth is eternal and not subject to the law of change.

He also stressed that the way to pay homage to him was not merely by offering flowers, incense, and lights, but by truly and sincerely striving to follow his teachings. This is how devotees are expected to celebrate Vesak: to use the opportunity to reiterate their determination to lead noble lives, to develop their minds, to practise loving-kindness and to bring peace and harmony to humanity.

VESAK IN JAPAN

In Japan, Vesak or hanamatsuri is also known as: *Kanbutsu-e*, *Goutan-e*, *Busshou-e*, *Yokubutsu-e*, *Ryuge-e*, *Hana-eshiki*. It is not a public holiday. It is based on a legend that a dragon appeared in the sky on his birthday and poured soma over him. It used to be celebrated on the 8th day of the fourth month in the Chinese Lunar Calendar, based on one of the legends that proclaims the day as Buddha's birthday. At present, the celebration is observed on April 8 of the Solar Calendar since the Meiji government adopted the western solar calendar as the official calendar. Since the 8th day of the fourth month in the lunar calendar commonly falls in May of the current solar calendar, it is now celebrated about a month earlier.

In Japan, the general populace are not practicing Buddhists (and may be called casual Buddhists), so most Buddhist temples provide a way to allow the general public to celebrate and participate in only the aspect of the day being Buddha's birthday, providing the statue of baby Buddha and allowing the populace to worship or pay respect by pouring *ama cha*, a tea made of Hydrangea. In Buddhist temples, monasteries and nunneries, more involved ceremonies are conducted for practicing Buddhists, priests, monks and nuns. Also, there are public festivals made out of the day in some areas.

Vesak in Sri Lanka

Vesak is celebrated as a religious and a cultural festival in Sri Lanka on the full moon of the month of May, for a duration of one week. During this week, the selling of alcohol and flesh is usually prohibited. Prisoners who are eligible for parole are often released. Celebrations include various religious and alms giving activities. Electrically lit pandols called *toranas* are erected in various locations in Colombo and elsewhere, most sponsored by donors, religious societies and welfare groups.

Each pandol illustrates a story from the 550 Jataka Katha or the 550 Past Life Stories of the Buddha. In addition, colourful lanterns called *Vesak koodu* are hung along streets and in front of homes. They signify the light of the Buddha, Dharma and the Sangha. Food stalls set up by Buddhist devotees called *dansälas* provide free food and drinks to passersby. Groups of people from various community organisations, businesses and government departments sing *bhakti gee* or Buddhist devotional songs. Colombo experiences a massive influx of public from all parts of the country during this week.

Vesak in Vietnam

In 1963, the South Vietnamese President Ngo Dinh Diem, a Catholic and younger brother of Archbishop Ngo Dinh Thuc banned the flying of the Buddhist flag. This led to a demonstration and flag-waving in defiance of the ban. Diem's forces opened fire on the Buddhist crowd, killing nine, sparking the Buddhist crisis, a period of civil disobedience against religious discrimination.

MAGHA PUJA

Mâgha Pûjâ or Makha Bucha is an important religious festival celebrated by Buddhists in Thailand, Cambodia, and Laos on the full moon day of the third lunar month (this usually falls in February). The full moon of the third lunar month, a month known in the Thai language as *Makha* (Pali: Mâgha). *Bucha*, also a Thai word, meaning to venerate or to honor. As such, Makha Bucha Day is for the veneration of Buddha and his teachings on the full moon day of the third lunar month.

The spiritual aims of the day are: not to commit any kind of sins; do only good; purify one's mind. Mâgha Pûjâ is a public holiday in Thailand and Laos - and is an occasion when Buddhists tend to go to the temple to perform merit-making activities.

Origin of Mâgha Pûjâ Day

Mâgha Pûjâ day marks the four auspicious occasions, which happened nine months after the Enlightenment of the Lord Buddha at Ve7uvana Bamboo Grove, near Râjagaha in Northern India. On that occasion, as recorded in the commentary to the Mahâsamayasutta, DN 20) four marvellous events occurred:

1. 1,250 enlightened disciples of the Buddha spontaneously gathered
2. Every one of those enlightened disciples had been given monastic ordination personally by the Lord Buddha
3. Those disciples knew to meet together without any previous appointment
4. It was the full-moon day.

The Lord Buddha gave an important teaching to the assembled monks on that day 2,500 years ago called the 'Ovâdapâtimokkha' which laid down the principles of the Buddhist teachings. In Thailand, this teaching has been dubbed the 'Heart of Buddhism'.

Celebration of Magha Puja Day

In the evening, each temple in Thailand holds a candle light procession called a *wian tian* (*wian* meaning circle; *tian* meaning candle). Holding flowers, incense and a lighted candle, the monks and congregation members circumambulate clockwise three times around the main chapel or pagoda in the temple - once for each of the Three Jewels – the Buddha, the Dharma, and the Sangha.

VASSA

Vassa also called Rains Retreat, is the traditional retreat during the rainy season lasting for three lunar months from July to October. During this time Buddhist monks remain in a single place, generally in their temples. In some monasteries, monks dedicate the Vassa to intensive meditation. During Vassa, many Buddhist lay people reinvigorate their spiritual training and adopt more ascetic practices, such as giving up meat, alcohol, or smoking (Vassa is sometimes known as "Buddhist Lent", though at least one prominent Theravada monk has objected to this usage). And in countries such as Thailand, the laity will often take monastic vows for period of Vassa and return to lay life afterwards. Commonly, the number of years a monk has spent in monastic life is expressed by counting the number of Vassas he has observed.

The Vassa retreat has largely been given up by Mahayana Buddhists, as Mahayana Buddhism has typically flourished in regions without a rainy season, however for Mahayana schools such as Zen and Tibetan Buddhism other forms of retreat are common. The observation of Vassa is said to originate with the Buddha himself. Gautama Buddha ordered his disciples to observe a pre-existing practice whereby holy men avoided travel for a three month period during the rainy season, in order to avoid damaging crops.

Vassa begins on the first day of the waning moon of the eighth lunar month; the preceding day is Asalha Puja. The focus of celebration by the laity is the first day of Vassa (or Wan Kao Pansa) during which worshippers donate candles and other necessities to temples, in a ceremony which has reached its most extravagant form in the Ubon Ratchathani Candle Festival. Vassa is followed by two of the major festivals of the year among Theravada Buddhists, Wan Awk Pansa and Kathina. The end of vassa is marked by joyous celebration. The following month, the Kathina ceremony is held, during which the laity gathers to make formal offerings of robe cloth and other requisites to the Sangha.

PAVARANA

Pavarana is a Buddhist holy day celebrated on the full moon of the eleventh lunar month. It marks the end of the month of Vassa, sometimes called "Buddhist Lent." This day marks the end of the rainy season in some Asian countries like Thailand, where Theravada Buddhism is practiced. On this day, each monk (Pali: *bhikkhu*) must come before the community of monks (*Sangha*) and atone for an offense he may have committed during the Vassa. Most Mahayana Buddhists do not observe Vassa, though many Son/Thien monks in Korea and Vietnam do observe an equivalent retreat of three months of intensive practice in one location.

In India, where Buddhism began, there is a three-month-long rainy season. According to the Vinaya (Mahavagga, Fourth Khandhaka, section I), in the time of the Buddha, once during this rainy season, a group of normally wandering monks sought shelter by co-habitating in a residence. In order to minimize potential inter-personal strife while co-habitating, the monks agreed to remain silent for the entire three months and agreed upon a non-verbal means for sharing alms. After this rains retreat, when the Buddha learned of the monks' silence, he described such a measure as "foolish." Instead, the Buddha instituted the Pavarana Ceremony as a means for dealing with potential conflict and breaches of disciplinary rules (Patimokkha) during the vassa season. The Buddha said:

'I prescribe, O Bhikkhus, that the Bhikkhus, when they have finished their Vassa residence, hold Pavâranâ with each other in these three ways: by what [offence] has been seen, or by what has been heard, or by what is suspected. Hence it will result that you live in accord with each other, that you atone for the offences (you have committed), and that you keep the rules of discipline before your eyes.

'And you ought, O Bhikkhus, to hold Pavâranâ in this way:

'Let a learned, competent Bhikkhu proclaim the following ñatti [motion] before the Samgha: "Let the Samgha, reverend Sirs, hear me. To-day is the Pavâranâ day. If the Samgha is ready, let the Samgha hold Pavâranâ."

'Then let the senior Bhikkhu adjust his upper robe so as to cover one shoulder, sit down squatting, raise his joined hands, and say: "I pronounce my Pavâranâ, friends, before the Samgha, by what has been seen, or by what has been heard, or by what is suspected; may you speak to me, Sirs, out of compassion towards me; if I see (an offence), I will atone for it. And for the second time, & c. And for the third time I pronounce my Pavâranâ (&c., down to) if I see (an offence), I will atone for it."

KATHINA

Kathina is a Buddhist festival which comes at the end of Vassa, the three-month rainy season retreat for Theravada Buddhists. The season during which a monastery may hold a 'Kathina' festival is one month long, beginning after the full moon of the eleventh month in the Lunar calendar (usually October). In order to hold a 'Kathina', a monastery must have had five monks in residence during the retreat period and only those who were present for the entire retreat are eligible to receive the robe cloth offered. It is a time of giving, for the laity to express gratitude to monks. Lay Buddhists bring donations to temples, especially new robes for the monks.

Thailand

Kathin in Thailand is the name for the robes of an ordained monk; the ceremony of *Kathina* is called *Thod Kathin*. The Thai lunar calendar reckons the day after the 11th full moon as *Waning 1, Evening, Moon 11*. The presentation of *Kathin* by the King of Thailand or HM representative is called *The Royal Kathin Ceremony* and often has been an occasion for one of Thailand's Royal Barge Processions.

UPOSATHA

The Uposatha is Buddhist Sabbath day, in existence from the Buddha's time (500 B.C.E.), and still being kept today in Buddhist countries. The Buddha taught that the Uposatha day is for "the cleansing of the defiled mind," resulting in inner calm and joy. On this day, disciples and monks intensify their practice, deepen their knowledge and express communal commitment through millennia-old acts of lay-monastic reciprocity.

Observance days

Depending on the culture and time period, uposatha days have been observed from two to six days each lunar month.

Theravada countries

In general, Uposatha is observed about once a week in Theravada countries in accordance with the four phases of the moon: the new moon, the full moon, and the two quarter moons in between. In some communities, only the new moon and full moon are observed as uposatha days. In Burma, Uposatha (called *ubot nei*) is observed by more pious Buddhists on the following days: waxing moon (*la hsan*), full moon (*la pyei nei*), waning moon (*la hsote*), and new moon (*la kwe nei*).

The most common days of observance are the full moon and the new moon. In pre-colonial Burma, Sabbath was a legal holiday that was observed primarily in urban areas, where secular activities like business transactions came to a halt. However, since colonial rule, Sunday has replaced the Uposatha day as the legal day of rest. All major Burmese Buddhist holidays occur on Uposatha days, namely Thingyan, the beginning of the Buddhist lent (beginning in the full moon of Waso, around July to the full moon of Thadingyut, around October). During this period, Uposatha is more commonly observed by Buddhists than during the rest of the year.

Mayahana countries

In Mahayana countries that use the Chinese calendar, the Uposatha days are observed six times a month, on the 8th, 14th, 15th, 23^{r} and final two days of each lunar month. In Japan, these six days are known as the roku sainichi. The word "uposatha" is derived from the Sanskrit word "upavasatha," which refers to the pre-Buddhistic fast day that preceded Vedic sacrifices.

In the Buddha's time, some ascetics used the new and full moon as opportunities to present their teachings. The Uposatha Day was instituted by the Buddha at the request of King Bimbisara, and the Buddha instructed the monks to give teachings to the laypeople on this day, and told the monks to recite the Patimokkha every second Uposatha day.

Practice

Lay Practice

On each uposatha day, devout lay people practice the Eight Precepts. For lay practitioners who live near a monastery, the uposatha is an opportunity for them to visit a local monastery, make offerings, listen to Dhamma talks by monks and participate in meditation sessions. For lay practitioners unable to participate in the events of a local monastery, the uposatha is a time to intensify ones own meditation and Dhamma practice, for instance, meditating an extra session or for a longer time, reading or chanting special suttas, recollecting or giving in some special way.

Monastic Practice

On the new-moon and full-moon uposatha, in monasteries where there are four or more bhikkhus, the local Sangha will recite the Patimokkha. Before the recitation starts, the monks will confess any violations of the disciplinary rules to another monk or to the Sangha. Depending on the speed of the Patimokkha chanter (one of the monks), the recitation may take from 30 minutes to over an hour. Depending on the monastery, lay people may or may not be allowed to attend.

Communal Reciprocity

Describing his experience of Uposatha day in Thailand, Khantipalo (1982a) writes:

"Early in the morning lay people give almsfood to the bhikkhus who may be walking on almsround, invited to a layman's house, or the lay people may take the food to the monastery. Usually lay people do not eat before serving their food to the bhikkhus and they may eat only once that day.... Before the meal the laity request the Eight Precepts [from the bhikkhus]..., which they promise to undertake for a day and night. It is usual for lay people to go to the local monastery and to spend all day and night there.... [In monasteries where] there is more study, [lay people] will hear as many as three or four discourses on Dhamma delivered by senior bhikkhus and they will have books to read and perhaps classes on Abhidhamma to attend.... In a meditation monastery..., most of their time will be spent mindfully employed — walking and seated meditation with some time given to helping the bhikkhus with their daily duties. So the whole of this day and night (and enthusiastic lay people restrict their sleep) is given over to Dhamma...."

Special uposatha days

There are five full-moon uposatha days of special significance:

- Visakha Puja or Vesak ("Buddha Day"): the most sacred Buddhist holiday, anniversary of the Buddha's birth, awakening and parinibbana.
- Asalha Puja ("Dhamma Day"): anniversary of the Buddha's delivering his first discourse, "Dhammacakka Sutta." The three-month-long Rains Retreat residence starts the following day.
- Pavarana Day: the end of the Rains Retreat residence during which time each monk atones before the Sangha for any offense they may have committed.
- Anapanasati Day: anniversary of the Buddha's delivering the "."
- Magha Puja ("Sangha Day"): anniversary of the assembling of 1250 monks in the Buddha's presence during which time he delivered the "Ovada-Patimokkha Gatha."

BUDDHIST VIEW OF MARRIAGE

While Buddhism neither encourages nor discourages marriage, it does offer some guidelines for it. While Buddhist practice varies considerably among its various schools, marriage is one of the few concepts specifically mentioned in the context of Úîla (Buddhist behavior discipline). The fundamental code of Buddhist ethics, the Pancasila (or five precepts), contains an admonishment of sexual misconduct, though what constitutes such misconduct from a Buddhist perspective varies widely depending on the local culture. The Digha Nikaya 31 (Sigalovada Sutta) describes the respect that one is expected to give to one's spouse.

Divorce

Divorce, although uncommon for Buddhists, is not prohibited. However, it is expected that if a couple enters into marriage and adheres to Buddhism's ethical prescriptions for marital and family life, that divorce will not be necessary or desired. If, however, a couple fails to follow the ethical prescriptions, is unable to live in peace, harmony, and mutuality with one another, or in the event of extreme circumstances, such as adultery or violence, it is deemed preferable for the marriage to be broken than for the marriage to destroy the couple or the family.

HUMAN BEINGS IN BUDDHISM

Human beings in Buddhism are the subjects of an extensive commentarial literature that examines the nature and qualities of a human life from the point of view of human beings' ability to achieve enlightenment. In Buddhism, human beings are just one type of sentient being, that is a being with a mindstream. In Buddhism, human beings have a very special status: only a human being can attain enlightenment as a fully enlightened Buddha. Enlightenment as an arhat can be attained from the realms of the Úuddhâvâsa deities. A bodhisattva can appear in many different types of lives, for instance as an animal or as a deva. Buddhas, however, are always human.

The status of life as a human being, at first glance, has nothing very special about it. In the hierarchy of Buddhist cosmology it is low but not entirely at the bottom. It is not intrinsically marked by extremes of happiness or suffering, but all the states of consciousness in the universe, from hellish suffering to divine joy to serene tranquility can be experienced within the human world. Human beings can be seen as highly favored, in that they have an immediate reason to seek out the Dharma and yet also have the means to listen to it and follow it.

Among the lower realms, Pretas, and dwellers in the Narakas are gripped by pain and fear, and can only endure their lot but cannot better themselves. Animals are intellectually unable to understand the Dharma in full. The way of life of the Asuras is dominated by violence and antithetical to the teachings of the Dharma, while most of the Devas simply enjoy reaping the fruits of their past actions and do not concern themselves with the future. When their past karmas have all had their result, these devas will fall into lower worlds and suffer again. The lowest sorts of devas deal with strife, love, and loss just as humans do, but even so they lack the spur of imminent mortality that can lead human beings to seek, not merely a better future life, but an escape from saCsâra altogether.

For this reason, life in the world of human beings is known as "the precious human rebirth". Born close to the pivot point of happiness and suffering, human beings have a unique capacity for moral choices with long-term significance. The human rebirth is said to be extremely rare. The *Bodhicaryâvatâra* compares it to a wooden cattle-yoke floating on the waves of the ocean, tossed this way and that by the winds and currents. The likelihood of a half-blind turtle, rising from the depths of the ocean to the surface once in a hundred years, putting its head through the hole in the yoke is considered greater than that of a being in saCsâra achieving rebirth as a human.

Among humans there are also better and worse conditions for attaining enlightenment. Besides being born as a human, the favorable conditions for obtaining enlightenment are:

- Being born a human at a time when a Buddha has arisen, has taught the Dharma, and has left a SaEgha that carries on the teachings; at such times there is a chance to learn the Dharma.

- Being born a human in countries where the Dharma is known. Buddhist commentaries contrast the "central lands" where Buddhism is known and can be practiced (originally just northern India, but now including a much larger portion of the globe) with "border countries" where Buddhism is unknown or cannot be practiced due to legal or practical impediments, for instance, a lack of qualified teachers. Technically a "central land" is one which possesses any one of the Buddhist upâsakas or upâsikâs.
- Being born a human who has the physical and intellectual capacity to grasp the basic message of the Dharma.
- Accepting the relationship between good or evil actions and their consequences, believing that good actions will lead to a happier life, a better rebirth or to enlightenment.
- Confidence in the moral teachings conveyed in the Vinaya.
- Avoiding crimes against people and against the Dharma.
- Having sincere compassion for other people.

Just as it is difficult to obtain birth as a human, it is also difficult to be born at the time when a Buddha's teaching is still available. Out of the infinite *kalpas* (incredibly long periods) in time, most have no Buddhas appearing in them at all. The present kalpa is called "Fortunate" because it is said that 1,000 Buddhas will appear in it, something that is very unusual. For this reason, Buddhist teachers say that one's present condition as a human being should be valued very highly, and not allowed to slide by, as the combination of existence as a human and the presence of a Buddha's teaching may not come again for a very long time.

Any human, in this view, who finds himself or herself in a position to learn the Dharma, would be remiss if he or she did not take advantage of it. This view also stands in contrast to those who would claim that, if one is to be reborn multiple times, there is no need to worry about one's actions in this life as they can always be amended in the future; rather, there is no assurance that in a long series of lives one will ever obtain the right circumstances for enlightenment, so it is important to seize the day. With regard to a fortunate human life, Pabongka Rinpoche said: "Instead of feeling so much regret when we lose our money, we should develop regret when we waste our human life."

Myth of human origins

According to the Aggañña Sutta (DN.27), human beings originated at the beginning of the current kalpa as deva-like beings reborn from the Âbhâsvara deva-realm. They were then beings shining in their own light, capable of moving through the air without mechanical aid, living for a very long time, and not requiring sustenance. Over time, they acquired a taste for physical nutriment, and as they consumed it, their bodies became heavier and more like human bodies; they lost their ability to shine, and began to acquire differences in their appearance.

Their length of life decreased, they differentiated into two sexes and became sexually active. Following this, greed, theft and violence arose among them, and they consequently established social distinctions and government and elected a king to rule them, called Mahâsammata, "the great appointed one". Some of the kings of India in the Buddha's day claimed descent from him.

Nature of the human realm

In the visionary picture of the human realm presented in Buddhist cosmology, human beings live on four continents which are, relatively speaking, small islands in a vast ocean that surrounds the axial world-mountain of Sumeru, and fills most of the earth's surface. The ocean is in turn surrounded by a circular mountain wall called Cakravâ

a (Sanskrit) or Cakkava7a (Pâli) which marks the horizontal limit of the earth. Because of the immenseness of the ocean, the continents cannot be reached from each other by ordinary sailing vessels, although in the past, when the cakravartin kings ruled, communication between the continents was possible by means of the treasure called the cakraratna (Pâli cakkaratana), which a cakravartin and his retinue could use to fly through the air between the continents.

The four Continents are:

- Jambudvîpa (Sanskrit) or Jambudîpa (Pâli) is also translated in Chinese) is located in the south and is the dwelling of ordinary human beings. It is said to be shaped "like a cart", or rather a blunt-nosed triangle with the point facing south. (This description probably echoes the shape of the coastline of southern India.) It is 10,000 yojanas in extent (Vibhajyavâda tradition) or has a perimeter of 6,000 yojanas (Sarvâstivâda tradition) to which can be added the southern coast of only 3 D 2 yojanas' length. The continent takes its name from a giant Jambu tree (Syzygium cumini), 100 yojanas tall, which grows in the middle of the continent. Every continent has one of these giant trees. All Buddhas appear in Jambudvîpa. The humans here are five to six feet tall and their length of life varies between 80,000 and 10 years.
- Pûrvavideha or Pubbavideha is located in the east, and is shaped like a semicircle with the flat side pointing westward (i.e., towards Sumeru). It is 7,000 yojanas in extent (Vibhajyavâda tradition) or has a perimeter of 6,350 yojanas of which the flat side is 2,000 yojanas long (Sarvâstivâda tradition). Its tree is the acacia. The humans here are about 12 feet tall and they live for 250 years.
- Aparagodânîya or Aparagoyâna is located in the west, and is shaped like a circle with a circumference of about 7,500 yojanas (Sarvâstivâda tradition). The tree of this continent is a giant Kadambu tree. The human

inhabitants of this continent do not live in houses but sleep on the ground. They are about 24 feet tall and they live for 500 years.

- Uttarakuru is located in the north, and is shaped like a square. It has a perimter of 8,000 yojanas, being 2,000 yojanas on each side. This continent's tree is called a kalpav[kca (Pâli: kapparukkha) or kalpa-tree, because it lasts for the entire kalpa. The humans of Uttarakuru are said to be extraordinarily wealthy. They do not need to labor for a living, as their food grows by itself, and they have no private property. They have cities built in the air. They are about 48 feet tall and live for 1,000 years, and they are under the protection of Vaiœravana.

WOMEN IN BUDDHISM

Women in Buddhism is a topic that can be approached from varied perspectives including those of theology, history, anthropology and feminism. As in other religions, the experiences of Buddhist women have varied considerably. According to Bernard Faure, "Buddhism is paradoxically neither as sexist nor as egalitarian as is usually thought". Scholars such as Faure and Miranda Shaw are in agreement that Buddhist Studies is in its infancy in terms of addressing gender issues. Shaw gave an overview of the situation in 1994:

In the case of Indo-Tibetan Buddhism, some progress has been made in the areas of women in early Buddhism, monasticism, and Mâhayâna Buddhism. Two articles have seriously broached the topic of women in Indian Tantric Buddhism, while somewhat more attention has been devoted to Tibetan nuns and lay yoginis.

However Khandro Rinpoche, a rare female lama in Tibetan Buddhism has pointed out:

When there is a talk about women and Buddhism, I have noticed that people often regard the topic as something new and different. They believe that women in Buddhism have become an important topic because we live in modern times and so many women are practicing the Dharma now. However, this is not the case. The female sangha has been here for centuries. We are not bringing something new into a twenty-five hundred-year-old tradition. The roots are there, and we are simply re-energizing them.

The founder of the religion, Gautama Buddha, permitted women to join his monastic community and fully participate in it, although there were certain provisos or *garudhammas*. As Susan Murcott comments, "The nun's sangha was a radical experiment for its time" Dr. Mettanando Bhikkhu (Dr. Mano Laohavanich), Chulalongkorn University, Bangkok, Thailand stated referring to the First buddhist council: "Their anti-women prejudice became institutionalized at that time with the eight garudhammas, the eight weighty restrictions.

There is no anti-women prejudice in Jainism and they survived in India; whereas Buddhism had prejudice and did not survive in India.". According to Ajahn Sujato, however, the early texts state that the most severe of the garudhammas, which states that every nun must bow to every monk, was instituted by the Buddha because of the customs of the time, and modern scholars doubt that the rule even goes back to the Buddha at all. Furthermore, an identical rule is found in Jainism.

According to Diana Paul, the traditional view of women in Early Buddhism is that they are inferior. Rita Gross agrees that "a misogynist strain is found in early Indian Buddhism. But the presence of some clearly misogynist doctrines does not mean that the whole of ancient Indian Buddhism was misogynist". The mix of positive attitudes to femininity with blatantly negative sentiment has led many writers to characterise early Buddhism's attitude to women as deeply ambivalent.

Some commentators on the *Aganna-Sutta* from the Pali Canon, a record of the teachings of Gautama Buddha, interpret it as showing women as responsible for the downfall of the human race. However, Buddhist interpretation is generally that it shows lust in general, rather than women, as causing the downfall. However, despite some less positive images of women in Early Buddhism, there are also examples in the Pali Canon demonstrating that from earliest times Buddhist philosophy represented clinging to beliefs based on gender as a hinderance to attaining nirvana, or enlightenment.

For example, in the *Bhikkhuni-samyutta*, found in the *Sagatha-vagga* of the Samyutta Nikaya, gender discrimination is stated to be the work of Mara, a personification of temptation from the Buddhist spiritual path. In the Soma Sutta, the bhikkhuni Soma states: "Anyone who thinks 'I'm a woman' or 'a man' or 'Am I anything at all?' — that's who Mara's fit to address", linking gender neutrality to the Buddhist concept of anatta, or "not-self", a strategy the Buddha taught for release from suffering. In a sutta titled "Bondage", the Buddha states that when either a man or a woman clings to gender identity, that person is in bondage.

Women's Spiritual Attainment

The various schools and traditions within Buddhism hold different views as to the possibilities of women's spiritual attainments. Feminist scholars have also noted than even when a woman's potential for spiritual attainment is acknowledged, records of such achievements may not be kept - or may be obscured by gender-neutral language or mis-translation of original sources by Western scholars.

Limitations on Women's Attainments in Buddhism

According to Bernard Faure, "Like most clerical discourses, Buddhism is indeed relentlessly misogynist, but as far as misogynist discourses go, it is one of the most flexible and open to multiplicity and contradiction." In the Buddhist tradition, positions of apparently worldly power are often a reflection of the spiritual achievements of the individual. For example, any gods are living in higher realms than a human being and therefore have a certain level of spiritual attainment. Cakravartins and Buddhas are also more spiritual advanced than an ordinary human being.

However, as Zen nun Heng-Ching Shih states, women in Buddhism are said to have five obstacles, namely being incapable of becoming a Brahma King, ‘Sakra‘, King ‘Mara‘, Cakravartin or Buddha. This is based on the statement of Gautama Buddha in the in the *Bahudhâtuka-sutta* of the Majjhima Nikaya in the Pali Canon that it is impossible that a woman should be “the perfectly rightfully Enlightened One’”, “the Universal Monarch”, “the King of Gods”, “the King of Death” or “Brahmaa’”.

Women and Buddhahood

Although early Buddhist texts such as the Cullavagga section of the Vinaya Pitaka of the Pali Canon contain statements from Gautama Buddha, the founder of Buddhism, that a woman can attain enlightenment,, it is also clearly stated in the *Bahudhâtuka-sutta* that there could never be a female Buddha. As Prof. Heng-Ching Shih states, women in Buddhism are said to have five obstacles, namely being incapable of becoming a Brahma King, ‘Sakra‘, King ‘Mara‘, Cakravartin or Buddha. This is based on the statement of Gautama Buddha in the *Bahudhâtuka-sutta* of the Majjhima Nikaya in the Pali Canon that it is impossible that a woman should be “the perfectly rightfully Enlightened One’”, “the Universal Monarch”, “the King of Gods”, “the King of Death” or “Brahmaa’”.

In Theravada Buddhism, the modern school based on the Buddhist philosophy of the earliest dated texts, Buddhahood is a rare event, happening only once in eons. The focus of practice is primarily on attaining Arhatship and the Pali Canon has examples of both male and female Arhats who attained nirvana. Yashodhara, the former wife of Buddha Shakyamuni, mother of his son Rahula, is said to have become an arhat after having joined the Bhikkhuni order of Buddhist nuns. In Mahayana schools, Buddhahood is the universal goal for Mahayana practitioners.

The Mahayana sutras, like the Pali Canon literature, maintain that a woman can become enlightened, only not in female form. For example, the *Bodhisattvabhûmi*, dated to the 4th Century, states that a woman about to attain enlightenment will be reborn in the male form. According to Miranda Shaw, “this belief had negative implications for women insofar as it communicated the insufficiency of the female body as a locus of enlightenment". However, in the tantric iconography of the Vajrayana practice path of Buddhism, female Buddhas do appear. Sometimes they are the consorts of the main yidam of a meditation mandala but Buddhas such as Vajrayogini, Tara and Simhamukha appear as the central figures of tantric sadhana in their own right.

Vajrayana Buddhism also recognizes many female yogini practitioners as achieving the full enlightenment of a Buddha, Miranda Shaw as an example cites sources referring to "Among the students of the adept Naropa, reportedly two hundred men and one thousand women attained complete enlightenment". Yeshe Tsogyal, one of the five tantric consorts of Padmasambhava is an example of a woman (Yogini) recognized as a female Buddha in the Vajrayana tradition.

According to Karmapa lineage however Tsogyel has attained Buddhahood in that very life. On the website of the Karmapa, the head of the Karma Kagyu school of Tibetan Buddhism, it is stated that Yeshe Tsogyal - some thirty years before transcending worldly existence - finally emerged from an isolated meditation retreat, (c.796-805 AD), as "a fully enlightened Buddha".

There are predictions from Sakyamuni Buddha to be found in the thirteenth chapter of the Mahayana Lotus Sutra, referring to future attainments of Mahapajapati and Yasodhara. In the 20th Century Tenzin Palmo, a Tibetan Buddhist nun in the Drukpa Lineage of the Kagyu school, stated "I have made a vow to attain Enlightenment in the female form - no matter how many lifetimes it takes".

Female Tulku Lineages

In the fifteenth century CE, Princess Chokyi-dronme (Wylie: *Chos-kyi sgron-me*) was recognized as the embodiment of the meditation deity and female Buddha in the Vajrayana tradition, Vajravarahi. Chokyi-dronme became known as Samding Dorje Pagmo (Wylie: *bSam-lding rDo-rje phag-mo*) and began a line of female tulkus, reincarnate lamas. At present, the twelfth of this line lives in Tibet.

Another female tulku lineage, that of Shugseb Jetsun Rinpoche (Wylie: *Shug-gseb rJe-btsun Rin-po-che*) (c. 1865–1951), began in the late nineteenth century CE. While she received teachings of all the Tibetan schools, Shugseb Jetsun Rinpoche was particularly known for holding a lineage of Chöd, the meditation practice of offering one's own body for the benefit of others. At the start of the twentieth century, Shugsheb Jetsun Rinpoche - also called Ani Lochen Chönyi Zangmo - founded the Shuksep or Shugsep (Wylie:*shug gseb*) nunnery located thirty miles from Lhasa on the slopes of Mount Gangri Thökar.

It became one of the largest and most famous nunneries in Tibet. Shugsep Nunnery, part of the Nyingma school of Tibetan Buddhism, has been re-established in Gambhir Ganj, India.In exile in India, the nuns of Shugsep are now determined to maintain the identity and traditions of their nunnery, and they continue the practices for which they were famous, particularly those of Longchen Nyingtig and Chöd.

Buddhist Ordination of Women

Gautama Buddha first ordained women as nuns five years after his enlightenment and five years after first ordaining men into the sangha. The first Buddhist nun was his aunt and foster mother Mahapajapati Gotami. Gautama Buddha refused Mahapajapati's request for ordination three times but when asked by Ananda if women could achieve nirvana and be arhats, confirmed that they could. Eventually Gautama concedes that, with certain provisos, women can be ordained. Bhikkhunis have to follow the eight rules of respect, which are vows called The Eight Garudhammas.

According to Peter Harvey "The Buddha's apparent hesitation on this matter is reminiscent of his hesitation on whether to teach at all", something he only does after persuasion from various devas. Since the special rules for female monastics were given by the founder of Buddhism they have been upheld to this day. Buddhists nowadays are still concerned with that fact, as shows an International Congress on Buddhist Women's Role in the Sangha held at the University of Hamburg, Germany, in 2007.

According to Thubten Chodron, the current Dalai Lama has said on this issue:

1. In 2005, the Dalai Lama repeatedly spoke about the bhikshuni ordination in public gatherings. In Dharamsala, he encouraged, "We need to bring this to a conclusion. We Tibetans alone can't decide this. Rather, it should be decided in collaboration with Buddhists from all over the world. Speaking in general terms, were the Buddha to come to this 21st century world, I feel that most likely, seeing the actual situation in the world now, he might change the rules somewhat...."
2. Later, in Zurich during a 2005 conference of Tibetan Buddhist Centers, His Holiness said, "Now I think the time has come; we should start a working group or committee" to meet with monks from other Buddhist traditions. Looking at the German bhikshuni, Ven. Jampa Tsedroen, he instructed, "I prefer that Western Buddhist nuns carry out this work...Go to different places for further research and discuss with senior monks (from various Buddhist countries). I think, first, senior bhikshunis need to correct the monks' way of thinking.
3. "This is the 21st century. Everywhere we are talking about equality....Basically Buddhism needs equality. There are some really minor things to remember as a Buddhist—a bhikshu always goes first, then a bhikshuni....The key thing is the restoration of the bhikshuni vow."

Alexander Berzin referred to the Dalai Lama having said on occasion of the 2007 Hamburg congress

"Sometimes in religion there has been an emphasis on male importance. In Buddhism, however, the highest vows, namely the bhikshu and bhikshuni ones, are equal and entail the same rights. This is the case despite the fact that in some ritual areas, due to social custom, bhikshus go first. But Buddha gave the basic rights equally to both sangha groups. There is no point in discussing whether or not to revive the bhikshuni ordination; the question is merely how to do so properly within the context of the Vinaya.- taken from Berzin Summary Report

FAMILY LIFE IN BUDDHISM

According to Diana Paul, Buddhism inherited a view of women whereby if they are not represented as mothers then they are portrayed as either lustful temptresses or as evil incarnate.

Motherhood

The status of motherhood in Buddhism has also traditionally reflected the Buddhist perspective that dukkha, or suffering, is a major characteristic of human existence. In her book on the Therigatha collection of stories of women arhats from the Pali Canon, Susan Murcott states: "Though this chapter is about motherhood, all of the stories and poems share another theme - grief. The mothers of this chapter were motivated to become Buddhist nuns by grief over the death of their children."

However, motherhood in Early Buddhism could also be a valued activity in its own right. Queen Maya, the mother of Gautama Buddha, the founder of Buddhism, had a certain following, especially in Lumbini, where she gave birth to him. Since Maya died some days after his birth, Gautama Buddha was brought up by a fostermother, his mother's sister Mahapajapati, who also had two children of her own.

She become the first Buddhist nun. Both of her children, her son Nanda and her daughter Sundari Nanda joined the Buddhist sangha of monastics. The wife of Gautama Buddha, Yasodhara, was the mother of one son named Rahula, meaning "fetter", who became a Buddhist monk at the age of seven and Yasodhara also eventually became a nun.

One of the attractions for women in Vajrayana Buddhism of following the path of a yogini rather than that of a bhikkhuṇi nun was the opportunity to practice amidst family life with a husband or spiritual consort and possibly have children. Also Yoginis -unlike nuns- were not obliged to shave their hair.

Machig Labdrön followed such a path, living in a monastery for a while but later leaving to unite with Topabhadra as her consort. According to Machig's namthar he cared for the children whilst she practiced and taught. Some of Machig's children followed her on the spiritual path, becoming accomplished yogins themselves. Tsultrim Allione, a recognised emanation of Machig Labdron, herself was a nun for four years but left to marry and have children. She has spoken of the contribution motherhood has made to her practice:

...in Buddhism the image of the mother as the embodiment of compassion is used a lot. She'll do anything for the children. As a mother I felt that depth of love and commitment and having somebody who I really would give my own life for - it was very powerful to have that kind of relationship. I also felt that I didn't really grow up until I had my children. There were ways that maturity was demanded of me and having children brought forth that maturity. So I wouldn't say my children were an inspiration in the sense of what I thought would have been a spiritual inspiration before I had children. More so I think meeting the challenges of motherhood with what I had learned made my practice very rich.

Love, Sexual Conduct and Marriage

In general, "While Buddhism regards the celibate monastic life as the higher ideal, it also recognizes the importance of marriage as a social institution". Some guidelines for marriage are offered. Although Buddhist practice varies considerably amongst its various schools, marriage is one of the few concepts specifically mentioned in the context of Úîla, the Buddhist formulation of core facets of spiritual discipline. The fundamental code of Buddhist ethics, The Five Precepts contains an admonishment against sexual misconduct, although what constitutes misconduct from the perspective of a particular school of Buddhism varies widely depending on the local culture.

In Early Buddhism, the Sigalovada Sutta of the Digha Nikaya in the Pali Canon describes the respect that one is expected to give to one's spouse. However, since the ideal of Early Buddhism is renunciation, it can be seen from examples such as the story of the monk Nanda and his wife Janapada Kalyâni that striving for the bliss of Nirvana is valued above love and marriage.

Despite having married her just that day, encouraged by his cousin Gautama Buddha, Nanda left his wife to become a bhikkhu in the Buddhist Sangha. In stories like this from the Pali Canon, love is generally perceived as part of attachment to samsara, the endless cycle of rebirth. Susan Murcott has pointed out that Early Buddhist attitudes to love and marriage generally reflect the Brahmanic ideals of India at the time... including the recent rise of the renunciate ideal and the associated decline in the status of love and marriage.

In Vajrayana Buddhism, a sexual relationship with a consort is seen in a technical way as being a spiritual practice in anuttarayoga tantra intended to allow the practitioners to attain realizations and attain enlightenment. The union of tantric consorts is depicted in the yab-yum iconography of meditation deities. In Buddhism the concept of love or metta is connected to the Buddha to come Maitreya.

Words

June Campbell writes in her book *Traveller in space* that Chandra Das in his *Tibetan English Dictionary* describes twenty synonyms for *woman*. The words used most often are kyemen (tibetan: skye.dman) meaning inferior birth and pumo (tibetan: bu.mo.) meaning female human being. There are others like tsamdenma (tibetan: mtshams.ldan.ma.), chingchema (tibetan: bching.byed.ma.), dodenma (tibetan: bdod.ldan.ma.), gaweshi (tibetan: dgah.wabi.gshi.) and tobmema (tibetan: stobs.med.ma.).

Throughout thc Mahâyâna world, Avalokiteúvara, who takes on both male and female form [e.g., Guan Yin, and Tara, a female Vajrayana yidam, are bodhisattvas who embody karuGâ, and Prajnaparamita is a female buddha who embodies wisdom.

His Holiness the Fourteenth Dalai Lama:

"Warfare has traditionally been carried out primarily by men, since they seem better physically equipped for aggressive behavior. Women, on the other hand, tend to be more caring and more sensitive to others' discomfort and pain. Although men and women have the same potentials for aggression and warm-heartedness, they differ in which of the two more easily manifests. Thus, if the majority of world leaders were women, perhaps there would be less danger of war and more cooperation on the basis of global concern – although, of course, some women can be difficult! I sympathize with feminists, but they must not merely shout. They must exert efforts to make positive contributions to society."

BUDDHIST SOCIALISM

Buddhist socialism is a political ideology which advocates socialism based on the principles of Buddhism. Buddhist socialists have called for state provision of the Buddhist requisites of food, shelter, clothing and medicine, for the abolition or amelioration of class distinctions, for campaigns for morality based on Buddhist traditions, and for workers and peasants to overcome the love of property. People who have been described as Buddhist socialists include Buddhadasa Bhikkhu, S. W. R. D. Bandaranaike, U Nu and Norodom Sihanouk.

The Dalai Lama Tenzin Gyatso has said that:

"Of all the modern economic theories, the economic system of Marxism is founded on moral principles, while capitalism is concerned only with gain and profitability. (...) The failure of the regime in the former Soviet Union was, for me, not the failure of Marxism but the failure of totalitarianism. For this reason I still think of myself as half-Marxist, half-Buddhist."

BUDDHIST ANARCHISM

Buddhism is rooted in three fundamental truths of the universe, the dharma seals, viz.:

1. Everything is in a constant state of change, nothing is permanent. (anicca)
2. That "suffering" exists everywhere in Samsara. (dukkha)
3. That everything is devoid of a "self." (anatta)

Thus, there can be no "perfect State"; from this Buddhist anarchists infer that it is only possible to try to approach an ideal community for all. Any man-made institution is impermanent as well as imperfect, as people and the world change constantly. Further, no material wealth or political power will grant people permanent happiness— unenlightened satisfaction is an illusion that only perpetuates samsara. Individual liberty, while a worthy goal for anarchists, is nevertheless incomplete, to the extent that it precludes our common humanity, since there is, ultimately, no "self" that is inherently distinct from the rest of the universe.

That being said, the aim of a *bodhisattva* is to try to minimize the amount of suffering that goes on during the lives of conscious beings. The socialist anarchist argues that both the state and capitalism generate oppression and, therefore, suffering. The former, the state, is an institution that frames the desire for power, and the latter, capitalism, the desire for material wealth. Trying to control other human beings, in the view of Buddhist anarchists, will only cause them to suffer, and ultimately causes suffering for those who try to control. Trying to hold on to and accumulate material wealth, likewise, increases suffering for the capitalist and those they do business with.

Compassion, for a Buddhist, springs from a fundamental selflessness. Compassion for humanity as a whole is what inspires the Buddhist towards activism; however, most, if not all, political groups tend to go against the Eightfold Path that steers Buddhist thought and action. Thus, anarchism, lacking a rigid ideological structure and dogmas, is seen as easily applicable for Buddhists. Those who have seen the conjunction of anarchism and Buddhism (in various ways) arguably include Uchiyama Gudo, Edward Carpenter, Ananda Coomaraswamy, Lala Hardayal, Liu Shipei, John Cage, Kenneth Rexroth, Allen Ginsberg, Diane di Prima, Gary Snyder, Jackson MacLow, Peter Lamborn Wilson, John Moore, Kerry Wendell Thornley, Max Cafard, William Batchelder Greene, as well as the pro-Situationist Ken Knabb and others.

The anarchist thinker Peter Kropotkin saw primitive Buddhist communities as embodying the principle of mutual aid, and Matthew Turner noted that some Buddhist priests were involved in the anarchist movement in Japan in the early part of the 20th century.

Differing Interpretations

Eisai, the founder of Rinzai school in Japan held quite a different view as regards the state (which is otherwise universally abhorred by all forms of anarchists) as shown in *Ko-zen-go-koku-ron* (*The Protection of the State by the Propagation of Zen*). This, however, has not prevented the promotion of Zen Anarchism as "whatever you make it" or of Anarchists as "scholar warriors" with little reference to Zen Buddhism itself, but rather promoting a literary and psychological view rooted in Japanese militaristic tradition. Parts of Japanese anarchism embraced this militarism and became ultra nationalists.

Anarchism and Hindu Fundamentalism

The Indian anarchist Har Dayal understood the realisation of ancient *Aryan* culture as anarchism, which he also saw as the goal of Buddhism. A prominent Sanskrit scholar influenced by Swami

Dayananda Saraswati (founder of Arya Samaj), he wished to create a movement which he saw as replicating a return to ancient vedic culture. He was active in the Industrial Workers of the World in San Francisco and was a central figure in the Ghadar movement which attempted to overthrow the British in India by reconciling Western concepts of social revolution - particularly those stemming from Mikhail Bakunin - with Buddhism..

It should be noted that the relationship between Buddhism and Hinduism remains a controversial issue. The controversy includes the usage of the term "Aryan", which does not necessarily carry racial connotations in Buddhism.

"Dharma Bums"

In the 1950s, California saw the rise of a strand of Buddhist anarchism emerging from the Beat movement. Gary Snyder and Diane di Prima were a product of this. Snyder was the inspiration for the character Japhy Rider in Jack Kerouac's novel the *The Dharma Bums* (1958). Snyder spent considerable time in Japan studying Zen Buddhism, and in 1961 published *Buddhist Anarchism* where he described the connection he saw between these two concepts originating in different parts of the world: "The mercy of the West has been social revolution; the mercy of the East has been individual insight into the basic self/void." He advocated "using such means as civil disobedience, outspoken criticism, protest, pacifism, voluntary poverty and even gentle violence" and defended "the right of individuals to smoke hemp, eat peyote, be polygymous, polyandrous or homosexual" which he saw as being banned by "the Judaeo-Capitalist-Christian-Marxist West".

Buddhism and the body

In contrast with many Indian religious traditions, Buddhism does not regard the body and the mind or spirit as being two entirely separate entities- there is no sense in Buddhism that the body is a "vessel" that is guided or inhabited by the mind or spirit. Rather, the body and mind combine and interact in a complex way to constitute an individual. Buddhist attitudes towards the body itself are complex, combining the distaste for sensual pleasure that characterizes the general Buddhist view towards desire with a recognition of both the individuals dependence on the body, and the utility of the body as an aide in the development of insight. Issues of gender, the mortification of the body, and the body as a source of troublesome desire are all addressed within the Buddhist scriptural tradition directly, while Buddhist attitudes towards other, more contemporary issues have continued to develop and change in response to the social and material changes in modern society.

Views on the Body Itself

The Place of the Body

The Buddhist tradition regards the body and the mind as being mutually dependent. The body or physical form (called *rupa*) is considered as one of the five *skandha*, the five interdependent components that constitute an individual. The Buddha taught that there is no separate, permanent, or unchanging self, and that a human being is an impermanent composite of interdependent physical, emotional and cognitive components.

Identifying either the body or the mind as a the self is dismissed as a mistaken view by the Buddha; in the Anatta-lakkhana Sutta, it is clearly stated that none of the five *skandha* should be regarded as the self. Traditional sources often emphasize the attitude that the body should be subordinate to the mind; scriptures depict the Buddha instructing followers to look beyond physical discomfort and leave their minds undisturbed.

Health and Mortification

Revulsion for the Body

Though perhaps less concerned with issues of purity and pollution than the Brahmanist tradition, certain views of the body recorded in Buddhist scriptures do depict the body as unwholesome and potentially an object of disgust. This is the "unwantedness" of a body in the tradition of Buddhism identified by some scholars. Reflecting on the loathsomeness of the is considered to be a particularly powerful method for countering attachment to sensual pleasures, such as sexuality or pride in appearance. Stories recorded in scriptures and in the biographies of Buddhist teachers particularly focus on the contemplation of the foulness of the female body as a remedy for sexual desire in a male religious practitioner.

The Value of the Body

In contrast to views of the body as disgusting or a source of unworthy desire, the Buddhist tradition does speak of the value of the body in the context of the preciousness of human birth, and the value of a healthy body as an aid to pursuing the Buddhist path. While contemplating the repulsiveness of the body is considered to be a powerful remedy for sensual attachment, this is a therapeutic perspective that is not necessarily intended to be carried over into other areas of life. In particular, the suitability of the human body for the pursuit of religious practice is praised in traditional sources, comparing favorably with the capacities of birth among the gods or the various chthonic realms.

Meditation and the body

Scriptures and meditation text depict a number of meditation method that focus particularly on the body. The passage of the breath through the body is a particularly common. Entire sutras devoted to contemplating breathing. Other meditations, used to counter attachment to sensuality, contemplate the frailty of the body - sickness, old age and death - to develop a sense of disgust with it. Analytic meditations- which break down the body into either its anatomical component or in terms of traditional elements- are intended to develop in the practitioner a knowledge of anatman, the Buddhist principle that no permanent enduring self exists within the individual.

The Body and Desire "the engine for sex exemplifies ignorant craving quintessentially,". Furthermore, "Sexual desire traps us; it renders us slaves to pleasure, slaves to our partners, slaves to the body itself. And it never brings satisfaction; rather, sex causes conflict, burns the mind, and brings us into bad company." Sex can be seen as a primary reason of continuing samsara, after all, it did bring us into our discontented existence. Nonetheless, sex is not forbidden and Buddhists are aware that laymen and women will still have sex, so "A symbiotic relationship between the monastic order and lay adherents has characterized Buddhism from the beginning, with a dual sexual ethical track: Buddhism has traditionally held celibate monasticism in the highest regard, but it has also seen marriage and family life as highly suitable for those who cannot commit themselves to celibacy, and as an arena in which many worthwhile qualities are nurtured.". For the laypeople, some guidelines regarding normal, ethical sexual behavior can be found. For example, sex should only be between married couples, it should not be done on religious holidays or within the area of sacred shrines, and there are some examples of sexual misconduct, like oral and anal sex.

GENDER AND THE BODY

Divine and Supernatural Bodies

There are a number of issues relating to the body that, though given little attention in traditional Buddhist sources, have assumed significant importance in the modern world. Contemporary Buddhist views on these issues vary greatly between different cultures and individuals, and may combine the reinterpretation of traditional views with a variety of other influences.

Addiction

Buddhist scriptures talk a great deal about the general idea of attachment to sensual pleasures, but do not directly address the issue of substance addiction as it is understood in contemporary society. Jataka stories and certain rules governing lay and monastic behavior do discuss the use of alcohol and intoxicants.

Suicide

The issue of suicide can be difficult to trace seen the Buddha words were not stated on what he thought about this topic. In Buddhism, suicide can be seen as immoral act or it can be justify under certain circumstances. "The topic of suicide has been chosen not only for its intrinsic factual and historical interest but because it spotlights certain key issues in the field of Buddhist ethics and doctrine".

This raises a lot of question whether suicide is right or wrong in Buddhism or if the Buddha believed that suicide can be condoned. Some Buddhist may say that only the Enlighten can commit suicide. "(suicide) can be either right or wrong depending on the state of mind of the person who suicides: the presence of desire (or fear) makes it wrong, and the absence of desire (or fear) makes it right". The story of Channa is one of the strongest stories, which question whether suicide can be justified.

"Channa was an unenlightened person (puthujjana) who, afflicted by the pain and distress of a serious illness, took his own life. This story however, raises a lot of questions whether the Buddha condoned suicide." "Channa was not an arhat until the point of death those who suggests that suicide is wrong for a non- arhat would have to accept that Channa was wrong to commit the act". It is said that there are some Buddhist who commit suicide and then become enlighten when they are about to kill themselves. The only person that can commit suicide is a bodhisattva. A bodhisattva might risk life and limb for the good of others.

To seek one death or to make death one's aim)even when the motive is compassionate, directed toward reducing suffering) is to negate in the most fundamental way the values and final goal of Buddhism by destroying what the traditional sources call the "precious human life" we have the rare god fortune to obtain.. It is also said, that a person who commits suicide will simply be reborn with the additional bad karma of the suicide to contend with.

BUDDHISM AND PSYCHOLOGY

Buddhism and psychology overlap in theory and in practice. Over the last century, three strands of interplay have evolved:

- **Descriptive Phenomenology:** Western and Buddhist scholars have found in Buddhist teachings a detailed introspective phenomenological psychology (particularly in the *Abhidhamma*).
- **Psychotherapeutic Meaning:** Humanistic psychotherapists have found in Buddhism's non-dualistic approach and enlightenment experiences (such as in Zen *kensho*) the potential for transformation, healing and finding existential meaning.
- **Clinical Utility:** Contemporary mental-health practitioners increasingly find ancient Buddhist practices (such as the development of mindfulness) of empirically proven therapeutic value.

Mindstream

Psychology is the study of the Psyche often rendered in English as mind. The principal and central teaching of Buddha Dharma is the 'consciousness continuum' or the Mindstream. As Mañjuúrîmitra states in Verse 62 of the *Bodhicittabhavana*, a seminal early text of Ati Yoga, here rendered into English by Kunpal Tulku (1995: unpaginated):

Yet no phenomena exists for either ordinary people or for enlightened Saints other than the continuum (santana) of their own mind (citta).

In human experience, a particular station of sentient beings, all phenomena or dharmas are mediated through and by the mind[stream]. Importantly, mind as embodied in the cartesian dualism of mind and body does not exist in the Buddha Dharma and instead is replaced with the mindstream which may be conveyed in a traditional metaphorical relationship where the mindstream is the flame of the candle of the skandha: where in exegetical commentary, the flame never touches the wick of the candle.

Buddhism's Phenomenological Psychology

The establishment of Buddhism predates the field of psychology by over two millennia; thus, any assessment of Buddhism in terms of psychology is necessarily a modern invention. One of the first such assessments occurred when British Indologists started translating Theravada Buddhism's *Abhidhamma* from Pali and Sanskrit texts. Long-term efforts to juxtapose abhidhammic psychology with Western empirical sciences have been carried out by such Vajrayana leaders as Chogyam Trungpa Rinpoche and the 14th Dalai Lama.

The earliest Buddhist writings are preserved in the three-part *Tipitaka* (Pali; Skt. *Tripitaka*). The third part (or *pitaka*, literally "basket") is known as the *Abhidhamma* (Pali; Skt. *Abhidharma*). Ven. Bhikkhu Bodhi, president of the Buddhist Publication Society, has synopsized the Abhidhamma as follows:

"The system that the Abhidhamma Pitaka articulates is simultaneously a philosophy, a psychology, and an ethics, all integrated into the framework of a program for liberation.... The Abhidhamma's attempt to comprehend the nature of reality, contrary to that of classical science in the West, does not proceed from the standpoint of a neutral observer looking outwards towards the external world. The primary concern of the Abhidhamma is to understand the nature of experience, and thus the reality on which it focuses is conscious reality.

For this reason the philosophical enterprise of the Abhidhamma shades off into a phenomenological psychology. To facilitate the understanding of experienced reality, the Abhidhamma embarks upon an elaborate analysis of the mind as it presents itself to introspective meditation. It classifies consciousness into a variety of types, specifies the factors and functions of each type, correlates them with their objects and physiological bases, and shows how the different types of consciousness link up with each other and with material phenomena to constitute the ongoing process of experience."

Western recognition of the phenomenological-psychological aspect of the Abhidhamma started over a century ago with the work of British Indologists.

Rhys Davids' Early Scholarship (1900):

In 1900, Indologist Caroline A. F. Rhys Davids published through the Pali Text Society a translation of the Theravada Abhidhamma's first book, the Dhamma Sangani, and entitled the translation, "Buddhist Manual of Psychological Ethics". In the introduction to this seminal work, Rhys Davids writes:

"... Buddhist philosophy is ethical first and last. This is beyond dispute. But among ethical systems there is a world of difference in the degree of importance attached to the psychological prolegomena of ethics.... [T]he Buddhists were, in a way, more advanced in the psychology of their ethics than Aristotle — in a way, that is, which would now be called scientific. Rejecting the assumption of a psyche and of its higher manifestations..., they were content to resolve the consciousness of the Ethical Man, *as they found it*, into a complex continuum of subjective phenomena.... The distinguishable groups of dhammâ — of states or mental psychoses — 'arise' in every case in consciousness, in obedience to certain laws of causation, physical and moral — that is, ultimately, as the outcome of antecedent states of consciousness.... It postulated other percipients as Berkeley did, together with, not a Divine cause or source of precepts, but the implicit Monism of early thought veiled by a deliberate Agnosticism.... [S]o Buddhism, from a quite early stage of its development, set itself to analyze and classify mental processes with remarkable insight and sagacity...."

Buddhism's psychological orientation is a theme Rhys Davids pursued for decades as evidenced by Rhys Davids (1914) and Rhys Davids (1936).

Trungpa Rinpoche and the Naropa Institute (1974)

In his introduction to his 1975 book, *Glimpses of the Abhidharma*, Chogyam Trungpa Rinpoche wrote:

"Many modern psychologists have found that the discoveries and explanations of the abhidharma coincide with their own recent discoveries and new ideas; as though the abhidharma, which was taught 2,500 years ago, had been redeveloped in the modern idiom."

Trungpa Rinpoche's book goes on to describe the nanosecond phenomenological sequence by which a sensation becomes conscious using the Buddhist concepts of the "five aggregates."

In 1974, Trungpa Rinpoche founded the Naropa Institute, now called Naropa University. Since 1975, this accredited university has offered degrees in "contemplative psychology."

The Dalai Lama and the Mind and Life dialogues (1987)

Every two years, since 1987, the Dalai Lama has convened "Mind and Life" gatherings of Buddhists and scientists. Reflecting on one Mind and Life session in March 2000, psychologist Daniel Goleman notes:

"Since the time of Gautama Buddha in the fifth century BC, an analysis of the mind and its workings has been central to the practices of his followers. This analysis was codified during the first millennium after his death within the system called, in the Pali language of Buddha's day, Abhidhamma (or Abhidharma in Sanskrit), which means 'ultimate doctrine'.... Every branch of Buddhism today has a version of these basic psychological teachings on the mind, as well as its own refinements".

PSYCHOTHERAPY AND ENLIGHTENMENT

British barrister Christmas Humphreys has referred to mid-twentieth century collaborations between psychoanalysts and Buddhist scholars as a meeting between "two of the most powerful forces operating in the Western mind today." Ever since, a variety of renowned teachers, clinicians and writers such as D.T. Suzuki, Carl Jung, Erich Fromm, Alan Watts and Jack Kornfield have attempted to bridge and integrate psychology and Buddhism in a manner that offers meaning, inspiration and healing. More recently, some traditional Buddhist practitioners have expressed concern that attempts to view Buddhism through the lens of Western psychology diminish the Buddha's liberating message.

Suzuki & Jung (1948)

A number of psychologists have identified a pivotal collaboration between Buddhism and psychology was when psychoanalyst Carl Jung wrote the foreword to Zen scholar Daisetz Teitaro Suzuki's *Introduction to Zen Buddhism*, first published together in 1948. In his foreword, Jung highlights the enlightenment experience of *satori* as the unsurpassed transformation to wholeness for Zen practitioners. And while acknowledging the inadequacy of Westerners' attempts to comprehend *satori* through the lens of Western intellectualism, Jung nonetheless contends:

"The only movement within our culture which partly has, and partly should have, some understanding of these aspirations [for such enlightenment] is psychotherapy. It is therefore not a matter of chance that this foreword is written by a psychotherapist.... Taken basically, psychotherapy is a dialectic relationship between the doctor and the patient.... The goal is transformation....".

Suzuki & Fromm (1957)

Referencing Jung and Suzuki's collaboration as well as the efforts of others, humanistic philosopher and psychoanalyst Erich Fromm noted:

"...[T]here is an unmistakable and increasing interest in Zen Buddhism among psychoanalysts".

Suzuki, Fromm and other psychoanalysts collaborated at a 1957 workshop on "Zen Buddhism and Psychoanalysis" in Cuernavaca, Mexico. In his contribution to this workshop, Fromm declares: "Psychoanalysis is a characteristic expression of Western man's spiritual crisis, and an attempt to find a solution". Fromm contends that, at the turn of the twentieth century, most psychotherapeutic patients sought treatment due to medical-like symptoms that hindered their social functioning. However, by mid-century, the majority of psychoanalytic patients lacked overt symptoms and functioned well but instead suffered from an "inner deadness":

"The common suffering is the alienation from oneself, from one's fellow man, and from nature; the awareness that life runs out of one's hand like sand, and that one will die without having lived; that one lives in the midst of plenty and yet is joyless".

Paraphrasing Suzuki broadly, Fromm continues:

"Zen is the art of seeing into the nature of one's being; it is a way from bondage to freedom; it liberates our natural energies;... and it impels us to express our faculty for happiness and love.

"...[W]hat can be said with more certainty is that the knowledge of Zen, and a concern with it, can have a most fertile and clarifying influence on the theory and technique of psychoanalysis. Zen, different as it is in its method from psychoanalysis, can sharpen the focus, throw new light on the nature of insight, and heighten the sense of what it is to see, what it is to be creative, what it is to overcome the affective contaminations and false intellectualizations which are the necessary results of experience based on the subject-object split".

Mainstream teachers and popularizers

In 1961, Philosopher and Orientalist Alan Watts wrote:

"If we look deeply into such ways of life as Buddhism and Taoism, Vedanta and Yoga, we do not find either philosophy or religion as these are understood in the West. We find something more nearly resembling psychotherapy.... The main resemblance between these Eastern ways of life and Western psychotherapy is in the concern of both with bringing about changes of consciousness, changes in our ways of feeling our own existence and our relation to human society and the natural world. The psychotherapist has, for the most part, been interested in changing the consciousness of peculiarly disturbed individuals. The disciplines of Buddhism and Taoism are, however, concerned with changing the consciousness of normal, socially adjusted people."

Since Watts's early observations and musings, there have been many other important contributors to the contemporary popularization of the integration of Buddhist meditation with psychology including Kornfield (1993), Joseph Goldstein, Tara Brach, Epstein (1995) and Nhat Hanh (1998).

Caveats regarding "Romantic Buddhism"

Tracing the roots of modern Western spiritual ideals from German Romantic Era philosopher Immanuel Kant through American psychologist and philosopher William James, Jung and humanistic psychologist Abraham Maslow, Thanissaro Bhikkhu (*undated*) identifies broad commonalities between "Romantic/humanistic psychology" and early Buddhism: beliefs in human (versus divine) intervention with an approach that is experiential, pragmatic and therapeutic.

However, Thanissaro asserts that there are also core differences between Romantic/humanistic psychology and Buddhism. Thanissaro implicitly deems those who impose Romantic/humanistic goals on the Buddha's message as "Buddhist Romantics." Recognizing the widespread alienation and social fragmentation of modern life, Thanissaro Bhikkhu writes:

"When Buddhist Romanticism speaks to these needs, it opens the gate to areas of dharma [the Buddha's teachings] that can help many people find the solace they're looking for. In doing so, it augments the work of psychotherapy....

"However, Buddhist Romanticism also helps close the gate to areas of the dharma that would challenge people in their hope for an ultimate happiness based on interconnectedness. Traditional dharma calls for renunciation and sacrifice, on the grounds that all interconnectedness is essentially unstable, and any happiness based on this instability is an invitation to suffering. True happiness has to go beyond interdependence and interconnectedness to the unconditioned.... [T]he gate [of Buddhist Romanticism] closes off radical areas of the dharma designed to address levels of suffering remaining even when a sense of wholeness has been mastered."

Buddhist Techniques in Clinical Settings

For over a millennium, throughout the world, Buddhist practices have been used for non-Buddhist ends. More recently, Western clinical psychologists, theorists and researchers have incorporated Buddhist practices in widespread formalized psychotherapies. Buddhist mindfulness practices have been explicitly incorporated into a variety of psychological treatments. More tangentially, psychotherapies dealing with cognitive restructuring share core principles with ancient Buddhist antidotes to personal suffering.

Mindfulness Practices

Fromm distinguishes between two types of meditative techniques that have been used in psychotherapy:

1. Auto-suggestion used to induce relaxation; and,
2. Meditation "to achieve a higher degree of non-attachment, of non-greed, and of non-illusion; briefly, those that serve to reach a higher level of being".

Fromm attributes techniques associated with the latter to Buddhist mindfulness practices. Two increasingly popular therapeutic practices using Buddhist mindfulness techniques are Jon Kabat-Zinn's Mindfulness-based Stress Reduction (MBSR) and Marsha M. Linehan's Dialectical Behavioral Therapy (DBT). Other prominent therapies that use mindfulness include Steven C. Hayes' Acceptance and Commitment Therapy (ACT) and, based on MBSR, Mindfulness-based Cognitive Therapy (MBCT).

Mindfulness Based Stress Reduction (MBSR):

Kabat-Zinn developed the eight-week MBSR program over a ten year period with over four thousand patients at the University of Massachusetts Medical Center. Describing the MBSR program, Kabat-Zinn writes:

"This 'work' involves above all the regular, disciplined practice of moment-to-moment awareness or *mindfulness,* the complete 'owning' of each moment of your experience, good, bad, or ugly. This is the essence of full catastrophe living."

Kabat-Zinn, a one-time Zen practitioner, goes on to write:

"Although at this time mindfulness meditation is most commonly taught and practiced within the context of Buddhism, its essence is universal.... Yet it is no accident that mindfulness comes out of Buddhism, which has as its overriding concerns the relief of suffering and the dispelling of illusions."

Not surprisingly, in terms of clinical diagnoses, MBSR has proven beneficial for people with depression and anxiety disorders; however, the program is meant to serve anyone experiencing significant stress.

Dialectical Behavioral Therapy (DBT):

In writing about DBT, Zen practitioner Linehan states:

"As its name suggests, its overriding characteristic is an emphasis on 'dialectics' – that is, the reconciliation of opposites in a continual process of synthesis.... This emphasis on acceptance as a balance to change flows directly from the integration of a perspective drawn from Eastern (Zen) practice with Western psychological practice."

Similarly, Linehan writes:

"Mindfulness skills are central to DBT.... They are the first skills taught and are [reviewed]... every week.... The skills are psychological and behavioral versions of meditation practices from Eastern spiritual training. I have drawn most heavily from the practice of Zen...."

Controlled clinical studies have demonstrated DBT's effectiveness for people with borderline personality disorder.

Cognitive restructuring

Dr. Albert Ellis, considered the "grandfather of cognitive-behavioral therapy" (CBT), has written:

"Many of the principles incorporated in the theory of rational-emotive psychotherapy are not new; some of them, in fact, were originally stated several thousands of years ago, especially by the Greek and Roman Stoic philosophers (such as Epictetus and Marcus Aurelius) and by some of the ancient Taoist and Buddhist thinkers."

To give but one example, Buddhism identifies anger and ill-will as basic hindrances to spiritual development. A common Buddhist antidote for anger is the use of active contemplation of loving thoughts. This is similar to using a CBT technique known as "emotional training" which Ellis describes in the following manner:

"Think of an intensely pleasant experience you have had with the person with whom you now feel angry. When you have fantasized such a pleasant experience and have actually given yourself unusually good, intensely warm feelings toward that person as a result of this remembrance, continue the process. Recall pleasant experiences and good feelings, and try to make these feelings paramount over your feelings of hostility."

BUDDHARUPA

Buddharûpa is the Sanskrit and Pali term used in Buddhism for statues or models of the Buddha.

Commonalities

Despite cultural and regional differences in the interpretations of texts about the life of the Buddha, there are some general guidelines to the attributes of a Buddharupa:

- Fingers and toes are elongated proportionately
- Long, aquiline nose
- Elongated earlobes
- Head protuberance
- Broad shoulders

The elongated earlobes are vestiges of his life as a prince, when he wore extravagant jewellery. The "head protuberance" symbolises the loose connection between the mind and the body of a Buddha or Bodhisattva.

Regional Variations

From a gaunt, seated ascetic to a laughing big-bellied wanderer, depictions of the Buddha vary widely across cultures.

Proportions

The Buddharupas of India, Tibet, and the other Buddhist cultures usually depict a well proportioned figure, but sometimes he is shown emaciated, in recollection of the Buddha's years of ascetic practices. Japanese Buddharupas are often very square and stolid, while Indian and Southeast Asian ones often have thinner figures. Many Westerners are familiar with the Hotei "Happy" or "Laughing" Buddharupa. He is depicted as fat and happy, often travelling or bearing wealth. This is a Chinese image, and is in fact a Chinese Buddhist monk who so completely and totally embodied the buddha-nature of all sentient beings that he was himself considered to be a Buddha.

Postures, Gestures and Artefacts

He is sometimes shown reclining, recalling the Buddha Shakyamuni's departure into final nirvana. Sometimes he is holding various symbolic objects, or making symbolic mudras (gestures). The clothing also varies; in China and Japan, where it is considered socially improper for monks and nuns to expose the upper arm, the Buddharupa has a tunic and long sleeves, much like the traditional monks and nuns, while in India they are often topless.

JAPANESE ART

Japanese art covers a wide range of art styles and media, including ancient pottery, sculpture in wood and bronze, ink painting on silk and paper, and a myriad of other types of works of art. It also has a long history, ranging from the beginnings of human habitation in Japan, sometime in the 10th millennium BC, to the present. Historically, Japan has been subject to sudden invasions of new and alien ideas followed by long periods of minimal contact with the outside world. Over time the Japanese developed the ability to absorb, imitate, and finally assimilate those elements of foreign culture that complemented their aesthetic preferences.

The earliest complex art in Japan was produced in the 7th and 8th centuries A.D. in connection with Buddhism. In the 9th century, as the Japanese began to turn away from China and develop indigenous forms of expression, the secular arts became increasingly important; until the late 15th century, both religious and secular arts flourished. After the Ônin War (1467-1477), Japan entered a period of political, social, and economic disruption that lasted for over a century. In the state that emerged under the leadership of the Tokugawa shogunate, organized religion played a much less important role in people's lives, and the arts that survived were primarily secular.

Painting is the preferred artistic expression in Japan, practiced by amateurs and professionals alike. Until modern times, the Japanese wrote with a brush rather than a pen, and their familiarity with brush techniques has made them particularly sensitive to the values and aesthetics of painting. With the rise of popular culture in the Edo period, a style of woodblock prints called *ukiyo-e* became a major art form and its techniques were fine tuned to produce colorful prints of everything from daily news to schoolbooks. The Japanese, in this period, found sculpture a much less sympathetic medium for artistic expression; most Japanese sculpture is associated with religion, and the medium's use declined with the lessening importance of traditional Buddhism.

Japanese ceramics are among the finest in the world and include the earliest known artifacts of their culture. In architecture, Japanese preferences for natural materials and an interaction of interior and exterior space are clearly expressed. Today, Japan rivals most other modern nations in its contributions to modern art, fashion and architecture, with creations of a truly modern, global, and multi-cultural (or acultural) bent.

Jômon art

The first settlers of Japan, the Jômon people (c 11000?–c 300 BC), named for the cord markings that decorated the surfaces of their clay vessels, were nomadic hunter-gatherers who later practiced organized farming and built cities with population of hundreds if not thousands. They built simple houses of wood and thatch set into shallow earthen pits to provide warmth from the soil. They crafted lavishly decorated pottery storage vessels, clay figurines called *dogu*, and crystal jewels.

Yayoi art

The next wave of immigrants was the Yayoi people, named for the district in Tokyo where remnants of their settlements first were found. These people, arriving in Japan about 350 BC, brought their knowledge of wetland rice cultivation, the manufacture of copper weapons and bronze bells (*dôtaku*), and wheel-thrown, kiln-fired ceramics.

Kofun art

The third stage in Japanese prehistory, the Kofun, or Tumulus, period (c AD 250–552), represents a modification of Yayoi culture, attributable either to internal development or external force. In this period, diverse groups of people formed political alliances and coalesced into a nation. Typical artifacts are bronze mirrors, symbols of political alliances, and clay sculptures called *haniwa* which were erected outside tombs.

Asuka and Nara art

During the Asuka and Nara periods, so named because the seat of Japanese government was located in the Asuka Valley from 552 to 710 and in the city of Nara until 784, the first significant invasion by Asian continental culture took place in Japan. The transmission of Buddhism provided the initial impetus for contacts between China, Korea and Japan. The Japanese recognized the facets of Chinese culture that could profitably be incorporated into their own: a system for converting ideas and sounds into writing; historiography; complex theories of government, such as an effective bureaucracy; and, most important for the arts, new technologies, new building techniques, more advanced methods of casting in bronze, and new techniques and media for painting.

Throughout the 7th and 8th centuries, however, the major focus in contacts between Japan and the Asian continent was the development of Buddhism. Not all scholars agree on the significant dates and the appropriate names to apply to various time periods between 552, the official date of the introduction of Buddhism into Japan, and 784, when the Japanese capital was transferred from Nara. The most common designations are the Suiko period, 552–645; the Hakuhô period, 645–710, and the Tenpyô period, 710–784.

The earliest Japanese sculptures of the Buddha are dated to the 6th and 7th century. They ultimately derive from the 1st-3rd century CE Greco-Buddhist art of Gandhara, characterized by flowing dress patterns and realistic rendering, on which Chinese and Korean artistic traits were superimposed.These indigenous characteristics can be seen in early Buddhist art in Japan and some early Japanese Buddhist sculpture is now believed to have originated in Korea, particularly from Baekje, or Korean artisans who immigrated to Yamato Japan.

Particularly, the semi-seated Maitreya form was adapted into a highly developed Korean style which was transmitted to Japan as evidenced by the Kôryû-ji Miroku Bosatsu and the Chûgû-ji Siddhartha statues. Although many historians portray Korea as a mere transmitter of Buddhism, the Three Kingdoms, and particularly Baekje, were instrumental as active agents in the introduction and formation of a Buddhist tradition in Japan in 538 or 552. They illustrate the terminal point of the Silk Road transmission of Art during the first few centuries of our era. Other examples can be found in the development of the iconography of the Japanese Fujin Wind God, the Niôguardians, and the near-Classical floral patterns in temple decorations.

The earliest Buddhist structures still extant in Japan, and the oldest wooden buildings in the Far East are found at the Hôryû-ji to the southwest of Nara. First built in the early 7th century as the private temple of Crown Prince Shôtoku, it consists of 41 independent buildings. The most important ones, the main worship hall, or *Kondô* (Golden Hall), and *Gojû-no-tô* (Five-story Pagoda), stand in the center of an open area surrounded by a roofed cloister. The *Kondô*, in the style of Chinese worship halls, is a two-story structure of post-and-beam construction, capped by an *irimoya*, or hipped-gabled roof of ceramic tiles.

Inside the *Kondô*, on a large rectangular platform, are some of the most important sculptures of the period. The central image is a Shaka Trinity (623), the historical Buddha flanked by two bodhisattvas, sculpture cast in bronze by the sculptor Tori Busshi (flourished early 7th century) in homage to the recently deceased Prince Shôtoku. At the four corners of the platform are the Guardian Kings of the Four Directions, carved in wood around 650. Also housed at Hôryû-ji is the Tamamushi Shrine, a wooden replica of a *Kondô*, which is set on a high wooden base that is decorated with figural paintings executed in a medium of mineral pigments mixed with lacquer.

Temple building in the 8th century was focused around the Tôdai-ji in Nara. Constructed as the headquarters for a network of temples in each of the provinces, the Tôdaiji is the most ambitious religious complex erected in the early centuries of Buddhist worship in Japan. Appropriately, the 16.2-m (53-ft) Buddha (completed 752) enshrined in the main Buddha hall, or *Daibutsuden*, is a Rushana Buddha, the figure that represents the essence of Buddhahood, just as the Tôdaiji represented the center for Imperially sponsored Buddhism and its dissemination throughout Japan. Only a few fragments of the original statue survive, and the present hall and central Buddha are reconstructions from the Edo period.

Clustered around the Daibutsuden on a gently sloping hillside are a number of secondary halls: the *Hokke-dô* (Lotus Sutra Hall), with its principal image, the Fukukenjaku Kannon (the most popular bodhisattva), crafted of dry lacquer (cloth dipped in lacquer and shaped over a wooden armature); the *Kaidanin* (Ordination Hall) with its magnificent clay statues of the Four Guardian Kings; and the storehouse, called the *Shôsôin*. This last structure is of great importance as an art-historical cache, because in it are stored the utensils that were used in the temple's dedication ceremony in 752, the eye-opening ritual for the Rushana image, as well as government documents and many secular objects owned by the Imperial family.

Heian art

In 794 the capital of Japan was officially transferred to Heian-kyô (present-day Kyoto), where it remained until 1868. The term *Heian period* refers to the years between 794 and 1185, when the Kamakura shogunate was established at the end of the Genpei War. The period is further divided into the early Heian and the late Heian, or Fujiwara era, the pivotal date being 894, the year imperial embassies to China were officially discontinued.

Early Heian art: In reaction to the growing wealth and power of organized Buddhism in Nara, the priest Kûkai (best known by his posthumous title Kôbô Daishi, 774-835) journeyed to China to study Shingon, a form of Vajrayana Buddhism, which he introduced into Japan in 806. At the core of Shingon worship are mandalas, diagrams of the spiritual universe, which then began to influence temple design. Japanese Buddhist architecture also adopted the stupa, originally an Indian architectural form, in its Chinese-style pagoda.

The temples erected for this new sect were built in the mountains, far away from the Court and the laity in the capital. The irregular topography of these sites forced Japanese architects to rethink the problems of temple construction, and in so doing to choose more indigenous elements of design. Cypress-bark roofs replaced those of ceramic tile, wood planks were used instead of earthen floors, and a separate worship area for the laity was added in front of the main sanctuary.

The temple that best reflects the spirit of early Heian Shingon temples is the Murô-ji (early 9th century), set deep in a stand of cypress trees on a mountain southeast of Nara. The wooden image (also early 9th c.) of Shakyamuni, the "historic" Buddha, enshrined in a secondary building at the Murô-ji, is typical of the early Heian sculpture, with its ponderous body, covered by thick drapery folds carved in the *hòmpa-shiki* (rolling-wave) style, and its austere, withdrawn facial expression.

Fujiwara art: In the Fujiwara period, Pure Land Buddhism, which offered easy salvation through belief in Amida (the Buddha of the Western Paradise), became popular. This period is named after the Fujiwara family, then the most powerful in the country, who ruled as regents for the Emperor, becoming, in effect, civil dictators. Concurrently, the Kyoto nobility developed a society devoted to elegant aesthetic pursuits. So secure and beautiful was their world that they could not conceive of Paradise as being much different. They created a new form of Buddha hall, the Amida hall, which blends the secular with the religious, and houses one or more Buddha images within a structure resembling the mansions of the nobility.

The *Hô-ô-dô* (Phoenix Hall, completed 1053) of the Byôdôin, a temple in Uji to the southeast of Kyoto, is the exemplar of Fujiwara Amida halls. It consists of a main rectangular structure flanked by two L-shaped wing corridors and a tail corridor, set at the edge of a large artificial pond. Inside, a single golden image of Amida (c. 1053) is installed on a high platform. The Amida sculpture was executed by Jôchô, who used a new canon of proportions and a new technique (*yosegi*), in which multiple pieces of wood are carved out like shells and joined from the inside.

Applied to the walls of the hall are small relief carvings of celestials, the host believed to have accompanied Amida when he descended from the Western Paradise to gather the souls of believers at the moment of death and transport them in lotus blossoms to Paradise. *Raigô* paintings on the wooden doors of the Hô-ô-dô, depicting the Descent of the Amida Buddha, are an early example of Yamato-e, Japanese-style painting, and contain representations of the scenery around Kyoto.

E-maki: In the last century of the Heian period, the horizontal, illustrated narrative handscroll, known as *e-maki* ("picture scroll"), came to the fore. Dating from about 1130, the illustrated 'Tale of Genji' represents one of the high points of Japanese painting. Written about the year 1000 by Murasaki Shikibu, a lady-in-waiting to the Empress Akiko, the novel deals with the life and loves of Genji and the world of the Heian court after his death.

The 12th-century artists of the *e-maki* version devised a system of pictorial conventions that convey visually the emotional content of each scene. In the second half of the century, a different, livelier style of continuous narrative illustration became popular. The *Ban Dainagon Ekotoba* (late 12th century), a scroll that deals with an intrigue at court, emphasizes figures in active motion depicted in rapidly executed brush strokes and thin but vibrant colors. *E-maki* also serve as some of the earliest and greatest examples of the *otoko-e* (Men's pictures) and *onna-e* (Women's pictures) styles of painting.

There are many fine differences in the two styles, appealing to the aesthetic preferences of the genders. But perhaps most easily noticeable are the differences in subject matter. *Onna-e*, epitomized by the Tale of Genji handscroll, typically deals with court life, particularly the court ladies, and with romantic themes. *Otoko-e*, on the other hand, often recorded historical events, particularly battles. The Siege of the Sanjô Palace (1160), depicted in the "Night

Attack on the Sanjô Palace" section of the Heiji Monogatari handscroll is a famous example of this style.

Kamakura art

In 1180 a war broke out between the two most powerful warrior clans, the Taira and the Minamoto; five years later the Minamoto emerged victorious and established a de facto seat of government at the seaside village of Kamakura, where it remained until 1333. With the shift of power from the nobility to the warrior class, the arts had to satisfy a new audience: men devoted to the skills of warfare, priests committed to making Buddhism available to illiterate commoners, and conservatives, the nobility and some members of the priesthood who regretted the declining power of the court. Thus, realism, a popularizing trend, and a classical revival characterize the art of the Kamakura period.

Sculpture: The Kei school of sculptors, particularly Unkei, created a new, more realistic style of sculpture. The two Niô guardian images (1203) in the Great South Gate of the Tôdai-ji in Nara illustrate Unkei's dynamic supra-realistic style. The images, about 8 m (about 26 ft) tall, were carved of multiple blocks in a period of about three months, a feat indicative of a developed studio system of artisans working under the direction of a master sculptor. Unkei's polychromed wood sculptures (1208, Kôfuku-ji, Nara) of two Indian sages, Muchaku and Seshin, the legendary founders of the Hossô sect, are among the most accomplished realistic works of the period; as rendered by Unkei, they are remarkably individualized and believable images.

Calligraphy and painting: The *Kegon Engi Emaki*, the illustrated history of the founding of the Kegon sect, is an excellent example of the popularizing trend in Kamakura painting. The Kegon sect, one of the most important in the Nara period, fell on hard times during the ascendancy of the Pure Land sects. After the Genpei War (1180-1185), Priest Myôe of Kôzan-ji sought to revive the sect and also to provide a refuge for women widowed by the war.

The wives of samurai had been discouraged from learning more than a syllabary system for transcribing sounds and ideas, and most were incapable of reading texts that employed Chinese ideographs (kanji). Thus, the *Kegon Engi Emaki* combines passages of text, written with a maximum of easily readable syllables, and illustrations that have the dialogue between characters written next to the speakers, a technique comparable to contemporary comic strips. The plot of the *e-maki*, the lives of the two Korean priests who founded the Kegon sect, is swiftly paced and filled with fantastic feats such as a journey to the palace of the Ocean King, and a poignant love story.

A work in a more conservative vein is the illustrated version of Murasaki Shikibu's diary. *E-maki* versions of her novel continued to be produced, but the nobility, attuned to the new interest in realism yet nostalgic for past days of wealth and power, revived and illustrated the diary in order to recapture the splendor of the author's times. One of the most beautiful passages illustrates the episode in which Murasaki Shikibu is playfully held prisoner in her room by two young courtiers, while, just outside, moonlight gleams on the mossy banks of a rivulet in the imperial garden.

Muromachi art

During the Muromachi period (1338-1573), also called the Ashikaga period, a profound change took place in Japanese culture. The Ashikaga clan took control of the shogunate and moved its headquarters back to Kyoto, to the Muromachi district of the city. With the return of government to the capital, the popularizing trends of the Kamakura period came to an end, and cultural expression took on a more aristocratic, elitist character. Zen Buddhism, the Ch'an sect0traditionally thought to have been founded in China in the 6th century CE, was introduced for a second time into Japan and took root.

Painting: Because of secular ventures and trading missions to China organized by Zen temples, many Chinese paintings and objects of art were imported into Japan and profoundly influenced

Japanese artists working for Zen temples and the shogunate. Not only did these imports change the subject matter of painting, but they also modified the use of color; the bright colors of Yamato-e yielded to the monochromes of painting in the Chinese manner, where paintings generally only have black and white or different tones of a single color.

Typical of early Muromachi painting is the depiction by the priest-painter Kao (active early 15th century) of the legendary monk Kensu (Hsien-tzu in Chinese) at the moment he achieved enlightenment. This type of painting was executed with quick brush strokes and a minimum of detail. 'Catching a Catfish with a Gourd' (early 15th century, Taizo-in, Myoshin-ji, Kyoto), by the priest-painter Josetsu (active c. 1400), marks a turning point in Muromachi painting. Executed originally for a low-standing screen, it has been remounted as a hanging scroll with inscriptions by contemporary figures above, one of which refers to the painting as being in the "new style."

In the foreground a man is depicted on the bank of a stream holding a small gourd and looking at a large slithery catfish. Mist fills the middle ground, and the Background Mountains appear to be far in the distance. It is generally assumed that the "new style" of the painting, executed about 1413, refers to a more Chinese sense of deep space within the picture plane. The foremost artists of the Muromachi period are the priest-painters Shubun and Sesshu. Shubun, a monk at the Kyoto temple of Shokoku-ji, created in the painting 'Reading in a Bamboo Grove' (1446) a realistic landscape with deep recession into space. Sesshu, unlike most artists of the period, was able to journey to China and study Chinese painting at its source. 'The Long Handscroll' is one of Sesshu's most accomplished works, depicting a continuing landscape through the four seasons.

Azuchi-Momoyama art

In the Momoyama period (1573-1603), a succession of military leaders, such as Oda Nobunaga, Toyotomi Hideyoshi, and

Tokugawa Ieyasu, attempted to bring peace and political stability to Japan after an era of almost 100 years of warfare. Oda, a minor chieftain, acquired power sufficient to take de facto control of the government in 1568 and, five years later, to oust the last Ashikaga shogun. Hideyoshi took command after Oda's death, but his plans to establish hereditary rule were foiled by Ieyasu, who established the Tokugawa shogunate in 1603.

Painting: The most important school of painting in the Momoyama period was that of the Kanô school, and the greatest innovation of the period was the formula, developed by Kano Eitoku, for the creation of monumental landscapes on the sliding doors enclosing a room. The decoration of the main room facing the garden of the Juko-in, a subtemple of Daitoku-ji (a Zen temple in Kyoto), is perhaps the best extant example of Eitoku's work. A massive *ume* tree and twin pines are depicted on pairs of sliding screens in diagonally opposite corners, their trunks repeating the verticals of the corner posts and their branches extending to left and right, unifying the adjoining panels. Eitoku's screen, 'Chinese Lions', also in Kyoto, reveals the bold, brightly colored style of painting preferred by the samurai.

Hasegawa Tohaku, a contemporary of Eitoku, developed a somewhat different and more decorative style for large-scale screen paintings. In his 'Maple Screen', now in the temple of Chishaku-in, Kyoto, he placed the trunk of the tree in the center and extended the limbs nearly to the edge of the composition, creating a flatter, less architectonic work than Eitoku, but a visually gorgeous painting. His sixfold screen, 'Pine Wood', is a masterly rendering in monochrome ink of a grove of trees enveloped in mist.

Art of the Edo period

The Tokugawa shogunate of the Edo period gained undisputed control of the government in 1603 with a commitment to bring peace and economic and political stability to the country; in large measure it was successful. The shogunate survived until 1867, when it was forced to capitulate because of its failure to deal with pressure from Western nations to open the country to foreign trade. One of the dominant themes in the Edo period was the repressive policies of the shogunate and the attempts of artists to escape these strictures.

The foremost of these was the closing of the country to foreigners and the accoutrements of their cultures, and the imposition of strict codes of behavior affecting every aspect of life, the clothes one wore, the person one married, and the activities one could or should not pursue. In the early years of the Edo period, however, the full impact of Tokugawa policies had not yet been felt, and some of Japan's finest expressions in architecture and painting were produced: Katsura Palace in Kyoto and the paintings of Tawaraya Sôtatsu, pioneer of the Rimpa school.

Architecture: Katsura Detached Palace, built in imitation of Genji's palace, contains a cluster of shoin buildings that combine elements of classic Japanese architecture with innovative restatements. The whole complex is surrounded by a beautiful garden with paths for walking.

Painting: Sôtatsu evolved a superb decorative style by re-creating themes from classical literature, using brilliantly colored figures and motifs from the natural world set against gold-leaf backgrounds. One of his finest works is the pair of screens The Waves at Matsushima in the Freer Gallery in Washington, D.C. A century later, Korin reworked Sôtatsu's style and created visually gorgeous works uniquely his own. Perhaps his finest are the screen paintings of red and white plum blossoms.

Sculpture The Buddhist monk Enkû carved 120,000 Buddhist images in a rough, individual style.

Woodblock prints and Bunjinga: The school of art best known in the West is that of the ukiyo-e paintings and woodblock prints of the demimonde, the world of the kabuki theater and the brothel district. Ukiyo-e prints began to be produced in the late 17th century, but in 1764 Harunobu produced the first polychrome print.

Print designers of the next generation, including Torii Kiyonaga and Utamaro, created elegant and sometimes insightful depictions of courtesans. In the West, erotic woodblock "prints" became popular because the material was not otherwise available. In that sense, such niche prints did more to promote Japanese art in the West than art studies.

In the 19th century the dominant figure was Hiroshige, a creator of romantic and somewhat sentimental landscape prints. The odd angles and shapes through which Hiroshige often viewed landscape, and the work of Kiyonaga and Utamaro, with its emphasis on flat planes and strong linear outlines, had a profound impact on such Western artists as Edgar Degas and Vincent van Gogh.

Another school of painting contemporary with ukiyo-e was Bunjinga, a style based on paintings executed by Chinese scholar-painters. Just as ukiyo-e artists chose to depict figures from life outside the strictures of the Tokugawa shogunate, Bunjin artists turned to Chinese culture. The exemplars of this style are Ike no Taiga, Yosa Buson, Tanomura Chikuden, and Yamamoto Baiitsu.

Meiji art

In the years after 1867, when Emperor Meiji ascended the throne, Japan was once again invaded by new and alien forms of culture. The introduction of Western cultural values led to a dichotomy in Japanese art, as well as in nearly every other aspect of culture, between traditional values and attempts to duplicate and assimilate a variety of clashing new ideas. This split remained evident in the late twentieth century, although much synthesis had by then already occurred, and created an international cultural atmosphere and stimulated contemporary Japanese arts toward ever more innovative forms.

By the early 20th century, European art forms were well introduced and their marriage produced notable buildings like the Tokyo Train Station and the National Diet Building that still exist today. Manga were first drawn in the Meiji period, influenced greatly by English and French political cartoons.

Painting: The first response of the Japanese to Western art forms was open-hearted acceptance, and in 1876 the Technological Art School was opened, employing Italian instructors to teach Western methods. The second response was a pendulum swing in the opposite direction spearheaded by Okakura Kakuzo and the American Ernest Fenollosa, who encouraged Japanese artists to retain traditional themes and techniques while creating works more in keeping with contemporary taste. Out of these two poles of artistic theory developed Yôga (Western-style painting) and Nihonga (Japanese painting), categories that remain valid to the present day.

Postwar period

After World War II, many artists began working in art forms derived from the international scene, moving away from local artistic developments into the mainstream of world art. But traditional Japanese conceptions endured, particularly in the use of modular space in architecture, certain spacing intervals in music and dance, a propensity for certain color combinations and characteristic literary forms. The wide variety of art forms available to the Japanese reflect the vigorous state of the arts, widely supported by the Japanese people and promoted by the government.

In the 1950s and 1960s, Japan's artistic avant garde included the internationally influential Gutai group, which originated or anticipated various postwar genres such as performance art, installation art, conceptual art, and wearable art. American art and architecture greatly influenced Japan. Though fear of earthquakes severely restricted the building of a skyscraper, technological advances let Japanese build larger and higher buildings with more artistic outlooks.

As Japan has always made little distinction between 'fine art' and 'decorative art', as the West is first beginning to do, it is important to note Japan's significant and unique contributions to the fields of art in entertainment, commercial uses, and graphic design. Cartoons imported from America led to anime that at first were derived exclusively from manga stories.

Today, anime abounds, and many artists and studios have risen to great fame as artists; Hayao Miyazaki and the artists and animators of Studio Ghibli are generally regarded to be among the best the anime world has to offer. Japan also flourishes in the fields of graphic design, commercial art (e.g. billboards, magazine advertisements), and in video game graphics and concept art.

Contemporary art in Japan

Japanese modern art takes as many forms and expresses as many different ideas as modern art in general, worldwide. It ranges from advertisements, anime, video games, and architecture as already mentioned, to sculpture, painting, and drawing in all their myriad forms. Many artists do continue to paint in the traditional manner, with black ink and color on paper or silk. Some of these depict traditional subject matter in the traditional styles, while others explore new and different motifs and styles, while using the traditional media. Still others eschew native media and styles, embracing Western oil paints or any number of other forms.

In sculpture, the same holds true; some artists stick to the traditional modes, some doing it with a modern flair, and some choose Western or brand new modes, styles, and media. Yo Akiyama is just one of countless modern Japanese sculptors. He works primarily in clay pottery and ceramics, creating works that are very simple and straightforward, looking like they were created out of the earth itself. Another sculptor, using iron and other modern materials, built a large modern art sculpture in the Israeli port city of Haifa, called *Hanabi* (Fireworks).

Takashi Murakami is arguably one of the most well-known Japanese modern artists in the Western world. Murakami and the other artists in his studio create pieces in a style, inspired by anime, which he has dubbed "superflat". His pieces take a multitude of forms, from painting to sculpture, some truly massive in size. But most if not all show very clearly this anime influence, utilizing bright colors and simplified details.

Performing arts

A remarkable number of the traditional forms of Japanese music, dance, and theater have survived in the contemporary world, enjoying some popularity through reidentification with Japanese cultural values. Traditional music and dance, which trace their origins to ancient religious use - Buddhist, Shintô, and folk - have been preserved in the dramatic performances of Noh, Kabuki, and bunraku theater.

Ancient court music and dance forms deriving from continental sources were preserved through Imperial household musicians and temple and shrine troupes. Some of the oldest musical instruments in the world have been in continuous use in Japan from the Jômon period, as shown by finds of stone and clay flutes and zithers having between two and four strings, to which Yayoi period metal bells and gongs were added to create early musical ensembles. By the early historical period (sixth to seventh centuries CE), there were a variety of large and small drums, gongs, chimes, flutes, and stringed instruments, such as the imported mandolin-like biwa and the flat six-stringed zither, which evolved into the thirteen-stringed koto.

These instruments formed the orchestras for the seventh-century continentally derived ceremonial court music (gagaku), which, together with the accompanying bugaku (a type of court dance), are the most ancient of such forms still performed at the Imperial court, ancient temples, and shrines. Buddhism introduced the rhythmic chants, still used, that underpin Shigin, and that were joined with native ideas to underlay the development of vocal music, such as in Noh.

Aesthetic concepts

Japanese art is characterized by unique polarities. In the ceramics of the prehistoric periods, for example, exuberance was followed by disciplined and refined artistry. Another instance is provided by two 16th-century structures that are poles apart: the Katsura Detached Palace is an exercise in simplicity, with an emphasis on natural materials, rough and untrimmed, and an affinity for beauty achieved by accident; Nikkô Tôshô-gû is a rigidly symmetrical structure replete with brightly colored relief carvings covering every visible surface. Japanese art, valued not only for its simplicity but also for its colorful exuberance, has considerably influenced 19th-century Western painting and 20th century Western architecture.

Japan's aesthetic conceptions, deriving from diverse cultural traditions, have been formative in the production of unique art forms. Over the centuries, a wide range of artistic motifs developed and were refined, becoming imbued with symbolic significance. Like a pearl, they acquired many layers of meaning and a high luster. Japanese aesthetics provide a key to understanding artistic works perceivably different from those coming from Western traditions. Within the East Asian artistic tradition, China has been the acknowledged teacher and Japan thc devoted student.

Nevertheless, several Japanese arts developed their own style, which can be differentiated from various Chinese arts. The monumental, symmetrically balanced, rational approach of Chinese art forms became miniaturized, irregular, and subtly suggestive in Japanese hands. Miniature rock gardens, diminutive plants (*bonsai*), and *ikebana* (flower arrangements), in which the selected few represented a garden, were the favorite pursuits of refined aristocrats for a millennium, and they have remained a part of contemporary cultural life. The diagonal, reflecting a natural flow, rather than the fixed triangle, became the favored structural device, whether in painting, architectural or garden design, dance steps, or musical notations.

Odd numbers replace even numbers in the regularity of a Chinese master pattern, and a pull to one side allows a motif to turn the corner of a three-dimensional object, thus giving continuity and motion that is lacking in a static frontal design. Japanese painters used the devices of the cutoff, close-up, and fade-out by the twelfth century in *yamato-e*, or Japanese-style, scroll painting, perhaps one reason why modern filmmaking has been such a natural and successful art form in Japan.

Suggestion is used rather than direct statement; oblique poetic hints and allusive and inconclusive melodies and thoughts have proved frustrating to the Westerner trying to penetrate the meanings of literature, music, painting, and even everyday language. The Japanese began defining such aesthetic ideas in a number of evocative phrases by at least the tenth or eleventh century. The courtly refinements of the aristocratic Heian period evolved into the elegant simplicity seen as the essence of good taste in the understated art that is called *shibui*.

Two terms originating from Zen Buddhist meditative practices describe degrees of tranquility: one, the repose found in humble melancholy (*wabi*), the other, the serenity accompanying the enjoyment of subdued beauty (*sabi*). Zen thought also contributed a penchant for combining the unexpected or startling, used to jolt one's consciousness toward the goal of enlightenment. In art, this approach was expressed in combinations of such unlikely materials as lead inlaid in lacquer and in clashing poetic imagery. Unexpectedly humorous and sometimes grotesque images and motifs also stem from the Zen *koan* (conundrum). Although the arts have been mainly secular since the Tokugawa period, traditional aesthetics and training methods, stemming generally from religious sources, continue to underlie artistic productions.

Artists

Traditionally, the artist was a vehicle for expression and was personally reticent, in keeping with the role of an artisan or entertainer of low social status. The calligrapher, a member of the Confucian literati class, or noble samurai class in Japan, had a higher status, while artists of great genius were often recognized in the Kamakura period by receiving a name from a feudal lord and thus rising socially. The performing arts, however, were generally held in less esteem, and the purported immorality of actresses of the early Kabuki theater caused the Tokugawa government to bar women from the stage; female roles in Kabuki and Noh thereafter were played by men.

After World War II, artists typically gathered in arts associations, some of which were long-established professional societies while others reflected the latest arts movement. The Japan Artists League, for example, was responsible for the largest number of major exhibitions, including the prestigious annual Nitten (Japan Art Exhibition). The P.E.N. Club of Japan (P.E.N. stands for prose, essay, and narrative), a branch of an international writers' organization, was the largest of some thirty major authors' associations. Actors, dancers, musicians, and other performing artists boasted their own societies, including the Kabuki Society, organized in 1987 to maintain this art's traditional high standards, which were thought to be endangered by modern innovation. By the 1980s, however, avant-garde painters and sculptors had eschewed all groups and were "unattached" artists.

Art Schools

There are a number of specialized universities for the arts in Japan, led by the national universities. The most important is the Tokyo Arts University, one of the most difficult of all national universities to enter. Another seminal center is Tama Arts University in Tokyo, which produced many of Japan's late twentieth- century innovative young artists. Traditional training in the arts, derived from Chinese traditional methods, remains; experts teach from their homes or head schools working within a master-pupil relationship. A pupil does not experiment with a personal style until achieving the highest level of training, or graduating from an arts school, or becoming head of a school. Many young artists have criticized this system as stifling creativity and individuality.

A new generation of the avant-garde has broken with this tradition, often receiving its training in the West. In the traditional arts, however, the master-pupil system preserves the secrets and skills of the past. Some master-pupil lineages can be traced to the Kamakura period, from which they continue to use a great master's style or theme. Japanese artists consider technical virtuosity as the *sine qua non* of their professions, a fact recognized by the rest of the world as one of the hallmarks of Japanese art. The national government has actively supported the arts through the Agency for Cultural Affairs, set up in 1968 as a special body of the Ministry of Education.

The agency's budget for FY 1989 rose to åÿ37.8 billion after five years of budget cuts, but still represented much less than 1 percent of the general budget. The agency's Cultural Affairs Division disseminated information about the arts within Japan and internationally, and the Cultural Properties Protection Division protected the nation's cultural heritage. The Cultural Affairs Division is concerned with such areas as art and culture promotion, arts copyrights, and improvements in the national language. It also supports both national and local arts and cultural festivals, and it funds traveling cultural events in music, theater, dance, art exhibitions, and filmmaking.

Special prizes are offered to encourage young artists and established practitioners, and some grants are given each year to enable them to train abroad. The agency funds national museums of modern art in Kyoto and Tokyo and the Museum of Western Art in Tokyo, which exhibit both Japanese and international shows. The agency also supports the Japan Academy of Arts, which honors eminent persons of arts and letters, appointing them to membership and offering åÿ3.5 million in prize money. Awards are made in the presence of the Emperor, who personally bestows the highest accolade, the Cultural Medal.

Private Sponsorship and Foundations

Arts patronage and promotion by the government are broadened to include a new cooperative effort with corporate Japan to provide funding beyond the tight budget of the Agency for

Cultural Affairs. Many other public and private institutions participate, especially in the burgeoning field of awarding arts prizes. A growing number of large corporations join major newspapers in sponsoring exhibitions and performances and in giving yearly prizes. The most important of the many literary awards given are the venerable Naoki Prize and the Akutagawa Prize, the latter being the equivalent of the Pulitzer Prize in the United States.

In 1989 an effort to promote cross-cultural exchange led to the establishment of a Japanese "Nobel Prize" for the arts, the Premium Imperiale, by the Japan Art Association. This prize of US$100,000 was funded largely by the mass media conglomerate Fuji-Sankei and was awarded on a worldwide selection basis. A number of foundations promoting the arts arose in the 1980s, including the Cultural Properties Foundation set up to preserve historic sites overseas, especially along the Silk Road in Inner Asia and at Dunhuang in China. Another international arrangement was made in 1988 with the United States Smithsonian Institution for cooperative exchange of high-technology studies of Asian artifacts.

The government plays a major role by funding the Japan Foundation, which provides both institutional and individual grants, effects scholarly exchanges, awards annual prizes, supported publications and exhibitions, and sends traditional Japanese arts groups to perform abroad. The Arts Festival held for two months each fall for all the performing arts is sponsored by the Agency for Cultural Affairs. Major cities also provides substantial support for the arts; a growing number of cities in the 1980s had built large centers for the performing arts and, stimulated by government funding, were offering prizes such as the Lafcadio Hearn Prize initiated by the city of Matsue.

A number of new municipal museums were also providing about one-third more facilities in the 1980s than were previously available. In the late 1980s, Tokyo added more than twenty new cultural halls, notably, the large Cultural Village built by Tokyo

Corporation and the reconstruction of Shakespeare's Globe Theatre. All these efforts reflect a rising popular enthusiasm for the arts. Japanese art buyers swept the Western art markets in the late 1980s, paying record highs for impressionist paintings and US$51.7 million alone for one blue period Picàsso.

Sacred art

Sacred art is imagery intended to uplift the mind to the spiritual. It can be an object to be venerated not for what it is but for what it represents; Catholics are taught that such venerated objects are more properly called sacramentals. Some Christians are still taught to regard all non-Christian cult images as "idols" that are worshiped in and of themselves, and do not consider them as "sacred art". The use of art in religion is essential, as it symbolizes understanding and feelings that words simply can't describe.

Christian European sacred art

This picture is about the Virgin Mary holding her child, Jesus commissioned by the Catholic Church during the Renaissance. It was during this time that Michelangelo Buonarotti painted the Sistine Chapel and carved the famous *Pietà*, Gianlorenzo Bernini created the massive columns in St. Peter's Basilica, and Leonardo da Vinci painted the *Last Supper*. Most Christian art is allusive, or built around themes familiar to the intended observer. One of the most common Christian themes is that of the Virgin Mary holding the infant Jesus. Another is that of Christ on the Cross.

For the benefit of the illiterate, an elaborate iconographic system developed to conclusively identify scenes: Saint Agnes depicted with a lamb, Saint Peter with keys, Saint Patrick with a shamrock. Each saint holds or is associated with attributes and symbols in sacred art. The genre of sacred art has lost much of its vigor since the Renaissance, but the themes are still popular, a 20th century example being Salvador Dalí's *Crucifixion* or the mystical image of *Corpus Hypercubus. After the Second World War some fine work was presented by major French artists* following the impuls of Father Marie-Alain Couturier: the Vence Chapel, the Église Notre-Dame de Toute Grâce du Plateau d'Assy, the Église du Sacré Cœur d'Audincourt.

Tibetan Buddhist Sacred art

Most Tibetan Buddhist artforms are related to the practice of Vajrayana or Buddhist tantra. Tibetan art includes thangkas and mandalas, often including depictions of Buddhas and bodhisattvas. Creation of Buddhist art is usually done as a meditation as well as creating an object as aid to meditation.

An example of this is the creation of a sand mandala by monks; before and after the construction prayers are recited, and the form of the mandala represents the pure surroundings (palace) of a Buddha on which is meditated to train the mind. The work is rarely, if ever, signed by t he artist. Other Tibetan Buddhist art includes metal ritual objects, such as the vajra and the phurba.

Islamic Sacred art

Because of the strict injunctions against such depictions of humans or animals which might result in idol-worship, Islamic art developed a unique character, utilizing a number of primary forms: geometric, arabesque, floral, and calligraphic, which are often interwoven. From early times, Muslim art has reflected this balanced, harmonious world-view. It focuses on spiritual essence rather than physical form. It offers no pictures of saints or illustrations of stories from the Qur'an, but rather expresses fundamental concepts such as the infinite nature of God through repetitive geometric designs without beginning or end.

BIBLIOGRAPHY

Auboyer, Jeannine, *Buddha: A Pictorial History of His Life and Legacy.* New York: Crossroad, 1983.

Bapat, P. V., ed., *2500 Years of Buddhism.* New Delhi: Government of India, Publications Division, 1956.

Basham, A. L., *History and Doctrines of the Ajivikas.* London: Luzac, 1951.

.............., *The Wonder That Was India.* New York: Grove Press, 1959.

Bechert, Heinz and Richard Gombrich, eds., *The World of Buddhism: Monks and Nuns in Society and Culture.* London: Thames and Hudson, 1984.

Cabezon, Jose Ignacia, ed., *Buddhism, Sexuality, and Gender.* Albany: SUNY Press, 1992.

Charles S. Prebish, ed., *Buddhism: A Modern Perspective.* University Park: Pennsylvania State University Press, 1975.

Conze, Edward, *Buddhism: Its Essence and Development.* New York: Harper Torchbooks, 1965.

..............., *Buddhist Scriptures.* Baltimore: Penguin, 1959.

............, *Buddhist Thought in India.* Ann Arbor: University of Michigan Press, 1967.

Conze, Edward, ed., *Buddhist Texts through the Ages.* New York: Harper Torchbooks, 1964.

Horner, I. B., *The Living Thoughts of Gotama the Buddha.* London: Cassell, 1948.

Jayatilleke, K. N., *Early Buddhist Theory of Knowledge.* London: George Allen & Unwin, 1963.

Joseph M. Kitagawa and Mark D. Cummings, ed., *Buddhism and Asian History.* New York: Macmillan, 1987.

Karetsky, Patricia Eichenbaum, *The Life of the Buddha: Ancient Scriptural and Pictorial Traditions.* Lanham: University Press of America, 1992.

Keown, Damein et.al., eds. *Buddhism and Human Rights.* London: Curzon, 1998.

Kohn, Michael H., trans., *The Shambhala Dictionary of Buddhism and Zen.* Boston: Shambhala, 1991.

Lamotte, Etienne, *History of Indian Buddhism: From the Origins to the Saka Era.* Louvain-La-Neuve: Institut Orientaliste, 1988.

Lopez, Donald S., Jr, ed., *Buddhist Hermeneutics.* Honolulu: University of Hawaii Press, 1988.

Lopez, Donald S., Jr., ed., *Buddhism in Practice.* Princeton: Princeton University Press, 1995.

Malalasekera, G. P., ed., *Encyclopedia of Buddhism.* Colombo: Government of Sri Lanka, 1961.

Morgan, Kenneth W., ed., *The Path of the Buddha.* New York: Ronald Press, 1974.

Nakamura, Hajime, *Gotama Buddha.* Los Angeles: Buddhist Books International, 1977.

Ñaṇamoli, Bhikkhu, *The Life of the Buddha.* Kandy, Sri Lanka: Buddhist Publication Society, 1972.

Narada Thera, *The Buddha and His Teachings.* Kandy, Sri Lanka: Buddhist Publication Society, 1988 (reprint).

Prebish, Charles S., ed. *Buddhist Ethics: A Cross-Cultural Approach.* Dubuque: Kendall/Hunt, 1992.

........................, ed., *Historical Dictionary of Buddhism.* Metuchen: Scarecrow Press, 1993.

Thomas, E. J., *The Life of the Buddha as Legend and History.* London: Routledge & Kegan Paul, 1927.

Warder, A. K, *Outline of Indian Philosophy.* Delhi: Motilal Banarsidass, 1971.

Warder, A. K., *Indian Buddhism,* 2nd ed. rev. Delhi: Motilal Banarsidass, 1980.

Warren, Henry C., *Buddhism in Translations.* New York: Atheneum, 1963.

INDEX

U

V

W

Y

Z